YAS

FRIENDS
OF ACPL

W9-AEM-312

Hiroshima

Fifty Years
of Debate

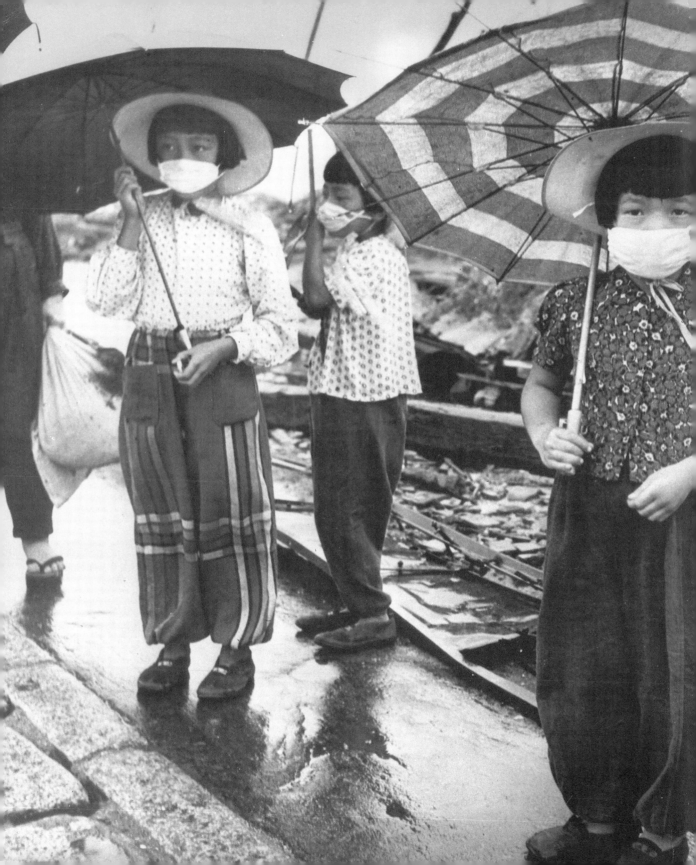

Hiroshima

Fifty Years
of Debate

BY ROBERT YOUNG

 **DILLON PRESS**
New York

Maxwell Macmillan Canada
Toronto

Maxwell Macmillan International
New York   Oxford   Singapore   Sydney

For Frank,
who knows a good idea when he hears one

Acknowledgments

I am grateful to Ray Byrne and Judy Mills for providing important background information, to Joyce Stanton for helping transform an idea into a book, and to my family for their constant support.

Photo Credits

Photo research by Debbie Needleman
Cover courtesy of UPI/Bettmann and the National Archives
UPI/Bettmann: frontispiece, 10, 15, 18, 22, 24, 36-37, 39, 44, 59, 61, 68; National Archives: 6, 13, 21, 26, 29, 32, 50-51, 67; The Bettmann Archive: 8; U.S. Army: 25; U.S. Army Military History Institute: 42; Reuters/Bettmann: 71.

Book design by Carol Matsuyama

Library of Congress Cataloging-in-Publication Data

Young, Robert, 1951-
    Hiroshima : fifty years of debate / by Robert Young.
        p. cm. — (Both sides)
    Includes bibliographical references and index.
    ISBN 0–87518–610–6
    1. Hiroshima-shi (Japan)—History—Bombardment, 1945—Juvenile literature. 2. Atomic bomb—Japan—Hiroshima-shi—Juvenile literature. [1. Hiroshima-shi (Japan)—History—Bombardment, 1945. 2. Atomic bomb—History.] I. Title. II. Series: Both sides (Dillon Press)
    D767.25.H6Y68   1994
    940.54'25—dc20   93-31261

Summary: A debate about the necessity of dropping the atomic bomb on Hiroshima. Covers the historical events that led up to the American action and the differing viewpoints on the part of historians, scientists, and political leaders.

Macmillan Publishing Company is part of the Maxwell Communication Group of Companies.

Dillon Press
Macmillan Publishing Company
866 Third Avenue
New York, NY 10022

Maxwell Macmillan Canada, Inc.
1200 Eglinton Avenue East
Suite 200
Don Mills, Ontario M3C 3N1

First edition

Printed in the United States of America

10 9 8 7 6 5 4 3 2 1

0-382-24713-2

★ ★ ★ Contents ★ ★ ★

Colonel Paul Tibbets
in the **Enola Gay**

ONE

August 6, 1945

In the early morning hours of August 6, 1945, on a tiny island called Tinian in the western Pacific, a small group of men posed for military photographers. The men were about to go on one of the most important missions of World War II.

Behind the men stood the *Enola Gay*, a B-29 bomber. B-29s were bigger, faster, and higher-flying than any bomber ever made. They could each carry 20,000 pounds of bombs nearly 6,000 miles. But there was something different about the *Enola Gay*. Instead of carrying many bombs, it was going to carry only one bomb. This one bomb was the most destructive weapon the world had ever known. It was an atomic bomb.

The atomic bomb, called "Little Boy," was the result of a top-secret program known as the Manhattan Project, which had its beginnings in 1939. Scientists used the latest knowledge about the

On the afternoon of August 5, 1945, Colonel Paul Tibbets, Jr., named the plane that would drop the first atomic bomb the next day. The name Tibbets chose was that of his mother, Enola Gay. She had encouraged him to become a pilot.

★ ★ ★ ★ ★

"Little Boy" was 10 feet long and 28 inches across. It got its nickname to distinguish it from the wider "Fat Man," another atomic bomb developed as part of the Manhattan Project. On August 9, 1945, "Fat Man" was dropped on the city of Nagasaki.

"Little Boy"

powerful forces created when atoms are split to try to develop a powerful weapon. Six years and two billion dollars later, the first atomic bomb was ready to be used in warfare.

At 2:45 A.M. the *Enola Gay*, carrying 12 men, 7,500 gallons of fuel, and the 9,000-pound bomb, was ready to go. After being cleared for takeoff, Colonel Paul Tibbets, the pilot, pushed the throttles and released the brakes. Knowing that he needed a long distance to get the heavy plane into the air, Tibbets used every inch of the 8,500-foot runway before lift-

ing the plane off the ground.

Fifteen minutes after takeoff, Captain William Parsons and his assistant, Second Lieutenant Morris Jeppson, went to work. Their job was to install the charge that would make the bomb explode. For safety reasons, the charge was kept separate from the bomb during takeoff.

Parsons lowered himself into the frigid bomb bay. While Jeppson held a flashlight and passed tools, Parsons carefully removed the rear plate of the bomb and put the charge into place. It was an 11-step procedure that took the two men about 30 minutes to complete. The bomb was almost ready to be detonated.

At about 5 A.M. the *Enola Gay* passed over the island of Iwo Jima, where two more planes joined it. The three created a V formation and headed northwest toward the islands that make up Japan.

An hour and a half later, Jeppson returned to the bomb bay. He unscrewed three small green plugs from the bomb and replaced them with red ones. The final electrical connections were complete. The atomic bomb was now fully armed and live.

When Colonel Tibbets was told the bomb was ready, he switched on the intercom and announced to the crew that they were carrying the world's first atomic bomb. Only a few of the 12 crew members

9

Nine of the twelve crew members of the Enola Gay

already knew that. The others believed that they were carrying an important bomb, but they weren't sure exactly what kind. Now there was no question about what their cargo was. What they didn't know was exactly where they would drop the weapon.

But that changed after 7 A.M., when the weather scout plane reached the city of Hiroshima. The message from the crew of the weather plane was that the skies were clear enough to see the aiming point for the bomb. Tibbets announced to his crew that they were heading to Hiroshima.

A half hour later, Captain Theodore Van Kirk,

A total of seven B-29s were needed for this mission. In addition to the *Enola Gay*, one plane would serve as a backup in case of any mechanical problems. Another plane preceded the *Enola Gay* and scouted the weather of Hiroshima. Two more scouted the weather of the other possible targets. The remaining two planes flew along with the *Enola Gay*. One carried instruments to measure the force of the blast; the other carried cameras to photograph it.

the navigator, told the crew they were ten minutes away from their aiming point, the Aioi Bridge. The *Enola Gay* was flying at 200 miles an hour, at 31,600 feet. A few minutes later Tibbets gave the order for the crew members to put on their glasses—black goggles that would protect their eyes from the bright flash of the bomb. When the bombing count-down began, they were to make sure their eyes were covered.

Major Thomas Ferebee, whose job was to drop the bomb at the proper place, leaned forward and pressed his left eye into the bombsight. He had studied photographs of the city and knew every inch of the landscape below them. He spotted the Ota River and then the Aioi Bridge.

When they got closer, Ferebee sent the bombing radio-tone signal through the intercom. The crew—except for the two pilots and Ferebee, who all need-ed to see clearly—pulled their goggles over their eyes. When the tone stopped, at 17 seconds after 8:15, the atomic bomb was automatically released.

The *Enola Gay*, suddenly 9,000 pounds lighter, lurched upward. Tibbets jerked the wheel forward and turned it hard to the right, which sent the plane into a sharp diving turn. He wanted to pick up speed and get as far away from the bomb as he could.

Forty-three seconds after it was released, and

From four cities—Hiroshima, Kokura, Niigata, and Naga-saki—Major General Curtis LeMay chose the target for the first atomic bomb. He selected Hiroshima because it contained many factories that made war materials. It was also the headquar-ters for the Japanese Second Army under Field Marshal Shunroku Hata. LeMay believed that Hiroshima, a city with a population of 300,000, was the only potential target without a prison-er-of-war camp in the area. But LeMay was wrong. Hiroshima Castle, located in the center of the city, held at least 23 American prisoners.

after having fallen for nearly 6 miles, the bomb exploded about 1,800 feet above ground. From the *Enola Gay* it looked like a pinkish, purplish flash that grew larger and larger. The tail gunner, Technical Sergeant George Robert Caron, saw a giant gray ball of air shooting toward them. Before he could shout a warning, the shock wave hit the plane, tossing the crew around like toys. Another shock wave hit them, but there were no injuries and the plane was not damaged.

On the ground at Hiroshima, it was another matter. At Ground Zero—the point on the ground directly below an exploding bomb—people and buildings were instantly vaporized in the blinding flash. The air, heated to 540,000 degrees F, or nearly as hot as the sun, and so compressed that it could be seen, pushed out in all directions faster than the speed of light. With the force of a tidal wave, the intensely heated air swept over the city and then, carrying dust and debris, rose in a mushroom-shaped cloud.

Thousands of people who were not turned into dust by the blast were left as charred corpses. Those who survived had their clothing scorched from their bodies and were badly burned. Some were trapped beneath collapsed buildings. All were shocked and dazed.

Survivors desperately looked for medical help,

An atomic bomb explodes because of the energy released by certain atoms. Uranium was placed at one end of a cannonlike tube. At the other end was an electrical fuse that set off a small explosion, which fired another piece of uranium through the tube. When the two pieces of uranium collided, they formed what scientists call a *critical mass. Critical* here means "large enough to produce a particular result": At this size, smaller parts of the atoms, called neutrons, begin bouncing into each other, causing a chain reaction and a huge explosion equaling 20,000 tons of dynamite.

The atomic bomb explodes over Hiroshima.

but there was little available. Most of the doctors and nurses had been killed. Only 3 hospitals of nearly 50 escaped destruction.

Hiroshima was devastated. Some 62,000 buildings were destroyed. Railroad tracks were twisted, power lines were bent, the city's water system was wrecked, and all forms of communication were knocked out. Fires raged throughout the city.

Finally, when it seemed as if calm might come to the city, it began to rain. But the rain was unlike any the people of Hiroshima had experienced before. The drops—a result of condensation of the water vapor in the bomb's cloud—were as big as a man's fingertips. The raindrops were black and left gray stains that wouldn't wash off people's skin. The drops had been polluted with deadly radioactive fallout from the explosion of the atomic bomb.

The attack on Hiroshima left thousands of people killed and injured. Early estimates were that about 68,000 people died and 72,000 were wounded. Later estimates varied, some increasing the number of dead to 200,000.

The estimates do not take into account the thousands of people who would later die as a result of exposure to the bomb's radiation. Also, numbers cannot possibly measure the pain and suffering the people of Hiroshima endured.

Was it really necessary for those people to ex-

The exact number of people killed and wounded at Hiroshima will probably never be known. The difference in the statistics reported results from the extreme confusion in the city following the explosion and different methods of calculating casualties. The number killed also depends on the point of view of the people collecting the statistics.

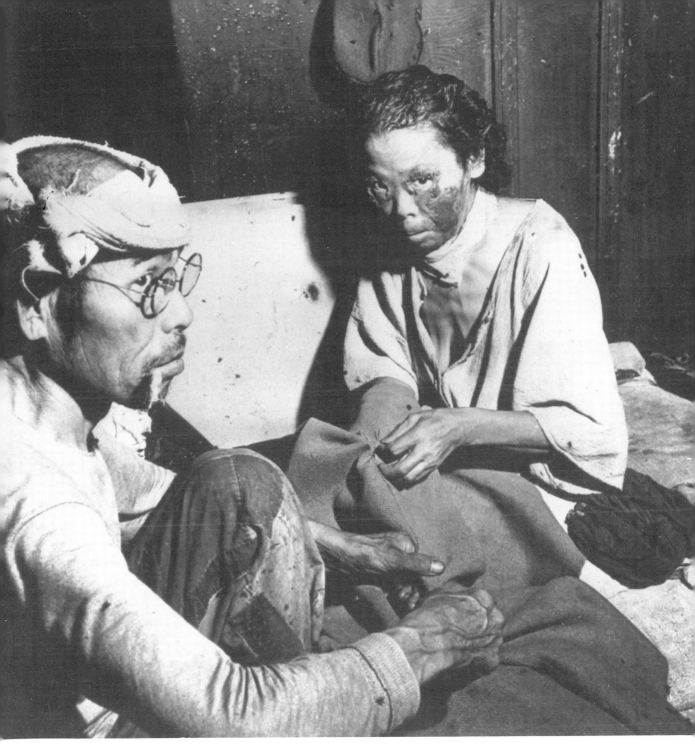

Two of the many thousands of victims of the bomb

perience such a nightmare? For many years it has been said that the United States had to drop the atomic bomb on Hiroshima to bring an end to World War II. Not everyone, however, shares this view. Some people believe that dropping the atomic bomb was not essential for ending the war. Some go even further and say that not only could the use of the bomb have been avoided but that the bomb made the world more dangerous. As with most important events in history, there is more than one point of view.

Hiroshima. Was dropping the bomb necessary, or could the fateful act have been avoided? This book will consider both sides of the issue. It will be up to you, however, to draw your own conclusions about one of the most significant events in the history of the world.

TWO

No Other Choice

According to many American political and military leaders, dropping the atomic bomb on Japan brought World War II to a swift end and saved American lives. To get a better understanding of this viewpoint, let's go back in time to the events that led up to Hiroshima.

World War II began because three countries—Germany, Italy, and Japan—developed dictatorships and started to expand their territories in the 1930s by invading other countries. The major Western democracies, Great Britain, France, and the United States, were distressed about what was happening but did not want to become involved in the conflicts. They remembered the costs—in lives as well as money—of World War I. World peace, they hoped, could be gained by agreements among nations.

By 1939, though, it was clear to England and France that agreements would not be enough. When

German dictator Adolf Hitler making a speech some months after his troops invaded Poland

Germany invaded Poland on September 1 of that year, both England and France declared war. The United States did not enter the war at this time but tried to help in other ways. It sold arms to Great Britain and other countries so they could defend themselves against Germany.

Europe wasn't the only area of conflict in the world. The Japanese believed that it was their destiny to control Asia. By 1939 they had taken over

Korea and parts of China. In September 1940, Japan sent troops into the French colony of Indochina (today known as Cambodia, Laos, and Vietnam). A few days later, Japan, Germany, and Italy signed an agreement called the Tripartite Pact, which called for these three countries to help each other if attacked. Japan, Germany, and Italy became known as the Axis powers. Countries that opposed the Axis powers were named the Allies.

Japan's move into Indochina as well as its agreement with Germany and Italy alarmed the Allies, especially the United States. The United States was concerned that Japan would move into other areas like Malaya and the East Indies (now called Indonesia) to obtain important natural resources. The Japanese needed resources such as oil, rubber, and tin to make war materials. Up to that time, Japan had been buying many of its resources from the United States. After warning the Japanese not to invade other countries, the United States restricted the sale of war materials to them. Sales were to be resumed when Japan withdrew its troops from Indochina.

Japan responded on December 7, 1941, by attacking America's Pacific fleet of ships anchored at Pearl Harbor on the Hawaiian island of Oahu. The Japanese knew that many Americans were isolationists, unwilling to get involved in matters outside their own country, and believed that if Japan could knock out the Pacific fleet quickly, the United States would not be willing or able to fight a war. Then no nation could stop Japan from taking over more territory in Asia.

The surprise attack began at 7:50 A.M., when the first of more than 350 Japanese planes began bombing American ships and planes on Oahu. In less than two hours, the attack was over, but the damage was tremendous. Eight battleships were sunk or crippled, 3 cruisers and 3 destroyers were ruined, 188 airplanes were destroyed, and 159 were damaged. The destruction was not limited to ships and planes: 2,403 Americans were killed and 1,178 were injured.

When the news of the attack reached the United States, Americans were shocked and angry. Instead of shrinking back, as the Japanese had expected, Americans were energized. The following day, December 8, 1941, the United States declared war on Japan. Three days later, Germany and Italy declared war on the United States. The United States was now an active participant in World War II and would have to split its fighting forces between Europe and Asia.

On the same day the Japanese bombed Pearl Harbor, they attacked other targets in Asia and out in the Pacific. Some of the targets were U.S. possessions, such as Guam, Midway Island, the Philip-

★ ★ ★ ★ ★

Lieutenant Commander Mitsuo Fuchida led the Japanese attack on Pearl Harbor. After he had dropped his bombs, Fuchida circled the area so he could report damage information to his commander. His was the last plane back to the aircraft carrier. After reporting on the damage, Fuchida urged that they attack again to finish off the fleet. The commander, however, decided against it.

December 7, 1941: Smoke and flames engulf Pearl Harbor.

President Franklin D. Roosevelt signs the declaration of war against Japan.

pines, and Wake Island. Other targets belonged to Great Britain, including Hong Kong and Malaya. Still another target was the independent country of Siam (now Thailand). Japan was successful in each of these attacks.

The challenge facing the United States was to stop the Japanese and to regain control of the area. But the United States had a big problem: It was not well prepared for war. And now it had to rebuild its Pacific fleet. On January 6, 1942, President Franklin Roosevelt announced a "victory program," an all-out effort to produce the weapons and materials needed to fight and win a war.

As the United States built its military arsenal, Japan continued its assaults in Asia. Within a few months, Japan controlled more than 1 million square miles of land, including most of the islands of the South Pacific. A corner of one of the Philippine

Within a few weeks of the attack on Pearl Harbor, $6 billion worth of planes and aircraft equipment was ordered by the U.S. government. Employment in the aircraft industry rose from 100,000 in 1940 to more than 2 million in 1944. As a result, the United States was able to produce nearly 300,000 airplanes during the war. One airplane factory, the largest in the world, covered 67 acres and could produce B-24 Liberators at the rate of one every hour. This tremendous production of war materials was a key factor in helping the Allies win the war.

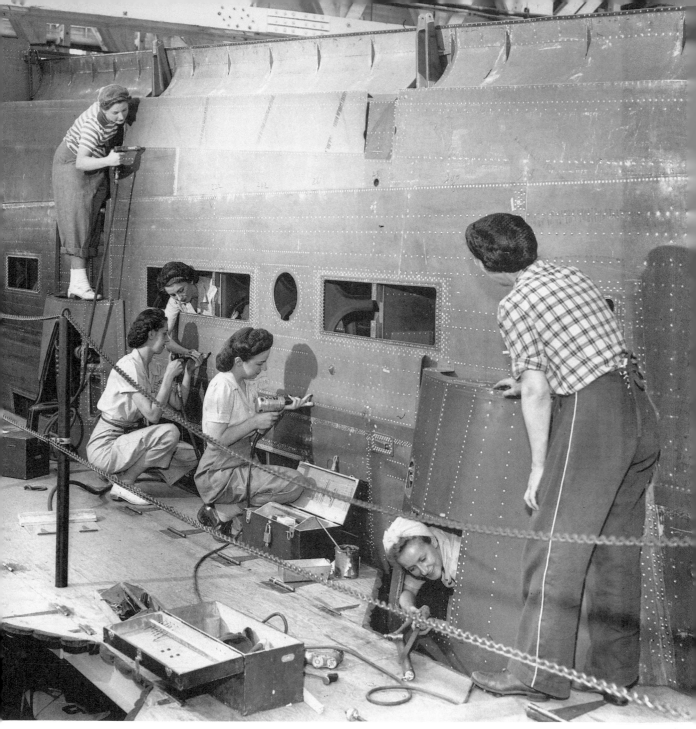

American women played an important role in building the nation's military arsenal.
Here, workers construct a transport plane that will carry 50 soldiers.

Islands was one of the few areas that had not fallen into Japanese hands.

The battle for the Philippines was fierce and bloody. Under General Douglas MacArthur, American and Filipino troops fought to defend the islands. But the well-equipped, well-trained Japanese army continued to push them back. Finally, after months of courageous fighting, 76,000 American and Filipino troops surrendered on April 9, 1942.

General Douglas MacArthur. After losing to the Japanese in the Philippines in 1942, he vowed to return to fight again.

With little food and water, the prisoners were forced to walk nearly 60 miles through the hot jungle up the Bataan Peninsula. They were jammed into poorly ventilated boxcars for a three-hour journey, and then made to walk 7 more miles to a prison camp. A few were able to escape into the jungle, but more than 10,000 prisoners died on what became known as the Bataan Death March.

Back in the United States, production of war

American prisoners of war during the grueling Bataan Death March

materials increased; so did the strength of the military. Although the United States could not concentrate all its efforts in the Pacific, it began to have some successes there. The turning point came on June 6, 1942, at the Battle of Midway. Japan had planned to use Midway Island as a base for taking over the Hawaiian Islands. But the United States had figured out Japan's secret code and knew an attack was coming. The Americans were ready and waiting for the Japanese to attack. When the battle was over, Japan had suffered its worse naval defeat in its history: 4 aircraft carriers and 1 cruiser sunk, 250 planes lost at sea, and 2,000 men killed.

Other successes followed for the Allies, but none came easily. Battles were fought in hot, steamy jungles filled with insects and diseases. The Japanese were fierce fighters and unafraid of death.

Slowly the Allied forces regained the Pacific islands from the Japanese. As the Japanese were pushed back, they began using more desperate methods of warfare. Pilots called kamikazes flew suicide missions in which they intentionally crashed their planes into Allied ships. Soldiers with explosives strapped to their bodies threw themselves into Allied command posts and under planes on the ground.

The fighting grew even more vicious, and the Japanese still refused to surrender. In February

Japanese soldiers lived by a centuries-old code known as Bushido, which means "way of the warrior." In this code, surrender was dishonorable and forbidden; suicide was required rather than submission to the enemy. Because of this view, prisoners of war held by the Japanese were treated with contempt. Some were killed, but most were put to work as slave laborers without adequate food, shelter, or medical care. Many prisoners slowly starved to death.

The term *kamikaze*, which means "divine wind," comes from the name of the typhoon that destroyed a fleet of enemy ships on their way to Japan during the Middle Ages. *Kamikaze* missions in World War II began in October 1944 at the Battle of Leyte Gulf in the Philippines. While these and later attacks shook Allied morale, they failed to sink any major warships. The reason is that kamikaze pilots were usually inexperienced, with many having received only seven days of training.

and March 1945, on the tiny island of Iwo Jima, more than 20,000 Japanese soldiers fought to their deaths. A little more than a month later, on the island of Okinawa, the fighting grew even more intense. Lying only 350 miles from Japan, Okinawa was the last line of defense for the Japanese. For the Allies, Okinawa was the final stop before the invasion of Japan.

Okinawa was a bloody battle—the bloodiest in the Pacific war—and it raged for three months. The Japanese used every kind of kamikaze attack imaginable. Not only planes but speedboats and submarines were used in suicide missions. There were even torpedo-shaped rockets, launched by airplanes and steered by Japanese pilots strapped to them and zooming to their deaths. Despite their efforts, the Japanese were badly beaten by the firepower of the Allies.

Okinawa was a costly battle. Nearly 50,000 Americans were killed or wounded, the worst casu-

The Marine Corps War Memorial near Arlington National Cemetery outside Washington, D.C., is based on a famous photograph taken during the battle for the island of Iwo Jima. The photograph shows five marines placing a flag on top of Mount Suribachi. The flag was meant to help boost the morale of the marines fighting in this bloody battle.

Marines raise the flag on Iwo Jima.

alties in the entire war. But for Japan the defeat was much worse: 110,000 men died. With such huge human losses combined with the heavy destruction of ships and planes, it seemed certain that the Japanese would surrender. But not only did the Japanese refuse to give up; they began to prepare all their citizens—including women and children—to defend their home islands.

In Europe, by the summer of 1945, Germany and Italy had been defeated by the Allies. The victors could now focus all their attention on defeating Japan. Military leaders made plans to invade the Japanese islands. The problem with an invasion was that so many people—Allied soldiers, mostly Americans—would have to die. There were many estimates of what America's losses might be, ranging from 50,000 to as high as a quarter of a million.

Was there an easier, less costly way of defeating the Japanese once and for all—something the Allies could do to shock the Japanese into surrendering? There was: the atomic bomb.

THREE

Ready to Surrender?

Dropping the atomic bomb on Japan was one choice the United States had in ending the war. But it was not the only choice. And, according to many important military, political, and scientific leaders, it certainly was not necessary.

Japan was interested in peace. As early as the summer of 1944, Japanese diplomats secretly spoke to leaders of neutral countries such as Sweden, Switzerland, and the Soviet Union. The Japanese hoped that these discussions would lead to talks of peace among the Allies. None resulted, however.

The Allies were not talking with Japan, but they were talking among themselves. On February 4, 1945, President Franklin Roosevelt met with British Prime Minister Winston Churchill and Soviet leader Joseph Stalin at Yalta, a resort city in the Ukraine republic of what used to be the Soviet Union. By this time it was certain that Germany would soon be

Allied leaders meet at Yalta: (from the left) British Prime Minister Winston Churchill, U.S. President Franklin Roosevelt, and Soviet Premier Joseph Stalin.

defeated. The leaders made final military plans and determined how German territory would be divided when they achieved victory. Stalin wanted eastern Europe to be under the influence of the Soviet Union. Because Roosevelt wanted the Soviet Union to help in the fight against Japan, he did not insist on guarantees for a free eastern Europe.

Japanese interest in peace increased in April 1945, when the Soviet Union declared it would not renew a neutrality agreement with Japan. Under this agreement, Japan and the Soviet Union had said they would not fight each other. If the Soviets were no longer going to be neutral, the Japanese reasoned, they would soon be fighting Japan.

U.S. relations with the Communist Soviet Union were complicated during World War II. When the war began, the Soviets and the Germans made an agreement not to fight against each other. The Germans broke that agreement in June 1941, when they invaded the Soviet Union. When the United States entered the war in December, the Soviets and the Americans became members of the Allies fighting against the Axis powers. Although they were fighting on the same side, there was mistrust between the Americans and the Soviets—the result of differences in political philosophy. Also, the Soviets had suffered huge losses—both soldiers and citizens—during the war, which made them even more wary of potential enemies. Tensions grew at the end of the war when Stalin established a Communist government in Poland and Soviet troops remained in countries they had freed from the Germans.

Taking part in the war against Japan would allow the Soviet Union to share in the Allied victory and gain territory for itself.

As the United States continued to intercept Japanese messages, the theme of those messages was clear. Japan was weakening and was willing to discuss plans for surrender. Still, the United States continued making military plans that included development and use of the atomic bomb as well as an invasion.

By the summer of 1945, Japan was near collapse. Hundreds of thousands of its troops had been killed in battle. Most of its ships had been sunk. Its air force was using what few planes it had left to fly kamikaze missions.

The Allied forces had captured control of islands close to Japan. From them, American B-29s launched bombing missions on Japan, inflicting immense damage on homes and factories as well as airfields. Thousands of men, women, and children were killed during these raids.

Japan was becoming desperate. It needed food for its people as well as materials and supplies to continue fighting. But it had little chance of getting help. Italy and Germany, its Axis partners, had been defeated by the Allies. In any case, it would be difficult to get supplies into the country. Japan's harbors were mined and blockaded by Allied ships.

Firebomb raids on the cities of Japan began in the spring of 1945. B-29s carried M-29 firebombs, which were dropped in clusters of 38 within a container. Each bomb weighed 6 pounds and was set to be released from the cluster at an altitude of 5,000 feet. The bombs exploded when they hit the ground, spreading a gasoline-jelly compound that set a raging fire. On the night of March 10, more than 300 B-29s carrying 1,667 tons of firebombs attacked Tokyo. Approximately 16 square miles of the city were burned, 83,000 people were killed, and another 40,000 were injured.

With the Japanese in such a difficult situation, and with such slim hope of victory, why didn't they surrender? The reason lay in the kind of surrender they would have been forced to accept. The Allies demanded an unconditional surrender, which meant that the victors would dictate all the terms.

Not only was surrendering dishonorable in the eyes of the proud Japanese, but unconditional surrender meant that the Allies could remove their emperor, whom they worshiped, from power. The Allies might try Emperor Hirohito as a war criminal. They might even execute him. The Japanese chose to fight on.

Why, then, didn't the Allies change the terms of surrender? Why didn't they make it possible for the emperor to keep his position after the war? One reason is that President Harry Truman, who took over after Roosevelt's death in April 1945, was told by his military advisers that yielding to the Jap-

American B-29s on a bombing mission in Japan pass Mount Fuji on their way to Tokyo.

In Japan, the emperor reigns but does not rule. He is more a spiritual leader than a political leader. Emperor Hirohito was believed to have been a descendant of the sun goddess. The Japanese people worshiped him as if he were a god. To protect their emperor, the Japanese were willing to fight to their deaths.

anese on any surrender terms would be seen as a sign of weakness by military leaders in Japan. They might even use this sign to encourage their troops to fight longer and harder.

Also, there was considerable political pressure on Truman. Allied casualties were running high, and the American people wanted the war ended as soon as possible. What would Americans have thought if the bomb had not been used and they discovered later that the war could have been ended sooner by using a new weapon?

Americans already had plenty of anger toward the Japanese for attacking Pearl Harbor. Hatred against the Japanese had even been directed against Americans of Japanese descent. As early as the spring of 1942, the U.S. government began re-

Franklin D. Roosevelt was president of the United States from 1933 to 1945. He was the only president in the history of the United States to be elected to four terms. When his fourth term began, in 1945, Roosevelt was in poor health. He attended the Yalta conference in February and reported the results of the conference to Congress on March 1. At the end of March he traveled to Warm Springs, Georgia, for a rest. On the morning of April 12, Roosevelt worked at his desk while an artist painted his portrait. Suddenly, the president fell over in his chair, complaining of a terrible headache. Within a few hours, Roosevelt was dead of a cerebral hemorrhage. He was deeply mourned by millions of Americans, whom he had led out of the Great Depression as well as through World War II.

Emperor Hirohito

moving 110,000 Japanese-Americans from their homes on the West Coast. These people, two-thirds of whom were native-born Americans, were considered to be a threat to the country and were moved to "relocation" camps where they lived under armed guards behind barbed wire. Property belonging to Japanese-Americans was sold at less than 10 percent of its real value.

Newspapers, magazines, and radio stations joined the government in successfully promoting anti-Japanese feelings among Americans. A public opinion poll in December 1943 revealed that by a margin of 14 to 1, southern Californians wanted Japanese-Americans deported. Another poll, taken in May 1945, showed that 70 percent of Americans were in favor of putting Emperor Hirohito in prison or executing him. Truman could not risk the loss of public support if he were to permit the war to go on or if he were to soften the terms of surrender.

Instead of working to end the war diplomatically, Truman made plans to end the war militarily. In July 1945 he went to the German city of Potsdam and met with Churchill and Stalin. While at the conference, Truman learned of the successful testing of the atomic bomb at Alamogordo, New Mexico. Now Truman had something Roosevelt had not had when he met with Stalin in Yalta: the most powerful weapon ever created.

The United States could use the atomic bomb to win the war without Soviet help. In doing so, the Americans could avoid further problems with an ally its government did not trust. The problem was that the Soviets were planning to live up to their agreement made at Yalta. They were preparing to enter the war against Japan.

On July 26, 1945, Truman issued a final demand to Japan. Again, it was for an unconditional surrender. Japanese Premier Suzuki answered with a statement that he would treat the demand with *mokusatsu*. This Japanese word can have many meanings, ranging from "contempt" to "no comment." The United States believed that the statement was a rejection of the demand.

On July 30 President Truman gave final approval to drop the atomic bomb. But not everyone who knew about the bomb was in agreement that it should be used. Many of the scientists who had worked on its development were opposed to its use. Some thought that the United States should warn the Japanese about the new weapon. Some called for a demonstration to the world of the bomb's tremendous power so that its use in Japan could perhaps be avoided.

Leaders close to the president opposed dropping the atomic bomb, too. Air Force Chief of Staff Henry "Hap" Arnold believed that the Japanese

President Harry Truman at the Potsdam conference, flanked by Stalin (left) and Churchill (right) and their interpreters

would soon surrender even if the bomb was not dropped or an invasion launched. Admiral William Leahy, Truman's chief of staff; Richard Bard, undersecretary of the navy; John McCloy, assistant secretary of war; and Joseph Grew, acting secretary of state, also felt that the bomb was not necessary.

Some historians say there is evidence that General Dwight Eisenhower, commander of Allied forces in Europe, was also opposed to using it.

On August 2 President Truman met with William Donovan, head of the Office of Strategic Services (OSS), an intelligence (spy) agency. Japanese diplomats had told Donovan that Suzuki was trying to get other Japanese leaders to agree to surrender and that they just needed a little more time.

But Japan was running out of time. Its apparent interest in peace would be ignored once more. So would the opposition of some scientists and advisers to the president. The atomic bomb would be dropped, even though, in the eyes of some knowledgeable people, it didn't have to be.

FOUR

Forced to Surrender

For the people who believed that dropping the atomic bomb was essential, it was clear that the Japanese were not ready to surrender. Why else would they continue to fight despite the staggering losses at Iwo Jima and Okinawa? Why else would they prepare 2.5 million soldiers and 28 million civilians to defend their homeland against an Allied invasion?

Japan was being controlled by a small group of

> The Japanese were determined to defend themselves against an invasion. They built bunkers and tunnels along their shoreline. More than 5,000 planes and hundreds of boats were loaded with explosives for kamikaze missions. Men, women, and children were trained to use bamboo spears and pitchforks to fight the enemy. Teenage girls were given woodworking awls to use as weapons. Citizens were told that if they didn't kill at least one enemy soldier, they didn't deserve to die. It was a great honor for the people of Japan to die for their country.

The Japanese had a strong fighting spirit.

Decisions in Japan during the war were made by a small group of leaders, which included the prime minister, the army and navy chiefs of staff, the ministers of the army and navy, and the foreign minister. Once the members of the group made a decision, they asked to meet with the emperor. The emperor listened to their decision, and then added his agreement. Agreement by the emperor gave decisions respectability.

military leaders. These men, known as militarists, believed that their country was destined to rule Asia and the Pacific. Even as Japan's chances for victory continued to slip away, the militarists hoped for help from heaven. They looked for a miracle like the divine wind, the typhoon that had saved their nation during the Middle Ages by destroying a fleet of enemy ships.

U.S. leaders knew that Japan was making efforts to achieve a peaceful end to the war. But, they reasoned, with the militarists in power, how serious were those efforts? And why didn't Japan contact the Allies directly? To many people, it seemed as though Japanese peace efforts were a trick to get the Allies to ease up on the fighting.

Japan was not to be trusted or easily forgiven. After all, it was Japan that had brought Americans into the war by launching a sneak attack at Pearl Harbor. It was Japan that had captured and mistreated so many soldiers and civilians. And it was Japan that had killed so many Allied troops.

President Truman believed, as did many other American military and political leaders, that he had an obligation to do whatever he could to end the war quickly and with as few Allied casualties as possible.

In light of Truman's duty, an important question becomes: How could Truman have justified *not* using the atomic bomb? The United States had spent a great deal of money—$2 billion—developing the bomb. It had been successfully tested, and strong evidence existed that this weapon could destroy its targets in Japan. Choosing not to use the bomb would have been an enormous waste of the time, money, and effort spent to develop it. It would have also been a waste of American lives, since without the bomb, most leaders believed, an invasion would be needed to bring an end to the war.

Some people have questioned why the atomic bomb was not first demonstrated to the people of Japan. The bomb could have been exploded in an unpopulated area—over a desert or an ocean. That way, its tremendous power could have been seen and Japan could have avoided more death and destruction by surrendering. This option was considered by the Target Committee, a group composed mainly of scientists who had worked on the bomb. In addition to suggesting targets for the bomb, the committee discussed concerns about its use.

After considering a demonstration of the bomb to the Japanese, the Target Committee rejected the idea. Its main reason was that if the bomb did not explode properly, the Japanese might be encouraged to continue fighting.

Another group, the Interim Committee, also considered the idea of demonstrating the bomb before using it. This committee, made up of government, military, and scientific leaders, agreed with the conclusion of the Target Committee. Also, they believed that the new weapon should make the maximum psychological impact possible on both Japan and the rest of the world. The Interim Committee wanted to show the world the power of the bomb, as well as shock the Japanese into surrender. Demonstrating the bomb beforehand would lessen its psychological effect.

Some people have questioned why the atomic bomb was dropped on a city that had so many civilians. Hiroshima was chosen because it was large and because it had not already been damaged by bombings. The full effects of the bomb would be clearly understood. Also, Hiroshima had factories producing war materials, and it was the headquarters of the Japanese Second Army.

That Hiroshima had so many civilians was a tragedy. But it certainly would not be the first city whose civilian population would be attacked; throughout World War II, civilians had been targets. As early as 1940, the German air force bombed major population centers in England. These bombings were followed by many other destructive ones in continental Europe and Asia. The purpose was to break the morale of the enemy and bring quick victory.

The morale of the people of Hiroshima was shattered when the atomic bomb was dropped on August 6, 1945. But because of the destruction as well as the chaos throughout the city, information about the bombing was slow to spread. Three days later, the United States dropped another atomic bomb on Japan. This time, the target was the city of Nagasaki.

On the same day the bomb was dropped on Nagasaki, the Japanese cabinet met to decide whether to accept the Allies' demand for unconditional surrender. The desire for peace was not unanimous, which meant that a decision could not be reached. The war minister, General Anami, was most strongly opposed to surrendering. He still believed the Japanese could win. Other leaders supported his position. It was necessary for every

On May 14, 1940, the Germans launched a massive air attack on the city of Rotterdam in the Netherlands, dropping thousands of 2,200-pound, delayed-action bombs. The raid killed more than 800 people, wounded thousands, and leveled nearly every building, leaving more than 78,000 people homeless.

Another destructive air attack took place on February 13 and 14, 1945, when more than 800 Allied planes dropped 2,600 tons of bombs on the city of Dresden, Germany. The firestorm caused by the attack destroyed the city and left at least 35,000 people dead.

Destruction at Nagasaki

> The mission for dropping the second atomic bomb was not as smooth as the first. Not long after takeoff, Major Charles Sweeney discovered that he would be unable to use the fuel from his reserve fuel tank. As a result, he was restricted in the amount of time he could keep his plane, *Bock's Car*, in the air.
>
> When Sweeney reached the spot where he was to meet other planes that were to escort him to the bombing site, they were not there. Finally, one showed up. Together they headed for the primary bomb site, Kokura, a port city on the northeast coast of the island of Kyushu. Because Sweeney found it covered by clouds, he ordered his crew to head for the secondary bomb site: Nagasaki.
>
> Dangerously low on fuel, Sweeney could make only one pass over the city. Since it was cloudy in Nagasaki, too, the decision was made to drop the bomb by radar. Just before the bomb was to be released, an opening appeared in the clouds, so the crew could see the city. The bomb was released immediately and exploded over Nagasaki at 11:02 A.M.
>
> Because hills blocked parts of the city from the blast, the death and destruction at Nagasaki were less than at Hiroshima. Still, more than 70,000 people were killed and more than 70,000 injured. Nearly one-fourth of the city's 52,000 homes were destroyed.

member of the cabinet to agree before a decision could be made final and taken to the emperor.

That evening Prime Minister Suzuki called a meeting of the War Council and the cabinet with the emperor. Each member had a chance to voice his opinion on the subject of continuing the war. They still could not come to a unanimous decision.

Then Prime Minister Suzuki did something that had not been done for a long time. He asked Emperor Hirohito to make the final judgment. For years the military and the government had been acting in the name of the emperor without actually asking his approval. Emperor Hirohito ruled that Japan should accept the Allied demand for unconditional surrender. The emperor said, "Continue fighting and we will be plunging the entire nation into further devastation and distress. I cannot bear any longer to see my innocent subjects tormented under the cruelties of war."

At long last—with the help of the atomic bomb—the war would finally be over. What better justification could there be for using the atomic bomb than history itself? Three days after the bomb was dropped on Hiroshima, Japanese leaders agreed to surrender.

FIVE

Another Reason for Dropping the Bomb

Since the Japanese agreed to surrender so soon after the second atomic bomb, on Nagasaki, was unleashed, many people assume that the new weapon of destruction brought a speedy end to World War II. Some historians, however, question whether dropping the atomic bomb was truly the cause for surrender.

Historians have learned about the discussions in Japan during the days after Hiroshima was bombed. Some militarist leaders were still optimistic about winning the war. Believing that the United States could have only one or two more atomic bombs to drop, they planned to protect themselves from further bombings by using anti-aircraft weapons.

To the militarists, the atomic bomb was just another American weapon designed to destroy their people. They must fight on to save their country and the Japanese race, they believed.

The militarists reasoned that the country could, and must, withstand more atomic bombings. They pointed out the tremendous damage done by American B-29s on Japanese cities. The firebombing campaign had destroyed more than 3 million homes, killed about 1 million people, and left about 15 million homeless. In comparison, the destruction done by an atomic bomb was not that great.

So if the atomic bomb did not cause the Japanese to surrender, what did? For many people, the most important factor was the entry of the Soviet Union into the war.

On August 8, 1945, the Soviet Union lived up to the agreement it had made at the Yalta conference. Stalin sent 1.6 million troops, along with 3,000 tanks, into Manchuria, a region in northeastern China that was under Japanese control. Nearly 6,000 Soviet bombers supported the attack by air. The Soviets pushed the Japanese back to within 100 miles of Peking (now Beijing).

The Japanese army numbered only about 600,000, a third of whom were newly drafted civilians. The army was not only short of men; it was short of ammunition and weapons. When the fighting ended, the Soviets reported killing 80,000 Japanese soldiers and losing about 8,000 of their own. Even for the die-hard militarists in Japan, the

Soviet Union's entry into the war came as a crushing blow.

For several months the Allies had hoped that the Soviet threat would influence the Japanese to seek peace. As early as April, United States intelligence studies reported that Soviet entry into the war would convince the Japanese that defeat was inevitable. British intelligence reports reflected the same conclusion.

According to President Truman's private journal, he thought that the fighting would be over once the Soviet Union declared war on Japan. After Stalin assured him that the Soviets would enter the war by August 15, Truman wrote, "Fini Japs when that comes about."

In writing to his wife about the Soviets' declaring war on Japan, Truman noted, "We'll end the war a year sooner now, and think of the kids who won't be killed!" Help from the Soviets was vital to Truman. In fact, he told several people that getting their assistance was his most important reason for going to the Potsdam conference.

With those beliefs, why did President Truman go ahead and authorize dropping the bomb on Japan? Why didn't the United States wait a few days until the Soviets declared war?

Waiting might have saved the city of Hiroshima from destruction. It might have stopped tens of thousands of Japanese people from being killed. It might have prevented pain and suffering to thousands of other Japanese men, women, and children.

Some historians believe that the atomic bomb was used to send a message to the Soviet Union, to show the Soviets how strong the United States was. It was a sort of warning for the Soviets to cooperate

Many books have been written about the survivors of the atomic blast at Hiroshima. One of the best-known stories tells of a girl named Sadako Sasaki, who was 2 years old when the bomb was dropped on her native city. Sadako grew to become a responsible and gentle 12-year-old. Her nickname was Monkey because she ran as though she were leaping through space.

During the winter she was in sixth grade, Sadako developed a lump on her neck that was diagnosed as leukemia, a blood disorder known as the "A-bomb disease." Sadako was treated with many drugs, but she continued to weaken.

One day a friend brought her a small piece of paper folded in the shape of a crane. She told Sadako a tale about a crane that lives for a thousand years. When a sick person folds a thousand cranes, the gods grant a wish and make her well. Sadako began to fold paper cranes with renewed hope.

However, her health continued to decline, and on October 25, 1955, Sadako Sasaki died. Her classmates were sad and angry at the death of their friend. They began a peace movement to honor her. They sent letters around the world telling about Sadako and her paper cranes. Then they built a statue in the Peace Memorial Park at Hiroshima to honor Sadako and the thousands of other children who suffered because of the atomic bomb. The statue is a life-size image of Sadako, with her hands raised to the sky. In them she holds a paper crane.

with the Allies. Some people even think it was a threat to the Soviet Union.

The strongest evidence that the bomb was used to send a message to the Soviets was the desire of the United States to end the war before the Soviets invaded Manchuria. Soon after Truman learned that the bomb had been successfully tested in the desert of New Mexico, his attitude about Soviet involvement in the war changed. On July 18, 1945, Truman wrote in his journal: "[I] believe Japs will fold up before Russia comes in. I am sure they will when Manhattan appears over their homeland." (Truman was referring to the Manhattan Project, as the development of the bomb was called.)

Truman's change in attitude toward the Soviet Union was noted by other political leaders. Secretary of State James Byrnes and British Prime Minister Churchill both commented that the United States was anxious to end the war without the help of the Soviet Union.

After Germany was defeated, scientists involved in the Manhattan Project felt increased pressure to get the bomb ready. Later, Albert Einstein spoke about his concerns in public, stating that the bomb was dropped because of "a desire to end the war in the Pacific by any means before Russia's participation."

It seems that dropping the bomb was less a

Albert Einstein with members of the U.S. military

measure to end World War II than to halt Soviet expansion, which the Allies saw looming on the horizon.

What were the results of dropping the atomic bomb over two Japanese cities? Did it save American lives? Did it intimidate the Soviet Union?

Some people believe that using the atomic bomb actually made the war last longer and cost more American lives. While the government waited until the bomb was ready, thousands of Americans were killed in battles on South Pacific islands. If Truman had taken the advice of Acting Secretary of State Joseph Grew in the spring of 1945 and changed the terms of surrender, the war might have ended then. This is of special significance because the most important part of the terms previously put forward by the Japanese and rejected by the United States—allowing the emperor to keep his position—was accepted when Japan finally surrendered.

As to whether the bomb helped intimidate the Soviet Union, there are a variety of opinions. Some people, like Secretary of State Byrnes, thought it made the Soviets more manageable. Many others disagree. According to John Foster Dulles, who later became secretary of state under President Eisenhower, it increased tensions between the two countries. General Eisenhower, on a trip to Moscow, observed that "before the atom bomb was used, I would have said, yes, I was sure we could keep the peace with Russia. Now I don't know. . . . People are frightened and disturbed all over. Everyone feels insecure again."

The insecurity of countries—other than the United States—led several of them to develop atomic bombs of their own. With the help of a British traitor, the Soviet Union exploded its first

General Dwight D. Eisenhower:
Was he opposed to dropping the bomb?

atomic bomb in 1949. The British, who felt they needed the atomic bomb to keep their place as a world power, exploded theirs in 1952. By the late 1950s, the United States and the Soviet Union had developed the hydrogen bomb, a weapon over 100 times more powerful than the atomic bomb. Other nations, such as China, France, Israel, South Africa, India, and Iraq, began working on nuclear weapons.

For many people, including scientists, historians, and political and military leaders, the atomic bomb was not necessary to end the war. For some, dropping the bomb was not only unnecessary; it made things worse. It made world peace a more difficult goal to achieve and contributed to the tensions among nations that continue to this day.

SIX

What Do You Think?

The war with Japan officially came to an end on September 2, 1945, but not without incident. On August 10, the day after Emperor Hirohito told Japanese leaders of his desire for peace, Japan sent a message to the Allies. Japan stated that it would accept the Allies' terms as long as the emperor would be allowed to continue in his position.

Japan's message brought mixed reactions from American leaders. Some, like Secretary of State Byrnes, argued that President Truman should reject Japan's offer of surrender. The Japanese should not be permitted to dictate the conditions of their surrender.

Others, including Secretary of War Henry Stimson, advised Truman to accept Japan's offer. The emperor, they reasoned, was the only person in Japan with the authority to order a peaceful surrender, the only person to get the Japanese to lay

63

down their arms with dignity. Also, the longer the war went on, the more the Soviets would be involved in the outcome.

After much discussion, Secretary of State Byrnes composed a carefully worded response to the Japanese. In it he stated that the surrender would have to be unconditional but that the status of the emperor would be decided by the supreme commander of the Allied forces and by a vote of the Japanese people.

For the Allies, the response was a brilliant one. It hinted that the emperor could be retained if all went well, yet it made no guarantees. President Truman approved the response, as did the leaders of the other Allied countries.

Japanese leaders still could not agree. Some of the militarists wanted a guarantee that the emperor would be retained. Others wanted to accept the response before the Allies changed their minds and made harsher surrender terms. Arguments among Japanese leaders went on for days.

Meanwhile, a small group of Japan's army and navy officers was plotting a rebellion. The officers' plan was to assassinate leaders who favored peace. Then they would convince the emperor to continue the war.

As the officers plotted, the cabinet met to consider the Allied response. Once again, there was no agreement. And once again, Prime Minister Suzuki called on the emperor to make the final decision. The emperor wept, then told the leaders to "bow to my wishes and accept the Allied reply."

Unwilling to ignore tradition, the cabinet agreed to the emperor's request. That night Emperor Hirohito recorded a message to the people of Japan, informing them of the surrender. When the recording was played over the radio the next day, August 15, the Japanese people listened in stunned silence. Then millions wept. Their emotions were a mixture of the humiliation that comes with losing a war and the relief that their suffering was over.

Surrender was especially difficult for people in the military. Vice Admiral Matome Ugaki, commander of the navy's Fifth Air Fleet, organized a kamikaze attack on the Allied forces at Okinawa. Some

Emperor Hirohito's message to the Japanese people was a historic one. Never before had the emperor broadcast a message to his people. The message was recorded at 11:30 on the evening of August 14 in a small studio in a government building. The message was recorded twice, each time on a 10-inch disc. Because of the rumors of a rebellion, the discs were put into a cloth bag and locked in a small safe until they were to be broadcast the next day. It was fortunate that precautions had been taken. During the night, rebels seized the building but could not find the discs. By morning, having failed to gain support for their rebellion, the conspirators gave up.

Japanese soldiers killed Allied soldiers who were being held as prisoners. Others quietly committed suicide.

Two weeks later, on Sunday, September 2, 1945, the formal surrender took place on board the USS *Missouri*, anchored in Tokyo Bay. General Douglas MacArthur, who had recently been appointed the supreme commander of the Allies, accepted the surrender from the representatives of Japan. After the surrender document had been signed, MacArthur stepped forward and spoke: "Let us pray that peace be now restored and that God will preserve it always." The war with Japan was finally over.

Because of the death and destruction it caused, the war in the Pacific would not be soon forgotten. Nearly 17 million people died, more than 20 million were wounded, and at least 10 million children were left orphans. Of the people of Hiroshima and Nagasaki, the ones who died instantly when the atomic bomb was dropped may have been the lucky

★ ★ ★ ★ ★ ★ ★ ★ ★ ★ ★ ★ ★ ★ ★

Secretary of the Navy James V. Forrestal was responsible for choosing the *Missouri*, one of the four largest battleships in the world, as the site for the surrender ceremonies. It was a choice that pleased President Truman. Besides being a symbol of American strength, the *Missouri* was named after Truman's home state and had been christened by his daughter, Margaret.

ones. Many thousands who survived the blast suffered from radiation sickness. Doctors found that the high doses of radiation people were exposed to caused a number of different problems. Damage to the immune system led to many kinds of illnesses. Damage to the cells produced a variety of cancers

Japanese officials on board the USS Missouri *formally surrender.*

A year after the bomb was dropped on Hiroshima, a young survivor returns to school.

as well as birth defects. Radiation can have effects for years and even generations.

What part did dropping the atomic bomb have on World War II? Was it necessary to drop an atomic bomb on Hiroshima and Nagasaki? As you have read, people differ in their opinions. Those who believe that dropping the atomic bomb was necessary make several points to support their view:

1. Without the atomic bomb, the Allies would have had to invade Japan. Dropping the bomb spared hundreds of thousands of soldiers' lives, and brought a quick end to the war.

2. The United States spent a tremendous amount of money developing the atomic bomb and was obligated to use it.

3. Japan was not trustworthy. The country was controlled by militarists who believed in death before surrender—no matter what.

4. Modern weapons changed the way wars were fought. Killing large numbers of civilians with a single bomb was no worse than killing large numbers of civilians with many smaller bombs.

People who believe that dropping the atomic bomb was not necessary use other points to support their view:

1. Japan was collapsing and would not have been able to continue the war much longer; an invasion would not have been needed.

2. Japan was making honest efforts to bring about a peace agreement.

3. President Truman was responding to the anti-Japanese feeling among Americans, and he did not want to risk losing public support.

4. President Truman was concerned about Soviet expansion and used the atomic bomb not to

For some Japanese soldiers, the war did not end on September 2, 1945. On tiny, remote islands in the Pacific, small groups of Japanese soldiers, some unaware the war had ended, continued to hide out for years after their country had surrendered. On one of the Mariana Islands, 19 Japanese surrendered in 1951. Two Japanese soldiers held out on a small Philippine island until they were discovered in 1972. One of them was killed by Philippine police; the other hid in the forest until his former commanding officer convinced him to give up in 1974, nearly 30 years after the war had ended!

end the war but to intimidate the Soviets with a show of American military strength.

Which side is correct? Either side might be correct, or perhaps the answer lies somewhere in between the two. You have read the arguments. Now consider them carefully. What do you think?

> Not all the results of World War II were negative. The war helped bring about positive changes as well. One of these changes was the formation of an international organization of countries. In 1945 the United Nations (UN) was created by 51 countries from around the world to "save succeeding generations from the scourge of war, which twice in our lifetime has brought untold sorrow to mankind." While the UN has not eliminated armed conflict, it has been a strong force in promoting peace and justice throughout the world.
>
> Another positive contribution of the war is the Peace Day celebration that is held on August 6 every year in the Peace Memorial Park in Hiroshima. Thousands of people from all over the world visit Hiroshima to remember the day the atomic bomb was dropped and to join together in their hope that such a tragedy will never happen again.

Peace Day in Hiroshima: Paper lanterns drift along the water, symbolizing the souls of the bomb victims.

71

★ ★ ★ Time Line ★ ★ ★

1930s Japan takes over territories in Asia

1939 **September 1** Germany invades Poland; World War II begins

1940 **September 27** Japan, Germany, and Italy sign the Tripartite Pact

1941 **July 26** United States stops trade with Japan

December 7 Japan attacks American bases at Pearl Harbor

December 8 United States declares war on Japan; enters World War II

1942 **January 6** President Roosevelt announces his "victory program" to produce weapons and materials to win the war

March Japanese-Americans living on the West Coast are sent to "relocation" camps

April 9 American and Filipino troops surrender on Bataan; Death March begins

June 6 Japan suffers its worse naval loss at the Battle of Midway

1944   **October 23** Kamikaze missions begin at the Battle of Leyte Gulf in the Philippines

November 7 Roosevelt is elected to a fourth term as president

1945   **February 4–11** Roosevelt, Churchill, and Stalin meet at Yalta; Soviets agree to enter war with Japan

March 10 American planes firebomb Tokyo

March 26 Japan is defeated at Iwo Jima

April 12 Franklin Roosevelt dies; Harry Truman becomes president

June 21 Japan is defeated at Okinawa

July 16 U.S. successfully tests first atomic bomb, at Alamogordo, New Mexico

July 17–August 2 Truman, Churchill, and Stalin meet at Potsdam

August 6 U.S. drops an atomic bomb on Hiroshima

August 8 Soviets declare war on Japan; invade Manchuria

August 9 U.S. drops an atomic bomb on Nagasaki; Japanese leaders agree to surrender

August 15 Emperor Hirohito's surrender message is broadcast to the people of Japan

September 2 Formal surrender ceremonies take place on board the USS *Missouri*

October 24 United Nations is established

★ ★ ★ Glossary ★ ★ ★

Allies—Great Britain, the United States, France, the Soviet Union, and other countries that joined against Japan, Germany, and Italy during World War II

Axis—The alliance of Japan, Germany, and Italy during World War II

Bushido—An ancient Japanese warrior code

casualties—People killed or wounded

cerebral hemorrhage—Burst blood vessels in the brain

chain reaction—A series of chemical reactions in which the products of each reaction start new reactions

condensation—The change from a gas to a liquid

cruiser—A small, fast warship with few guns

descendant—An individual proceeding from an ancestor

destroyer—A medium-sized warship, armed with guns and torpedoes

dictatorship—A country ruled by a person or small group of people with absolute power and unlimited authority

diplomatically—According to the rules of diplomacy; using words rather than weapons

fallout—Tiny radioactive particles that fall to the earth following a nuclear explosion

isolationist—One who is unwilling to get involved in matters outside one's own country

kamikazes—Japanese soldiers who made suicide crash attacks

leukemia—Cancer of the blood

militarists—Japanese leaders who wanted to expand their country's territory by military means

navigator—A person who directs the course of an airplane or ship and who keeps track of its location

neutron—A particle in the nucleus of an atom that has no electric charge

radiation—Rays and particles given off by radioactive elements

radioactive—Spontaneously emitting rays or particles

unconditional—Without conditions or limitations; absolute

uranium—A heavy, silver-white metal used to make atomic weapons

vaporized—Changed into a streamlike mist

★ For Further Reading ★

If you would like to learn more about World War II and the dropping of the atomic bomb, here are some articles and books that were helpful in creating *Hiroshima: Fifty Years of Debate.*

ARTICLES

Alperovitz, Gar. "Why the United States Dropped the Bomb." *Technology Review* (August/September 1990).

Granfeld, Mary. "Hiroshima's Lost Americans." *People* (August 6, 1990).

Isaacson, Walter. "Why Did We Drop the Bomb?" *Time* (August 19, 1985).

Mitchell, Greg. "The Photographer and the Flash." *Progressive* (August 1990).

Morris, Mary. "Hiroshima: Peace Enshrined." *New York Times Magazine* (March 3, 1991).

Morrison, Samuel Eliot. "Why Japan Surrendered." *Atlantic Monthly* (October 1960).

Stimson, Henry. "The Decision to Use the Atomic Bomb." *Harper's* (February 1947).

BOOKS

Campbell, John, ed. *The Experience of World War II.* New York: Oxford University Press, 1989.

Claypool, Jane. *Turning Points of World War II: Hiroshima and Nagasaki.* New York: Franklin Watts, 1984.

Coerr, Eleanor. *Sadako and the Thousand Paper Cranes.* New York: Dell, 1977.

Ferrall, Robert H. *Off the Record: The Private Papers of Harry S Truman.* New York: Harper & Row, 1980.

Hersey, John. *Hiroshima.* New York: Knopf, 1946.

Hoyt, Edwin P. *Japan's War.* New York: McGraw-Hill, 1986.

Maruki, Toshi. *Hiroshima No Pika.* New York: Lothrop, Lee & Shepard, 1980 (pb).

Miller, Merle. *Plain Speaking.* New York: Berkley, 1973.

Morimoto, Junko. *My Hiroshima.* New York: Viking Penguin, 1987 (pb).

Nardo, Don. *World War II: The War in the Pacific.* San Diego: Lucent Books, 1991.

Reader's Digest Association, ed., *The World at Arms: The Reader's Digest Illustrated History of World War II.* London: Reader's Digest Association, 1989.

Spector, Ronald H. *Eagle Against the Sun.* New York: Macmillan, 1985.

Wheeler, Keith. *The Fall of Japan.* Chicago: Time-Life, 1983.

★ ★ ★ ★ Index ★ ★ ★ ★

★ ★ About the Author ★ ★

Robert Young has been fascinated with the past ever since he walked through the house in which George Washington once lived. Besides writing books that help bring history alive, Robert job-shares a teaching position and visits schools to speak about writing. The author of ten books for children and teachers, Robert lives in Eugene, Oregon, with his wife, Sara, and their son, Tyler.

WASHINGTON'S FAREWELL ADDRESS:
THE VIEW FROM THE 20th CENTURY

Washington's Farewell Address:
THE VIEW FROM THE 20th CENTURY

Edited with an Introduction by
Burton Ira Kaufman

Chicago | Quadrangle Books | 1969

Library of Congress Catalog Card Number: 72-84110

Grateful acknowledgement is made to publishers and individuals
as noted herein for permission to reprint copyrighted materials.

INTRODUCTION

It is a popular view among historians that George Washington was concerned more with domestic matters during his first term, and more with foreign affairs during his second. In many ways this view is valid. When Washington first became President in 1789, he faced the Herculean task of organizing the government with only those institutions established during the Confederation as guidelines. Moreover, he had to determine the basic policies of the new nation at a critical juncture in its history. In both tasks he was generally successful. During his first four years in office Washington defined the role of the executive, formulated the functions of the Cabinet, and set administrative precedents which still operate today. At the same time his administration established an elaborate judicial system, organized the nation's finances on a sound basis, encouraged manufacturing, and fostered the growth of commerce. Matters of foreign policy during his first term were limited essentially to issues springing from the Revolution. These included England's refusal to evacuate her posts in the Northwest Territory, Spain's encroachments on soil claimed by the United States in the Southwest, and that same nation's refusal to open the Mississippi River to American commerce. Except for a brief threat of war in 1790 over rival English and Spanish claims to Nookta Sound, one which could have resulted in the trespass of alien troops across American soil, the administration faced no serious international crisis.

During Washington's second administration, however, the situation was quite different. The French Revolution, which had begun with the storming of the Bastille in 1789, erupted into a major European conflict. In 1792 the French officially transformed their nation into a republic, went to war against Austria, and declared the "war of peoples against all kings." The following year they guillotined their deposed monarch, Louis XVI, and added England and Spain to their list of enemies. Since the United States was allied to France by a treaty of 1778, this European conflagration, in its threat to involve the new nation, for the next three years (1793-96) constituted the principal problem facing Washington's second administration.

Despite the emphasis placed on domestic issues in Washington's first term and on foreign issues in his second, these two areas of concern were naturally and constantly interrelated. They both posed similar questions about the development of the United States, including ones on the role of popular government and the powers of central administration. In fact, the country was sharply divided over these issues. One group, the Federalists, was interested primarily in establishing order and stability. Favoring strong central government, they supported only administration programs which they expected would keep the nation on a sound economic and political basis. Thus, while many of them had at first welcomed the French Revolution, they were quickly horrified by the execution of Louis XVI and the reign of terror (and chaos) which followed. They came to back England and her allies in their struggle against France. Not only did the Federalists wish to draw economically closer to the former mother country, they felt that the government in London represented the forces of order in contrast to the mob rule of France.

The Anti-Federalists, on the other hand, regarded administration programs as undemocratic and unconstitutional because, by placing great power in the hands of a few, they deprived local government of much of its influence. Emphasizing liberty rather than authority, they opposed any strong national government which, they feared, would escape from popular control and endanger individual liberties. Thus the Anti-Federalists were sympathetic to the French Revolution because they associated it with the cause of liberty. Retaining their attachment to France despite Louis XVI's execution, they supported that country in her battle against England.

War in Europe, then, merely exacerbated political differences already evident during Washington's first administration and furthered the cleavage between Federalists and Anti-Federalists. In so doing, it also prepared the way for the formation of political parties. Washington himself was greatly disturbed by the growing division within the nation. While his programs made him seem more sympathetic to the Federalist viewpoint, he actually tried to steer a middle course between the two opposing groups. In foreign policy, particularly in regard to the European struggle, he attempted to maintain strict neutrality. In fact, in 1793 he issued a proclamation of neutrality in which he made clear his administration's determination, despite the treaty commitments to France, not to become involved in the war.

Washington's neutralist intentions notwithstanding, the President appeared to Anti-Federalists to be drawing closer to England. Any doubt of this inclination seemed removed by the signing of Jay's Treaty in 1794. Washington had sent Chief Justice John Jay to England in an attempt to settle major differences with the London government and avert the possibility of war. Although peace was assured as a result of the treaty, opponents of the agreement, particularly Anti-Federalists, regarded it as a total betrayal of America's interests. Internal dissension increased and the President himself became the target of personal abuse.

Washington had considered retirement ever since 1792. While he had been persuaded by James Madison and others to accept a second term as President, the attacks on his administration convinced him not to seek reelection again. Determined to retire, he decided to deliver a farewell address to the nation before his successor was chosen. It was given to the newspapers on September 19, 1796. Referring in his address to the partisanship and division in the country, he counseled against party strife, sectional animosity, and foreign intrigue. "The Great Rule of Conduct for us, in regard to foreign nations," he remarked,

> is in extending our commercial relations to have with them as little *political* connection as possible.—So far as we have already formed engagements let them be fulfilled, with perfect good faith. Here let us stop.

Almost immediately, the first President's valedictory became one of the major documents of American foreign policy. This development was not surprising. Even before he died, Washington was being transformed into a mythical figure. He became the father of his country, the model of nobility and perfect character, and the fountain of eternal wisdom. Following his death in 1799 and throughout the nineteenth century, his biographers perpetuated the Washington myth, regarding his writings as absolute truth.

Thus, as Washington's final testament to the nation, his Farewell Address received especial notice. It was constantly used to justify a policy of total abstention from world affairs. Again, this use was not surprising. Concerned with the development of their own nation, most nineteenth-century Americans preferred to have few official ties with the rest of the world. They found ample support for that position in Washington's warnings against political alliances. By the end of the nineteenth century, historians and diplomats alike considered the President's valedictory as the classic statement of American isolationism.

Even during this time, however, a few statesmen who expected the United States to play a leading role in world affairs refused to accept the limitations imposed by traditional interpretations of the Farewell Address. They questioned the assumption that Washington had intended his country indefinitely to pursue an isolationist policy. This view received increased attention during the last decade of the nineteenth century. America was then on the threshold of the imperialist venture which finally resulted in the acquisition of the Philippine Islands. Those who favored a greater international role for the United States, in some cases including retention of the Philippines, rejected the isolationists' contention that they were advocating a course which violated Washington's doctrines. Aware of the importance Americans still attached to the Farewell Address, they even cited it as support of their program of overseas expansion.

While Washington's valedictory continued to be used during the twentieth century by opponents of America's international commitments, the nation's emergence as a world power led numerous internationally minded historians to challenge that position. In fact, they were so successful in destroying the myths attached to Washington's address that it is now commonplace to view it as something less than a plea against world involvement. Because the first President spoke in generalities, however, these same historians continued to argue over what he really meant. Was he speaking to future generations or addressing himself to present circumstances? Was he articulating a broad program or a limited policy? Indeed, was he concerned primarily with foreign affairs or with the domestic political struggle between Federalists and Anti-Federalists?

Important in themselves, these questions have far-reaching implications about the basis of early American foreign policy. Until recently the conduct of diplomacy during the early republic has been treated in largely negative terms. Moreover, while most historians have generally regarded the Federalist era as the golden age of American statesmanship, they have viewed its diplomatic endeavors in a political vacuum. In their interpretation, America merely reacted to the power struggle between England, Spain, and France. Europe's distresses became this country's advantages. But while America was able passively to capitalize on the European situation, it lacked any firm guidelines on which to conduct an active policy (except perhaps to remain aloof from European imbroglios—again, however, essentially a passive course). Thus the Federalist era established no framework on which to base future foreign policy.

Other studies of the Federalist period, especially more recent ones, emphasize influences on the nation's early policy-makers different from the European situation in the late eighteenth and early nineteenth centuries. Several writers stress the importance of the domestic political situation, particularly the bitter struggle between Federalists and Anti-Federalists. In contrast, a number of scholars suggest that distinct attitudes toward foreign affairs had been developing since the colonial period; these attitudes, they maintain, eventually became the basis for American foreign

policy. Unlike traditional interpretations, this view emphasizes
a conceptual framework for the conduct of foreign policy. But
even those sharing this view disagree about the factors which
influenced the nation's diplomats. Some scholars stress the importance of American nationalism; others the influence of British
mercantilism; and still others the impact of enlightenment ideas.

All these different viewpoints are reflected in twentieth-century
interpretations of the Farewell Address. As a result, the debate
over its meaning involves basic questions about the nature of
early American foreign policy. Were early American diplomats
merely reacting to European distresses? Were political considerations or other domestic matters of paramount importance in policy
formulation? Were the foundations of later American diplomacy
already evident in the country's early history? If so, on what
assumptions did they rest?

Another issue related to the debate over the meaning of the
Farewell Address concerns Washington's character and his role
in American history. While most scholars regard the first President as one of the nation's finest leaders, some emphasize his
virtues of character over his impact on the events of his day
(with, of course, the exception of his command of the Revolutionary armies.) His speeches and correspondence, most of which
reflect his determination to follow a middle course between, even
conciliate, opposing political factions, appear to these historians
to be replete with superficial counsel and platitudes; they seem
to lack the vision, depth, and scope of interest evident in the
writings of Alexander Hamilton, Thomas Jefferson, and James
Madison. These historians therefore admire Washington's sense
of purpose and sobriety at a time when the nation's future was
in doubt, but they find him far less significant as a creative historical figure, especially when compared with the other founding
fathers.

Treatment of Washington in this fashion is also reflected in
twentieth-century interpretations of his Farewell Address. In delivering his valedictory, the first President is viewed alternately
as an advocate of a traditional policy of aloofness from European affairs; as a Federalist tool in their campaign against the
Anti-Federalists; or as a parrot of ideas formulated by Hamilton,
the real author of the address. In none of these cases is Washington regarded as an innovative leader of the nation.

Those writers who emphasize the influence of nationalism or mercantile thought on the nation's foreign policy portray the first President in yet another light. They relate their interpretation of policy to the nation's concern with westward expansion. Since Washington's interest in the settlement and development of the West has been long documented, these historians regard him more favorably than most. In some cases, they even consider him a visionary who had a far-reaching sense of America's destiny in the world. Several of those holding this view, including this writer, interpret the Farwell Address as an expression of Washington's ideas on the new nation's future.

Debate over Washington's Farewell Address thus involves consideration of his impact on history. Was he a President of high character but little imagination who followed policy conceived by others? Was he a political figurehead manipulated by the real power behind the throne, Alexander Hamilton? Or was he an imaginative figure, one with a well-defined concept of the course his nation should follow which he both pursued during his own administration and urged the nation to follow after he left office?

The selections in this volume cover the various interpretations of the Farewell Address since the United States emerged as a world power at the turn of this century. They are arranged chronologically in three sections, each with an introduction which places the essays in historiographical perspective.

CONTENTS

The Farewell Address

United States, September 17, 1796.

Friends and Fellow-Citizens:

The period for a new election of a citizen to administer the Executive Government of the United States being not far distant, and the time actually arrived when your thoughts must be employed in designating the person who is to be clothed with that important trust, it appears to me proper, especially as it may conduce to a more distinct expression of the public voice, that I should now apprise you of the resolution I have formed to decline being considered among the number of those out of whom a choice is to be made.

I beg you at the same time to do me the justice to be assured that this resolution has not been taken without a strict regard to all the considerations appertaining to the relation which binds a dutiful citizen to his country; and that in withdrawing the tender of service, which silence in my situation might imply, I am influenced by no diminution of zeal for your future interest, no deficiency of grateful respect for your past kindness, but am supported by a full conviction that the step is compatible with both.

The acceptance of and continuance hitherto in the office to which your suffrages have twice called me have been a uniform sacrifice of inclination to the opinion of duty and to a deference for what appeared to be your desire. I constantly hoped that it would have been much earlier in my power, consistently with motives which I was not at liberty to disregard, to return to that retirement from which I had been reluctantly drawn. The strength of my inclination to do this previous to the last election had even led to the preparation of an address to declare it to you; but mature reflection on the then perplexed and critical posture of our affairs with foreign nations, and the unanimous advice of persons entitled to my confidence, impelled me to abandon the idea.

I rejoice that the state of your concerns, external as well as internal, no longer renders the pursuit of inclination incompatible with the sentiment of duty or propriety, and am persuaded, whatever partiality may be retained for my services, that in the present circumstances of our country you will not disapprove my determination to retire.

The impressions with which I first undertook the arduous trust were explained on the proper occasion. In the discharge of this trust I will only say that I have, with good intentions, contributed toward the organization and administration of the Government the best exertions of which a very fallible judgment was capable. Not unconscious in the outset of the inferiority of my qualifications, experience in my own eyes, perhaps still more in the eyes of others, has strengthened the motives to diffidence of myself; and every day the increasing weight of years admonishes me more and more that the shade of retirement is as necessary to me as it will be welcome. Satisfied that if any circumstances have given peculiar value to my services they were temporary, I have the consolation to believe that, while choice and prudence invite me to quit the political scene, patriotism does not forbid it.

In looking forward to the moment which is intended to terminate the career of my political life my feelings do not permit me to suspend the deep acknowledgment of that debt of gratitude which I owe to my beloved country for the many honors it has conferred upon me; still more for the steadfast confidence with which it has supported me, and for the opportunities I have thence enjoyed of manifesting my inviolable attachment by services faithful and persevering, though in usefulness unequal to my zeal. If benefits have resulted to our country from these services, let it always be remembered to your praise and as an instructive example in our annals that under circumstances in which the passions, agitated in every direction, were liable to mislead; amidst appearances sometimes dubious; vicissitudes of fortune often discouraging; in situations in which not unfrequently want of success has countenanced the spirit of criticism, the constancy of your support was the essential prop of the efforts and a guaranty of the plans by which they were effected. Profoundly penetrated with this idea, I shall carry it with me to my grave as a strong incitement to unceasing vows that Heaven may continue to you the choicest tokens of its beneficence; that your union and brotherly affection may be perpetual; that the free Constitution which is the work of your hands may be sacredly maintained; that its administration in every department may be stamped with wisdom and virtue; that, in fine, the happiness of the people of these States, under the auspices of liberty, may be made complete by so careful a preservation and so prudent a use of this blessing as will acquire to them the glory of recommending it to the applause, the affection, and adoption of every nation which is yet a stranger to it.

Here, perhaps, I ought to stop. But a solicitude for your welfare which can not end but with my life, and the apprehension of danger natural to that solicitude, urge me on an occasion like the present to offer to your solemn contemplation and to recommend to your frequent review some sentiments which are the result of much reflection, of no inconsiderable observation, and which appear to me all important to the permanency of your felicity as a people. These will be offered to you with the more freedom as you can only see in them the disinterested warnings of a parting friend, who can possibly have no personal motive to bias his counsel. Nor can I forget as an encouragement to it your indulgent reception of my sentiments on a former and not dissimilar occasion.

Interwoven as is the love of liberty with every ligament of your hearts, no recommendation of mine is necessary to fortify or confirm the attachment.

The unity of government which constitutes you one people is also now dear to you. It is justly so, for it is a main pillar in the edifice of your real independence, the support of your tranquillity at home, your peace abroad, of your safety, of your prosperity, of that very liberty which you so highly prize. But as it is easy to foresee that from different causes and from different quarters much pains will be taken, many artifices employed, to weaken in your minds the conviction of this truth, as this is the point in your political fortress against which the batteries of internal and external enemies will be most constantly and actively (though often covertly and insidiously) directed, it is of infinite moment that you should properly estimate the immense value of your national union to your collective and individual happiness; that you should cherish a cordial, habitual, and immovable attachment to it; accustoming yourselves to think and speak of it as of the palladium of your political safety and prosperity; watching for its preservation with jealous anxiety; discountenancing whatever may suggest even a suspicion that it can in any event be abandoned, and indignantly frowning upon the first dawning of every attempt to alienate any portion of our country from the rest or to enfeeble the sacred ties which now link together the various parts.

For this you have every inducement of sympathy and interest. Citizens by birth or choice of a common country, that country has a right to concentrate your affections. The name of American, which belongs to you in your national capacity, must always exalt the just pride of patriotism more than any appellation derived from local discriminations. With slight shades of difference, you have the same religion, manners, habits, and political principles. You have in a common cause fought and triumphed together. The independence and liberty you possess are the work of joint councils and joint efforts, of common dangers, sufferings, and successes.

But these considerations, however powerfully they address themselves to your sensibility, are greatly outweighed by those which apply more immediately to your interest. Here every portion of our country finds the most commanding motives for carefully guarding and preserving the union of the whole.

The *North,* in an unrestrained intercourse with the *South,* protected by the equal laws of a common government, finds in the productions of the latter great additional resources of maritime and commercial enterprise and precious materials of manufacturing industry. The *South,* in the same intercourse, benefiting by the same agency of the *North,* sees its agriculture grow and its commerce expand. Turning partly into its own channels the seamen of the *North,* it finds its particular navigation invigorated; and while it contributes in different ways to nourish and increase the general mass of the national navigation, it looks forward to the protection of a maritime strength to which itself is unequally adapted. The *East,* in a like intercourse with the *West,* already finds, and in the progressive improvement of interior communications by land and water will more and more find, a valuable vent for the commodities which it brings from abroad or manufactures at home. The *West* derives from the *East* supplies requisite to its growth and comfort, and what is perhaps of still greater consequence, it must of necessity owe the *secure* enjoyment of indispensable *outlets* for its own productions to the weight, influence, and the future maritime strength of the Atlantic side of the Union, directed by an indissoluble community of interest as *one nation.* Any other tenure by which the *West* can hold this essential advantage, whether derived from its own separate strength or from an apostate and unnatural connection with any foreign power, must be intrinsically precarious.

While, then, every part of our country thus feels an immediate and particular interest in union, all the parts combined can not fail to find in the united mass of means and efforts greater strength, greater resource, proportionably greater security from external danger, a less frequent interruption of their peace by foreign nations, and what is of inestimable value, they must derive from union an exemption from those broils and wars between themselves which so frequently afflict neighboring countries not tied together by the same governments, which their own rivalships alone would be sufficient to produce, but which opposite foreign alliances, attachments, and intrigues would stimulate and embitter. Hence, likewise, they will avoid the necessity of those overgrown military establishments which, under any form of government, are inauspicious to liberty, and which are to be regarded as particularly hostile to republican liberty. In this sense it is that your union ought to be considered as a main prop of your liberty, and that the love of the one ought to endear to you the preservation of the other.

These considerations speak a persuasive language to every reflecting and virtuous mind, and exhibit the continuance of the union as a primary object of patriotic desire. Is there a doubt whether a common government can embrace so large a sphere? Let experience solve it. To listen to mere speculation in such a case were criminal. We are authorized to hope that a proper organization of the whole, with the auxiliary agency of governments for the respective subdivisions, will afford a happy issue to the experiment. It is well worth a fair and full experiment. With such powerful and obvious motives to union affecting all parts of our country, while experience shall not have demonstrated its impracticability, there will always be reason to distrust the patriotism of those who in any quarter may endeavor to weaken its bands.

In contemplating the causes which may disturb our union it occurs as matter of serious concern that any ground should have been furnished for characterizing parties by *geographical* discriminations—*Northern* and *Southern, Atlantic,* and *Western*—whence designing men may endeavor to excite a belief that there is a real difference of local interests and views. One of the expedients of party to acquire influence within particular districts is to misrepresent the opinions and aims of other districts. You can not shield yourselves too much against the jealousies and heartburnings which spring from these misrepresentations; they tend to render alien to each other those who ought to be bound together by fraternal affection. The inhabitants of our Western country have lately had a useful lesson on this head. They have seen in the negotiation by the Executive and in the unanimous ratification by the Senate of the treaty with Spain, and in the universal satisfaction at that event throughout the United States, a decisive proof how unfounded were the suspicions propagated among them of a policy in the General Government and in the Atlantic States unfriendly to their interests in regard to the Mississippi. They have been witnesses to the formation of two treaties—that with Great Britain and that with Spain—which secure to them everything they could desire in respect to our foreign relations toward confirming their prosperity. Will it not be their wisdom to rely for the preservation of these advantages on the union by which they were procured? Will they not henceforth be deaf to those advisers, if such there are, who would sever them from their brethren and connect them with aliens?

To the efficacy and permanency of your union a government for the whole is indispensable. No alliances, however strict, between the parts can be an adequate substitute. They must inevitably experience the infractions and interruptions which all alliances in all times have experienced. Sensible of this momentous truth, you have improved upon your first essay by the adoption of a Constitution of Government better calculated than your former for an intimate union and for the efficacious management of your common concerns. This Government, the offspring of our own choice, uninfluenced and unawed, adopted upon full investigation and mature deliberation, completely free in its principles, in the distribution of its powers, uniting security with energy, and containing within itself a provision for its own amendment, has a just claim to your confidence and your support. Respect for its authority, compliance with its laws, acquiescence in its measures, are duties enjoined by the fundamental maxims of true liberty. The basis of our political systems is the right of the people to make and to alter their constitutions of government. But the constitution which at any time exists till changed by an explicit and authentic act of the whole people is sacredly obligatory upon all. The very idea of the power and the right of the people to establish government presupposes the duty of every individual to obey the established government.

All obstructions to the execution of the laws, all combinations and associations, under whatever plausible character, with the real design to direct, control, counteract, or awe the regular deliberation and action of the constituted authorities, are destructive of this fundamental principle and of fatal tendency. They serve to organize faction; to give it an artificial and extraordinary force; to put in the place of the delegated will of the nation the will of a party, often a small but artful and enterprising minority of the community, and, according to the alternate triumphs of different parties, to make the public administration the mirror of ill-concerted and incongruous projects of faction rather than the organ of consistent and wholesome plans, digested by common counsels and modified by mutual interests.

However combinations and associations of the above description may now and then answer popular ends, they are likely in the course of time and things to become potent engines by which cunning, ambitious, and unprincipled men will be enabled to subvert the power of the people, and to usurp for themselves the reins of government, destroying afterwards the very engines which have lifted them to unjust dominion.

Toward the preservation of your Government and the permanency of your present happy state, it is requisite not only that you steadily discountenance irregular oppositions to its acknowledged authority, but also that you resist with care the spirit of innovation upon its principles, however specious the pretexts. One method of assault may be to effect in the forms of the Constitution alterations which will impair the energy of the system, and thus to undermine what can not be directly overthrown. In all the changes to which you may be invited remember that time and habit are at least as necessary to fix the true character of governments as of other human institutions; that experience is the surest standard by which to test the real tendency of the existing constitution of a country; that facility in changes upon the credit of mere hypothesis and opinion exposes to perpetual change, from the endless variety of hypothesis and opinion; and remember especially that for the efficient management of your common interests in a country so extensive as ours a government of as much vigor as is consistent with the perfect security of liberty is indispensable. Liberty itself will find in such a government, with powers properly distributed and adjusted, its surest guardian. It is, indeed, little else than a name where the government is too feeble to withstand the enterprises of faction, to confine each member of the society within the limits prescribed by the laws, and to maintain all in the secure and tranquil enjoyment of the rights of person and property.

I have already intimated to you the danger of parties in the State, with particular reference to the founding of them on geographical discriminations. Let me now take a more comprehensive view, and warn you in the most solemn manner against the baneful effects of the spirit of party generally.

This spirit, unfortunately, is inseparable from our nature, having its root in the strongest passions of the human mind. It exists under different shapes in all governments, more or less stifled, controlled, or repressed; but in those of the popular form it is seen in its greatest rankness and is truly their worst enemy.

The alternate domination of one faction over another, sharpened by the spirit of revenge natural to party dissension, which in different ages and countries has perpetrated the most horrid enormities, is itself a frightful despotism. But this leads at length to a more formal and permanent despotism. The disorders and miseries which result gradually incline the minds of men to seek security and repose in the absolute power of an individual, and sooner or later the chief of some prevailing faction, more able or more fortunate than his competitors, turns this disposition to the purposes of his own elevation on the ruins of public liberty.

Without looking forward to an extremity of this kind (which nevertheless ought not to be entirely out of sight), the common and continual mischiefs of the spirit of party are sufficient to make it the interest and duty of a wise people to discourage and restrain it.

It serves always to distract the public councils and enfeeble the public administration. It agitates the community with ill-founded jealousies and false alarms; kindles the animosity of one part against another; foments occasionally riot and insurrection. It opens the door to foreign influence and corruption, which find a facilitated access to the government itself through the channels of party passion. Thus the policy and the will of one country are subjected to the policy and will of another.

There is an opinion that parties in free countries are useful checks upon the administration of the government, and serve to keep alive the spirit of liberty. This within certain limits is probably true; and in governments of a monarchical cast patriotism may look with indulgence, if not with favor, upon the spirit of party. But in those of the popular character, in governments purely elective, it is a spirit not to be encouraged. From their natural tendency it is certain there will always be enough of that spirit for every salutary purpose; and there being constant danger of excess, the effort ought to be by force of public opinion to mitigate and assuage it. A fire not to be quenched, it demands a uniform vigilance to prevent its bursting into a flame, lest, instead of warming, it should consume.

It is important, likewise, that the habits of thinking in a free country should inspire caution in those intrusted with its administration to confine themselves within their respective constitutional spheres, avoiding in the exercise of the powers of one department to encroach upon another. The spirit of encroachment tends to consolidate the powers of all the departments in one, and thus to create whatever the form of government, a real despotism. A just estimate of that love of power and proneness to abuse it which predominates in the human heart is sufficient to satisfy us of the truth of this position. The necessity of reciprocal checks in the exercise of political power, by dividing and distributing it into different depositories, and constituting each the guardian of the public weal against invasion by the others, has been evinced by experiments ancient and modern, some of them in our country and under our own eyes. To preserve them must be as necessary as to institute them. If in the opinion of the people the distribution or modification of the constitutional powers be in any particular wrong, let it be corrected by an amendment in the way which the Constitution designates. But let there be no change by usurpation; for though this in one instance may be the instrument of good, it is the customary weapon by which free governments are destroyed. The precedent must always greatly overbalance in permanent evil any partial or transient benefit which the use can at any time yield.

Of all the dispositions and habits which lead to political prosperity, religion and morality are indispensable supports. In vain would that man claim the tribute of patriotism who should labor to subvert these great pillars of human happiness—these firmest props of the duties of men and citizens. The mere politician, equally with the pious man, ought to respect and to cherish them. A volume could not trace all their connections with private and public felicity. Let it simply be asked, Where is the security for property, for reputation, for life, if the sense of religious obligation *desert* the oaths which are the instruments of investigation in courts of justice? And let us with caution indulge the supposition that morality can be maintained without religion. Whatever may be conceded to the influence of refined education on minds of peculiar structure, reason and experience both forbid us to expect that national morality can prevail in exclusion of religious principle.

It is substantially true that virtue or morality is a necessary spring of popular government. The rule indeed extends with more or less force to every species of free government. Who that is a sincere friend to it can look with indifference upon attempts to shake the foundation of the fabric? Promote, then, as an object of primary importance, institutions for the general diffusion of knowledge. In proportion as the structure of a government gives force to public opinion, it is essential that public opinion should be enlightened.

As a very important source of strength and security, cherish public credit. One method of preserving it is to use it as sparingly as possible, avoiding occasions of expense by cultivating peace, but remembering also that timely disbursements to prepare for danger frequently prevent much greater disbursements to repel it; avoiding likewise the accumulation of debt, not only by shunning occasions of expense, but by vigorous exertions in time of peace to discharge the debts which unavoidable wars have occasioned, not ungenerously throwing upon posterity the burden which we ourselves ought to bear. The execution of these maxims belongs to your representatives; but it is necessary that public opinion should cooperate. To facilitate to them the performance of their duty it is essential that you should practically bear in mind that toward the payment of debts there must be revenue; that to have revenue there must be taxes; that no taxes can be devised which are not more or less inconvenient and unpleasant; that the intrinsic embarrassment inseparable from the selection of the proper objects (which is always a choice of difficulties), ought to be a decisive motive for a candid construction of the conduct of the Government in making it, and for a spirit of acquiescence in the measures for obtaining revenue which the public exigencies may at any time dictate.

Observe good faith and justice toward all nations. Cultivate peace and harmony with all. Religion and morality enjoin this conduct. And can it be that good policy does not equally enjoin it? It will be worthy of a free, enlightened, and at no distant period a great nation to give to mankind the magnanimous and too novel example of a people always guided by an exalted justice and benevolence. Who can doubt that in the course of time and things the fruits of such a plan would richly repay any temporary advantages which might be lost by a steady adherence to it? Can it be that Providence has not connected the permanent felicity of a nation with its virtue? The experiment, at least, is recommended by every sentiment which ennobles human nature. Alas! is it rendered impossible by its vices?

In the execution of such a plan nothing is more essential than that permanent, inveterate antipathies against particular nations and passionate attachments for others should be excluded, and that in place of them just and amicable feelings toward all should be cultivated. *The nation which indulges toward another an habitual hatred or an habitual fondness is in some degree a slave. It is a slave to its animosity or to its affection, either of which is sufficient to lead it astray from its duty and its interest.* Antipathy in one nation against another disposes each more readily to offer insult and injury, to lay hold of slight causes of umbrage, and to be haughty and intractable when accidental or trifling occasions of dispute occur.

Hence frequent collisions, obstinate, envenomed, and bloody contests. The nation prompted by ill will and resentment sometimes impels to war the government contrary to the best calculations of policy. The government sometimes participates in the national propensity, and adopts through passion what reason would reject. At other times it makes the animosity of the nation subservient to projects of hostility, instigated by pride, ambition, and other sinister and pernicious motives. The peace often, sometimes perhaps the liberty, of nations has been the victim.

So, likewise, a passionate attachment of one nation for another produces a variety of evils. Sympathy for the favorite nation, facilitating the illusion of an imaginary common interest in cases where no real common interest exists, and infusing into one the enmities of the other, betrays the former into a participation in the quarrels and wars of the latter without adequate inducement or justification. It leads also to concessions to the favorite nation of privileges denied to others, which is apt doubly to injure the nation making the concessions by unnecessarily parting with what ought to have been retained, and by exciting jealousy, ill will, and a disposition to retaliate in the parties from whom equal privileges are withheld; and it gives to ambitious, corrupted, or deluded citizens (who devote themselves to the favorite nation) facility to betray or sacrifice the interests of their own country without odium, sometimes even with popularity, gilding with the appearances of a virtuous sense of obligation, a commendable deference for public opinion, or a laudable zeal for public good the base or foolish compliances of ambition, corruption, or infatuation.

As avenues to foreign influence in innumerable ways, such attachments are particularly alarming to the truly enlightened and independent patriot. How many opportunities do they afford to tamper with domestic factions, to practice the arts of seduction, to mislead public opinion, to influence or awe the public councils! Such an attachment of a small or weak toward a great and powerful nation dooms the former to be the satellite of the latter. Against the insidious wiles of foreign influence (I conjure you to believe me, fellow-citizens) the jealousy of a free people ought to be *constantly* awake, since history and experience prove that foreign influence is one of the most baneful foes of republican government. But that jealousy, to be useful, must be impartial, else it becomes the instrument of the very influence to be avoided, instead of a defense against it. Excessive partiality for one foreign nation and excessive dislike of another cause those whom they actuate to see danger only on one side, and serve to veil and even second the arts of influence on the other. Real patriots who may resist the intrigues of the favorite are liable to become suspected and odious, while its tools and dupes usurp the applause and confidence of the people to surrender their interests.

The great rule of conduct for us in regard to foreign nations is, in extending our commercial relations to have with them as little *political* connection as possible. So far as we have already formed engagements let them be fulfilled with perfect good faith. Here let us stop.

Europe has a set of primary interests which to us have none or a very remote relation. Hence she must be engaged in frequent controversies, the causes of which are essentially foreign to our concerns. Hence, therefore, it must be unwise in us to implicate ourselves by artificial ties in the ordinary vicissitudes of her politics or the ordinary combinations and collisions of her friendships or enmities.

Our detached and distant situation invites and enables us to pursue a different course. If we remain one people, under an efficient government, the period is not far off when we may defy material injury from external annoyance; when we may take such an attitude as· will cause the neutrality we may at any time resolve upon to be scrupulously respected; when belligerent nations, under the impossibility of making acquisitions upon us, will not lightly hazard giving us provocation; when we may choose peace or war, as our interest, guided by justice, shall counsel.

Why forego the advantages of so peculiar a situation? Why quit our own to stand upon foreign ground? Why, by interweaving our destiny with that of any part of Europe, entangle our peace and prosperity in the toils of European ambition, rivalship, interest, humor, or caprice?

It is our true policy to steer clear of permanent alliances with any portion of the foreign world, so far, I mean, as we are now at liberty to do it; for let me not be understood as capable of patronizing infidelity to existing engagements. I hold the maxim no less applicable to public than to private affairs that honesty is always the best policy. I repeat, therefore, let those engagements be observed in their genuine sense. But in my opinion it is unnecessary and would be unwise to extend them.

Taking care always to keep ourselves by suitable establishments on a respectable defensive posture, we may safely trust to temporary alliances for extraordinary emergencies.

Harmony, liberal intercourse with all nations are recommended by policy, humanity, and interest. But even our commercial policy should hold an equal and impartial hand, neither seeking nor granting exclusive favors or preferences; consulting the natural course of things; diffusing and diversifying by gentle means the streams of commerce, but forcing nothing; establishing with powers so disposed, in order to give trade a stable course, to define the rights of our merchants, and to enable the Government to support them, conventional rules of intercourse, the best that present circumstances and mutual opinion will permit, but temporary and liable to be from time to time abandoned or varied as experience and circumstances shall dictate; constantly keeping in view that it is folly in one nation to look for disinterested favors from another; that it must pay with a portion of its independence for whatever it may accept under that character; that by such acceptance it may place itself in the condition of having given equivalents for nominal favors, and yet of being reproached with ingratitude for not giving more. There can be no greater error than to expect or calculate upon real favors from nation to nation. It is an illusion which experience must cure, which a just pride ought to discard.

In offering to you, my countrymen, these counsels of an old and affectionate friend I dare not hope they will make the strong and lasting impression I could wish—that they will control the usual current of the passions or prevent our nation from running the course which has hitherto marked the destiny of nations. But if I may even flatter myself that they may be productive of some partial benefit, some occasional good—that they may now and then recur to moderate the fury of party spirit, to warn against the mischiefs of foreign intrigue, to guard against the impostures of pretended patriotism—this hope will be a full recompense for the solicitude for your welfare by which they have been dictated.

How far in the discharge of my official duties I have been guided by the principles which have been delineated the public records and other evidences of my conduct must witness to you and to the world. To myself, the assurance of my own conscience is that I have at least believed myself to be guided by them.

In relation to the still subsisting war in Europe my proclamation of the 22d of April, 1793, is the index to my plan. Sanctioned by your approving voice and by that of your representatives in both Houses of Congress, the spirit of that measure has continually governed me, uninfluenced by any attempts to deter or divert me from it.

After deliberate examination, with the aid of the best lights I could obtain, I was well satisfied that our country, under all the circumstances of the case, had a right to take, and was bound in duty and interest to take, a neutral position. Having taken it, I determined as far as should depend upon me to maintain it with moderation, perseverance, and firmness.

The considerations which respect the right to hold this conduct it is not necessary on this occasion to detail. I will only observe that, according to my understanding of the matter, that right, so far from being denied by any of the belligerent powers, has been virtually admitted by all.

The duty of holding a neutral conduct may be inferred, without anything more, from the obligation which justice and humanity impose on every nation, in cases in which it is free to act, to maintain inviolate the relations of peace and amity toward other nations.

The inducements of interest for observing that conduct will best be referred to your own reflections and experience. With me a predominant motive has been to endeavor to gain time to our country to settle and mature its yet recent institutions, and to progress without interruption to that degree of strength and consistency which is necessary to give it, humanly speaking, the command of its own fortunes.

Though in reviewing the incidents of my Administration I am unconscious of intentional error, I am nevertheless too sensible of my defects not to think it probable that I may have committed many errors. Whatever they may be, I fervently beseech the Almighty to avert or mitigate the evils to which they may tend. I shall also carry with me the hope that my country will never cease to view them with indulgence, and that, after forty-five years of my life dedicated to its service with an upright zeal, the faults of incompetent abilities will be consigned to oblivion, as myself must soon be to the mansions of rest.

Relying on its kindness in this as in other things, and actuated by that fervent love toward it which is so natural to a man who views in it the native soil of himself and his progenitors for several generations, I anticipate with pleasing expectation that retreat in which I promise myself to realize without alloy the sweet enjoyment of partaking in the midst of my fellow-citizens the benign influence of good laws under a free government—the ever-favorite object of my heart, and the happy reward, as I trust, of our mutual cares, labors, and dangers.

Go. Washington

Part I
The Farewell Address
and America's Rise
to World Power

JOHN QUINCY ADAMS and William Henry Seward were among nineteenth-century leaders who refused to accept an isolationist interpretation of the Farewell Address. Recognized as two of America's finest secretaries of state, Adams and Seward felt that the nation's expansion would someday rank it among the great world powers. Thus they challenged the assumption that the first President had wished permanently to limit America's international involvement. Commenting on the Farewell Address, Seward remarked,

> It may well be said that Washington did not enjoin us [to follow a program of noninvolvement] as a perpetual policy. On the contrary, he inculcated [noninvolvement] as the policy to be pursued until the Union of the States, which is only another form of expressing the integrity of the nation, should be established, its resources should be developed, and its strength adequate to the chances of national life, should be matured and perfected.[1]

Seward's suggestion that Washington had been concerned more with the nation's development than with avoidance of world commitments is echoed in biographies of the first President written by Woodrow Wilson and Henry Cabot Lodge at the end of the century. These future political rivals were both in the vanguard of the growing expansionist movement of the 1890's. In their biographies they attempted to show that Washington had himself been an expansionist who believed the nation was destined to play an important role in world affairs. Referring to Washington's second annual message to Congress, Wilson noted:

> Steps were urged to create a navy; to develop an army with permanent organization and equipment; and the President insisted upon vigorous action at the frontiers against the western Indians. This was part of his cherished policy. It was his way of fulfilling the vision that had long ago come to him, of a nation spreading itself down the western slopes of the mountains and over the broad reaches of land that looked towards the Mississippi.[2]

Wilson's views are also evident in interpretations of the Farewell Address made during the great debate over retention of the Philippine Islands. For two years after the Spanish-American War of 1898 this issue held the center of the political stage. Prominent Americans from all walks of life aligned themselves on both sides of the question. Those who opposed annexation were not motivated by humanitarian scruples or constitutional concerns; rather, these anti-imperialists opposed retention simply because they felt such action was contrary to America's political doctrines, especially the principle of noninvolvement in world affairs. In support of their position they naturally referred to the Farewell Address.[3]

The Reverend Robert Ellis Jones, president of Hobart College and a strong supporter of keeping the Philippines, in 1899 tried to weaken the anti-imperialist contention that the first President's valedictory had prohibited a vigorous foreign policy. Former Secretary of State Richard Olney, himself an exponent of an expansionist policy, had established the basis for Jones's position a year earlier by arguing that Washington had never counseled against any action in the national interest, including United States involvement in world affairs at the appropriate time.[4]

Jones merely extends Olney's argument one step further. In speaking against permanent alliances, Jones maintains, Washington had not advocated a policy binding on future generations. Concerned for the weakness of the new nation in 1796, he had felt it unwise to make any alliances until the country became politically and economically more mature; he was aided in this decision by the fact that strong powers never negotiated on an equal basis with weak ones. But, Jones maintains, because the United States was the strongest nation in the world in 1899, Washington's advice in the Farewell Address was no longer applicable. Furthermore the first President had never spoken out against *temporary* alliances. As the country grew more powerful, he had expected it to take its place among the family of nations. Finally, Jones points out, the only possibility of making a permanent alliance in 1899 was with England. Such an alliance was both unnecessary and unlikely because of the ideological and political bonds which already united the two countries.

Having shown that the Farewell Address did not directly apply to the situation in 1899, Jones then argues that, indirectly at least, it actually supported retention of the Philippines. The first President, he maintains, had recognized that the United States could achieve its destined greatness only if it remained outside the European balance of power. As a corollary and extension of this viewpoint, however, he then cites the Monroe Doctrine of 1823 which excluded the entire Western Hemisphere from the European power struggle. Since, unfortunately, Europe still sought to colonize and dominate South America, one way for America to prevent such a takeover would be to seize the offensive and establish itself as a neutral power in the Far East, an area which Europe was also seeking to dominate. By serving as a rallying point for the forces of a more beneficient international system, America could then prevent the extension of European despotism. According to Jones, the nation's commitment in the Orient would thus fulfill Washington's prophecy that his country would one day play a vital, worthwhile role in world affairs.

While America's colonial venture lasted only a few years, many citizens remained convinced that the country should continue to play an influential role in international matters and a controlling role in the world's underdeveloped areas, particularly in Latin America and the Far East. Soon after the opening of World War I in 1914, Professor Roland G. Usher of Washington University, a respected historian and frequent contributor to periodicals, predicted an inevitable clash between the victor and the United States for control of Latin American trade; the clash would result from the victor's search for new markets to recover from the ravages of war and America's attempt to secure its economic welfare. The nation's economic growth, Usher noted, was beginning to slacken because of the end of mass immigration and the gradual disappearance of virgin lands which had hitherto provided markets for the nation's goods. Consequently, he implied, America should now assert the Monroe Doctrine against Europe, not on ethical or moral grounds, as some wished, but because of the exigencies of the nation's economy.[5]

As an expansionist Usher berates those who believed the Farewell Address justified a policy of American isolationism. In delivering his valedictory, Usher maintains Washington had been primarily defending his policy of neutrality rather than advocating as isolationist doctrine. But his message was much more than a condemnation of European involvement. In Usher's view, Washington's policy had been based only on the nation's (temporary) weakness; thus the first President had purposely limited himself to speaking out against permanent political alliances. Washington had never opposed either American economic involvement in the world or temporary political alliances, both of which were necessary for the nation's development. He had expected that his counsel against even permanent alliances would be invalidated once the nation became stronger.

NOTES

1. John Bassett Moore, *A Digest of International Law* (8 vols., Washington, 1906), VI, 18. For Adams' view of the address, see James D. Richardson, ed., *Messages and Papers of the Presidents* (11 vols., Washington, 1896), II, 337.

2. Woodrow Wilson, *George Washington* (New York, 1896), p. 295. See also Henry Cabot Lodge, *George Washington* (2 vols., Boston, 1899), II, 6-10.

3. Fred H. Harrington, "The Anti-Imperialist Movement in the United States, 1898-1900," *Mississippi Valley Historical Review,* XXII (September 1935), 211-12.

4. Richard Olney, "International Isolation of the United States," *The Atlantic Monthly,* LXXXI (May 1898), 577-88.

5. Roland G. Usher, *Pan-Americanism: A Forecast of the Inevitable Clash Between the United States and Europe's Victor* (New York, 1915), pp. 151-65, 351-53, 363-64, 382, 388.

Washington's Farewell Address and Its Applications

BY ROBERT ELLIS JONES

If our orators and public prints correctly interpret its contents and meaning, the Farewell Address is a most comprehensive and elastic document. It has been interpreted as outlining our national policy for centuries to come. By some it is assumed that it contains warnings against imperialism and extra-continental expansion, that it counsels non-interference in European affairs, and that it urges us to remain a hermit nation. By others it is held to be a number of other things quite contradictory. . . .

I have long hoped to see some one reclaim the Address from this turmoil of confusion by telling us what Washington actually said; but so far I have been almost entirely disappointed. . . . I shall, therefore, lay before the reader . . . the substance [of the message].

The Address begins with an announcement of the writer's un-

Reprinted from *Forum*, XXVIII (September 1899), 13-28.

willingness to be nominated as President for the third time. There follows a plea for the fostering of a national unity which should override and destroy the separative tendencies of fancied sectional interests, and for a government of the whole "of as much vigor as is consistent with the perfect security of liberty. . . ."

The third section depicts the pernicious effects of party spirit; and while it recognizes that partisanship is "inseparable from our nature, having its root in the strongest passions of the human mind," it counsels its severe repression. The fourth section is comprised of short paragraphs advocating various things as essential to political prosperity, such as religion and morality, the general diffusion of knowledge, and the maintenance of public credit. The next section has to do with the relations of the United States with foreign nations. The Address ends with a solemn leave-taking of public responsibilities and fellow-patriots.

I shall now more minutely review the section that especially concerns us—the fifth, which treats of foreign relations. I shall quote parts of it which present its argument and express its spirit.

The section begins by urging impartiality toward foreign Powers.

> Observe good faith and justice towards all nations. . . . In the execution of such a plan, nothing is more essential than that permanent, inveterate antipathies against particular nations and passionate attachments for others should be excluded. . . . The nation which indulges towards another an habitual hatred, or an habitual fondness, is in some degree a slave . . . to its animosity or to its affection, either of which is sufficient to lead it astray from its duty and its interest . . .

Such feelings offer to foreign influences the opportunity

> to tamper with domestic factions, to practise the arts of seduction, to mislead public opinion, to influence or awe the public councils! Such an attachment of a small or weak, towards a great and powerful nation, dooms the former to be the satellite of the latter. . . . Jealousy, [of foreign influence] to be useful, must be impartial; else it becomes the instrument of the very influence to be avoided.

This is the general thesis, which the section proceeds to elaborate:

> The great rule of conduct for us, in regard to foreign nations, is, in extending our commercial relations, to have with them as little political connection as possible. . . . It is our true policy to

steer clear of permanent alliances with any portion of the foreign world . . . even our commercial policy should hold an equal and impartial hand; neither seeking nor granting exclusive favors or preferences . . .

He then states that his administration has been guided by these principles, especially in the matter of the Proclamation of April, 1793, establishing the neutrality of the United States in the war between France and England. Finally, he takes leave of the responsibilities so long and nobly borne, and retires into private life, the grandest figure of his own, and perhaps of any age.

As we read the earlier sections of the Address, those treating of national unity, party spirit, religion, learning, and public credit, we feel that they convey general warnings. Washington had in mind certain current problems and pressing dangers; but he had predominantly in view the permanent assailments peculiar to popular government. Governmental systems founded on the popular will are always menaced by certain tendencies "inseparable from our nature," and "rooted in the strongest passions of the human mind."

But when we reach the section specially concerning us, we find different premises and a different movement of thought. Party rancor, blind local selfishness . . . *are* weaknesses almost inseparable from our nature. But can the same be said of permanent antipathies against particular nations and passionate attachment for others? Are they also rooted in the strongest passions of the human mind? I trow not. The tendency of each nation to consider itself the greatest and most enlightened on earth *is* rooted in one of the strongest passions of the human mind— self-conceit. Americans are accused of having arrogant, national conceit; and we indict France and England and Germany of the same folly. No modern nation has fanciful impulsions to love one fellow-nation and to hate another causelessly. The broadly human tendency is for each nation to love and vaunt itself inordinately. No nation welcomes "the insidious wiles of foreign influence," or rejoices at the prospect of becoming "the satellite" of another Power, however strong. The fifth section is not directed against any general and constant human weakness. Considered as a merely general warning, it is unintelligible.

It is not a general warning: it is the discussion of a definite historical situation, first describing it, then outlining the policy and expedients by which it might be met. It is specific advice for a specific crisis. It is an argument regarding the relation of the United States to France and England, then at war, and a defence of Washington's policy in the matter. Read in the light of current events, its every word is definite and full of the vitality of fact. Let me briefly sketch the situation.

The War of the Revolution was still vividly in mind: its exasperations died hard—all the more slowly because England long refused to give up the Western posts and secretly fomented Indian outrages. Rudeness and stupidity characterized her diplomacy. She seemed bent upon humiliating us. When war with France broke out, our seamen were impressed and made to serve British guns, our commerce was harassed, and our very national existence was endangered. War with England on our own account was the natural recourse; but we were not ready.

What wonder, then, that many Americans were anxious to have their country throw herself into the arms of France? She had helped us in the Revolution, and stood for liberty in Europe. French fashions and modes of thought, French terms of speech, were current everywhere. Nothing would serve the grateful admirers of France but a fixed alliance with her, linking our fortunes with hers for good or ill. Any other course or counsel was held as rank ingratitude. It is hard for us to realize the extent of this French madness. The antics of M. Edmond Genêt, the French Envoy,[1] had justification in the conduct of our people. It was a time for apprehension when Thomas Jefferson could vacillate between attachment to France and his duty as Secretary of State; when James Monroe, our Minister to Paris, could wear a Liberty Cap and allow himself to be publicly embraced by the Representatives of the People; and when Edmund Randolph could enter into questionable commerce with Fauchet, the French Ambassador.[2]

Washington saw that peace almost at any price was indispensable to the consolidation of our strength. He realized further that England and the United States had common interests and traditions and a common destiny. He divined that France was republican in name alone, and that the dictator had already come. Our country was between Scylla and Charybdis: its animosity toward England, its gratitude to France, were alike freighted deep with danger. Alliance with either meant that it should become the vassal of one European Power and the victim of another.

Mark with what trenchant intensity Washington denounces prevailing unwise policies and unwiser men. Referring to England:

> Antipathy in one nation against another disposes each more readily to offer insult and injury, to lay hold of slight causes of umbrage, and to be haughty and intractable when accidental or trifling occasions of dispute occur. Hence frequent collisions, obstinate, envenomed, and bloody contests. The nation, prompted by ill-will and resentment, sometimes impels to war the government, contrary to the best calculations of policy. The government sometimes participates in the national propensity, and adopts, through passion, what reason would reject. . . . The peace often, sometimes perhaps the liberty, of nations has been the victim.

He next turns to France and her American partisans:

> So, likewise, a passionate attachment of one nation for another produces a variety of evils. Sympathy for the favorite nation, facilitating the illusion of an imaginary common interest, in cases where no real common interest exists, and infusing into one the enmities of the other, betrays the former into a participation in the quarrels and wars of the latter, without adequate inducement or justification . . . it gives to ambitious, corrupted, or deluded citizens (who devote themselves to the favorite nation) facility to betray or sacrifice the interest of their own country, without odium, sometimes even with popularity; gilding, with the appearance of a virtuous sense of obligation, a commendable deference for public opinion, or a laudable zeal for public good, the base or foolish compliances of ambition, corruption, or infatuation.

These are not the generalities of a theorist; nor are the words aimed at the failings of humanity at large. Their but half-concealed exasperation has specific personages in mind: every word has the impetus of some definite event.

If further proof were needed of the specific character of the argument, it would be furnished by the enumeration of the immediate benefits likely to follow upon a wise policy. We read thus: "If we remain one people, under an efficient government, the period is not far off when we may defy material injury from external annoyance"—as from Spain at New Orleans, or from England on our Indian frontier. We may hope, in the second place, "soon to cause the neutrality we may at any time resolve upon to be scrupulously respected"—that is, we should be able to build a navy, making it dangerous to harry our commerce, in the hope of drawing us into an alliance. Third, we shall reach a stage "when belligerent nations, under the impossibility of making acquisitions upon us, will not lightly hazard the giving us provocation"—as France and England had no hesitation in doing daily. And last, the time will soon come "when we may choose peace or war, as our interest, guided by justice, shall counsel."

These benefits were plainly not to be the ultimate results of national life, but almost immediate achievements; and in about eighteen years they were accomplished facts. The War of 1812 caused our neutrality and autonomy to be respected. That war put us unmistakably outside the suction of the European vortex called "the Balance of Power," which Washington feared and hated far more than he did France or England, the leaders, for the time being, of the two opposing groups constituting this baleful system.

European statesmen sought to range the nations into two camps of about equal strength, thus hoping to prevent any one people from becoming predominant. It was important, for the maintenance of this scheme, that the United States should become attached to one battalion or another, lest she should become the incalculable and troublesome third factor in international affairs. Neutrals . . . were not wanted. Until 1812, Europe had not despaired of putting the United States into its so-called Balance, hoping, as John Adams said, "to use them for make-weight candles in weighing out its pounds." The term "Balance of Power" could be substituted for the words "foreign influence" throughout the Address. The freedom of the United States from the influence and compulsion of the Balance of Power was Washington's supreme purpose.

National autonomy and a distinctively American character were the conclusion of the argument; but the starting point and premise of it were the temporary weakness of the United States, and the danger of her being crushed between the upper and nether millstones of the rivalries of Europe. The Address proceeds to argue thus:

> Europe has a set of primary interests which to us have none,

or a very remote relation. Hence she must be engaged in frequent controversies, the causes of which are essentially foreign to our concerns. Hence, therefore, it must be unwise in us to implicate ourselves by artificial ties, in the ordinary vicissitudes of her politics, or the ordinary combinations and collisions of her friendships or enmities.

Our detached and distant situation invites and enables us to pursue a different course.

Washington reckoned with the effective separation by the Atlantic Ocean. The barrier of the Atlantic was plainly providential. He said of it, on another occasion: "The Atlantic enables us to maintain a state with respect to European nations which otherwise could not be preserved by human wisdom."

The section concludes, as has been said, with a reference to the Neutrality Proclamation of 1793 (of which it is primarily a discussion and defence), and with a statement of the purpose underlying all Washington's official acts. He says:

With me, a predominant motive has been to endeavor to gain time to our country to settle and mature its yet recent institutions, and to progress, without interruption, to that degree of strength and consistency which is necessary to give it, humanly speaking, the command of its own fortunes.

Washington's letter of October 9, 1795, to Patrick Henry is even more explicit. He says:

My ardent desire is, and my aim has been . . . to keep the United States free from political connections with any other country, to see them independent of all and under the influence of none. In a word, I want an *American* character, that the powers of Europe may be convinced we act for *ourselves,* and not for others. This in my judgment is the only way to be respected abroad and happy at home; and not, by becoming the partisans of Great Britain or France, create dissensions, disturb the public tranquillity, and destroy, perhaps forever, the cement which binds the union.

Washington was the first Nationalist. Long after his death politicians were still pro-English and pro-French. The later Federalists were as madly English as the early Anti-Federalists had been madly French. An independent American nationality may be said to be the creation of the Farewell Address.

The Address is usually summarized as "advice to steer clear of European entanglements." Most people imagine, therefore, that it pleads for national isolation and advises against alliances of any kind with the European world. Helpful relations are not entanglements: entanglements are injurious relationships from which it is difficult to withdraw. Washington considered as entangling any European alliance in which the United States should be an unequal partner and dependent—any connection which should make this country the vassal of any other. He condemned anything which subjects the will and policy of one country to the will and policy of another. He deprecated the passionate attachments and hatreds which make weak nations the satellites of strong ones. His constant effort was to foster "that degree of strength and consistency which is necessary to give it, humanly speaking, the command of its own fortunes."

In the second place, any equal alliance which is permanent would be entangling. However advantageous an alliance on equal terms may be, the relative strength of nations is continually changing; and thus fixed alliances result at last in the virtual annexation of the weaker country by the stronger. The weaker no longer commands its own fortunes. That Washington contemplated equal, temporary alliances, but feared fixed ones, is clear from his own words: "It is our true policy to steer clear of permanent alliances with any portion of the foreign world. . . . we may safely trust to temporary alliances for extraordinary emergencies."

It is assumed that Washington urged non-intervention in European affairs, and neutrality under all circumstances whatsoever; but his words do not warrant it. He says: "It must be unwise for us to implicate ourselves, by artificial ties, in the ordinary vicissitudes of her [Europe's] politics, or the ordinary combinations and collisions of her friendships or enmities"; distinctly implying that events might weave for us ties with Europe which are not artificial, but natural and unavoidable. While we were to stand aloof from "ordinary" European combinations, there might arise "extraordinary emergencies" forcing us to interfere.

Washington believed, also, that the United States might wisely become a member of a European coalition. The reader will remember that it was given as one of the results of a wise neutrality that "belligerent nations, under the impossibility of making ac-

quisitions upon us, will not lightly hazard the giving us provocation." The sentence seems to end somewhat too abruptly to please
the ear. It is not surprising, then, to find that in the first draft
it was finished thus: "Belligerent European nations will not lightly
hazard giving us provocation *to throw our weight into the opposite scale.*" The words "to throw our weight into the opposite
scale" were, upon revision, erased; but they clearly show that in
Washington's mind armed intervention in Europe was a possibility. Washington expected that, if it were necessary for reprisal
upon a persistent European enemy, we might throw our sword
into the European Balance. Washington was no gentle dreamer
or theory-spinning humanitarian, but a warrior from his youth.

It is assumed that the Address surveyed the far future of national life; but it does no more than enter the vestibule of that
future. Washington was convinced that American conditions
would constantly change for the better; so that any permanent
arrangements, based on weakness and lack of development, would
soon become disastrous bonds. He pleads for commercial treaties
—"the best that present circumstances and mutual opinions will
permit, but temporary, and liable to be, from time to time, abandoned or varied, as experience and circumstances shall dictate.
. . ." Temporary arrangements in politics and commerce, fitted
to temporary conditions, form the burden of his argument.

Washington's concern was to insure an unhampered future.
He realized that the permanent conditions of our national development had not yet been established, and, therefore, gave little
advice about them; but he was determined that a glorious future
should not be discounted by a fatuous acceptance of the limitations of present weakness.

It is curious how little he indulged in prophecy. He does,
however, speak of the United States as "a free, enlightened, and,
at no distant period, a great nation." In a letter to LaFayette
he says, that "these United States shall one day have weight in
the scale of empire." He also describes himself as "a member
of an infant empire."

What has the fifth section of the Address, concerning foreign
relations, shown itself to be? It is not a warning against extra-
continental expansion; the subject is not mentioned. It does not
glimpse the bogey of imperialism. The general course and career
of the nation when fully grown are not considered. It does not

contain Cassandra-like warnings of coming ill. . . . Washington felt no such stirrings of the prophetic soul; and his contemporaries saw in him not a prophet, but merely a statesman defending a specific measure—the Neutrality Proclamation of 1793.

The Address did furnish specific advice to meet specific temporary conditions. It counselled a weak, isolated, immature nation not to make a permanent alliance with any strong foreign Power, thereby becoming its subject and satellite. It urged neutrality until national character and political individuality should be consolidated, and institutions and resources fully developed. When all this should have come to pass, it looked to see the United States take her equal place in the family of nations, and, having full command of her own fortunes, make temporary alliances with foreign Powers, or, if need be, on extraordinary occasions, throw herself into one side or the other of the European Balance, as her interest and dignity should dictate.

It is more than time to ask, What present application has the Farewell Address? What part of the fifth section still remains in force? Evidently only so much of it as has foundation in conditions still unchanged. If premises have been destroyed by the march of circumstances, the original conclusions therefrom are invalid.

The premise of national weakness no longer stands: we are the richest, strongest people in the world. National isolation is done away with. The Atlantic affords no barrier, but has become a ferry crossed at every whim. London and New York are now nearer to each other than Boston and Philadelphia were a century ago. Quickened transportation and communication have contracted the world. When we read in the Address that "Our national situation enables us to pursue a course of self-withdrawal from European affairs," the words have an almost mocking sound.

When we remember also that the armed collisions of the day in Africa and China are really struggles for markets and cheap, raw materials, Washington's "great rule of conduct for us, in regard to foreign nations," namely, to extend our commercial relations while having "with them as little political connection as possible," seems the naïve expedient of an ignorant and unworldly soldier. But ignorant or unworldly Washington was not. He clearly saw that, without the barrier of a protracted Atlantic voyage, our withdrawal from political Europe could not be main-

tained by any human wisdom. Washington would not have talked
of detachment from Europe and of ocean greyhounds in the
same breath.

We cannot now make an unequal alliance if we would. We
cannot become the satellite of any stronger Power. All that
stands is a dissuasion from permanent alliances with any Power.
It would still be folly to espouse the quarrels of another people,
regardless of our own interests. It is still "our true policy to steer
clear of permanent alliances with any portion of the foreign
world." We may still "safely trust to temporary alliances for
extraordinary emergencies."

The only practical application of this remainder of Washington's advice is to a fixed alliance between the United States and
England, which few imagine can ever come to pass. Grateful as
we are to England for recent kindnesses, a fixed alliance is undesirable and unnecessary. A unity of ideals, interests, traditions,
blood, language, and religion makes the artificial bonds of a paper
treaty superfluous.

There is a slim, permanent reminder of Washington's advice;
but to cite the whole fifth section as applicable to the situation
in Cuba and the Philippines is to evince an astonishing ignorance
of its real purport. The Address has directly put a restricted bearing on the present situation; and there is not a desire anywhere
to go contrary to it. It is difficult to see why Anti-Expansionist
orators and journalists have thought it an oracle to swear by.
There is but one explanation—few of them have read it.

So much for the direct application. But has the Address any
indirect bearing on our present problems?

To find an answer let us ask, What was Washington's position,
broadly stated? It was that unhindered internal development is
necessary to the consolidation of political individuality; that distinctively national character is stunted and destroyed by foreign
influences; that, as a monarchical environment is unfavorable to
Republican institutions, it is a vital necessity for the United
States to stand outside the Balance of Power of the European
nations.

The War of 1812 reaffirmed these contentions with powder,
lead, and steel. Europe was effectually warned off, and it appeared that the sacredness of American nationality had been at
last established; for after 1812 no European Power dreamed of

the United States as a safe mark for coercion or intrigue.

Ten years later the Allied Powers (Russia, Austria, France, and Prussia) sought to reinstate Spain in her rebellious South American colonies. This movement called forth President Monroe's famous Message of 1823, in which he declared that the United States would consider any attempt of the Allied Powers to "extend their system to any portion of this hemisphere as dangerous to our peace and safety," and that such interposition could not be regarded "in any other light than as a manifestation of an unfriendly spirit toward the United States." The Monroe Doctrine extended the area from which European influence was excluded: South America must also, for our benefit and her own, stand outside the system of the European Powers.

Was this extension of Washington's anti-foreign-influence doctrine justifiable? Had that doctrine any such rightful scope as to embrace a hemisphere in its prohibitions? Are we irrevocably committed to maintain the autonomy of South America? Is there danger to our institutions in the future occupation of South America by European Powers?

An academic discussion as to whether the Monroe Doctrine is virtually contained in the Address, and whether it should still be maintained, would be almost silly. The Monroe Doctrine is not a theory, but a fact of national procedure. It is not a mere political figment, but a strenuous mode of national action. It has been explicit for seventy-five years, and was implied in the Revolution and in the War of 1812. The expulsion of the French and Austrians from Mexico,[3] and the halting of the British advance in Venezuela,[4] reaffirmed it; and now in Cuba it has received a heightened application. President Monroe said, European sovereignty shall not be extended on this hemisphere. President McKinley said, European sovereignty may not be endlessly abused on this hemisphere. The national right of self-development was recognized in both cases. All large, national measures spring from the necessities of self-preservation, which take small account of bloodless theory. It is trivial to discuss the technical correctness of Monroe's deductions from the Address. We may as well accept them as the utterances of that national consciousness which makes our destiny as it chooses, without regard to theorists or doctrinaires.

Under Washington's guidance in 1776, and under his inspiration in 1812, we shook ourselves free from foreign influence. Later we protected our Spanish-American neighbors from European domination. The result of loyalty to Washington's principles is that at last the Balance of the European Powers seems to most of us a faint, shadowy, and unreal thing.

But shadowy, unreal, or futile the Balance of Power is not. In Europe it has never ceased to operate. It plays off dual against triple alliances; it burdens the nations with gigantic armaments; it maintains the "great assassin," the Sultan, lest in the division of Turkey some one Power should get the lion's share. After every war it intervenes to prevent the victor from upsetting the equivalence of power artificially created. The partition of Africa has been its preoccupation for the last ten years. The other day France and England were ready to fly at each other's throats about Fashoda and the control of the Upper Nile. The partition of the Orient is now in full swing. One part of China after another is seized by Europe, without as much as "by your leave" to its rightful masters. The command of Chinese markets, the exploitation of Chinese resources, and the maintenance of equivalent power in the Orient call all Europe to arms.

The partition of Africa was the work of the last ten years; the partition of Asia will occupy the present decade; and the partition of South America is not far distant, unless something arrests the spread of the system of equivalence. European nations look with longing eyes upon South America, the best and richest undeveloped territory. The European press reiterates that overcrowded Europe cannot rightfully be kept out of it; that Europeans have a right to go into it, and to carry with them their own laws, institutions, and political allegiances. Germany cherishes the ultimate annexation of Brazil as a part of her settled plan.

This world-including German plan is most impressive. It comprises: (1) the annexation of Syria, in order to be at hand to grab as large as possible a part of Turkey, when at last that country falls to pieces; and (2) the absorption of Holland, in order to Prussianize the Dutch East Indies (Java, Sumatra, and Borneo), which command the China Seas, the Indian Ocean, and Australasia, and in order also to appropriate the Dutch West Indies, with the view of influencing the world-commerce one day to pour through the Caribbean Sea and the Isthmian Canal, and helping forward the annexation of Brazil. Let Germany get a foothold in Brazil, and her rivals will claim their share; and South America will become another area of balanced hostilities. These designs are no mere fancies; and Germany's recent interference in Manila seems not so stupid, when it is recognized, as it is by every one in Europe, that a strong, neutral, non-European Power in the Philippines would be fatal to Germany's future Oriental supremacy, of which she hopes to make the Dutch East Indies the base and centre.

Now why should not the Powers of Europe occupy and appropriate South America for development, its own people being incompetent to do so? We must give some better answer than that the Monroe Doctrine prohibits it. We must not play the dog in the manger.

A sufficient answer is, that, with the exception of England, no great European Power has any capacity for colonization or for the advancement of new or backward countries. Successful colonial administration is as little understood on the Continent of Europe as constitutional liberty seems to be. French and German colonies alike fail to be self-supporting; they are not the creations of trade and agriculture, but of governmental initiative. All alike are burdened by numerous civil and military officials, out of all proportion to the colonists and the financial interests involved. . . . The commercial methods of the European Powers, England excepted, are unintelligent: they are monopolistic, and they consider colonies as freeholds to be exploited, to furnish revenue, raw materials, and exclusive markets to the mother-country. Continental Europe is not competent to develop South America in any large and liberal and intelligent way. Africa and Asia should satisfy them.

There is another valid reason why South America should remain as she is. It is not proved that her peoples are hopelessly incapable of self-development. Venezuela, backward as she is, is still in advance of British Guiana. The European assertion of the right to take control of South America rests upon the assumption that the latter's states are moribund and incapable of progress; but no one can tell when a hitherto backward nation will leap to great heights of power and prosperity. Japan, for example, is a source of astonishment and admiration. Thirty-five years ago Mexico was held hopeless. . . . To-day, Mexico leads the nations in rate of progress. . . . It is at least probable that the South American states will yet produce types of civic capacity which will amply repay the waiting of their long infancy. Freedom from European domination is as necessary for them as it was for us. And if they are backward, France and Germany have not made such successes of their colonial affairs as to prove that without their guidance the future of South America is hopeless.

European domination in South America would still be dangerous to our interests. The principles of the Address still hold. The enemy is the old one, the Balance of Power. Its menace is greater now than in 1823. If the European Balance comes into South America, with the power and *prestige* gained from partitioning the world between its members, we shall have unfriendly neighbors amply able and willing to assail our interests and thwart our purposes.

Let our minds dwell upon the immense power and *prestige* of a supposed European coalition which had succeeded in partitioning the earth between its members. Could we stand before it unconcerned? Our national optimism would at last turn pale. The Continental Powers would delight to humiliate and thwart us. How much they love us recent events have shown. England alone prevented their intervention in behalf of Spain. There is no doubt that a Europeanized South America would be injurious to our peace and prosperity.

I want again to look away from our own immediate interests. Would it advance civilization if the whole world should be dominated by a monopolistic, military, and largely incompetent system? Is the higher civilization of individual liberty, industrialism, and free exchanges to be retarded in opening up new areas of the earth? The doings of the concerted Powers in the last few years show that the halting of their system is a necessity for civilization. . . . A system which crushes out national individuality makes the world poorer by reducing its races to one conventional type. The world has need of every variety of character and capacity which new peoples can contribute. By such accessions alone can it keep its powers fresh and vigorous.

How may the system of European equivalence be halted? By the presence in the East of a strong nation, standing outside the system of powers, but friendly to each of them; forming a centre around which may rally all the forces which make for a new,

more intelligent, and more generous international order. Such a
neutral Power in the Orient would support liberal and enlightened
England in her struggle for open markets; it would save Japan
from the Russian Bear, who sharpens his claws and waits; and
Holland would rejoice in an alliance which would rescue her
from any fears of German annexation.

Some readers have already mentally objected, that "England
is a member of the Balance of Power; that she was futile in
Armenia and Crete; that she herself partitions Africa, and is
taking her share of China." They also remember that Venezuela
is in South America, and are disposed to ask, What reason is
there to think that England would rally to new and better order?
England became involved in the Balance during the eighteenth
century, and has long been trying to escape from it. An English
Prime Minister, Canning, suggested the Doctrine of 1823 to Monroe and aided it diplomatically. England's dominance in Africa
is the reward of competency: she has a right to it. Venezuela
is a dead issue. Jameson's raid[5] was promptly disavowed. England
has been reluctantly forced to her recent steps in China; she
would gladly restrict her expansion if she could. She took our
side, as I have said, against all the continent in our war with
Spain; and she has brought forth fruits meet for repentance in
Crete. She would welcome a new and better order.

Our providential overthrow of Spain in the Philippines implies
grave responsibilities. Our retention or relinquishment of the
Philippines is a most portentous matter. Should we give them up,
the islands would become the arena of Asia. If they become
the prize of any European Power, the Oriental Balance will be
destroyed; and blood will flow to reestablish it. If we keep them,
all this can be prevented; and it is likely that, in a free and friendly
coalition of commercial and constitutional nations, the old, im-
moral scheme of European equivalence will meet its match and
master, and Washington's prophecy, that "these United States
shall one day have weight in the scale of Empire," will be
gloriously fulfilled.

The same judicial reader is disposed to say to me, "You are
now becoming sentimental and are deserting the ground of fact
as well as the principles of the Address. All that concerns you
is to show that our own interests would be endangered by the

European occupation of South America. You must also show the relation of the holding of the Philippines to South American autonomy. Vague, international humanitarianism cannot weigh in this discussion." I am quite content to argue on facts, and on the principles of the Address.

Please consider the following facts: the accomplished partition of Africa and Asia; the undoubted desire of Europe to appropriate South America; the ill-concealed Continental hostility to the United States; and our traditional maintenance of the autonomy of South America as necessary to our own peace.

We are fully warranted in considering a European advance on South America as a possibility, and in forestalling it in any way we can. Great, national struggles may be anticipated and prevented by the early occupation of advanced strategical positions, and by the knitting of virtual alliances strong enough to dissuade from the meditated attack. The partition of South America may best be prevented by halting European equivalence in the Orient. Germany can best be repelled from Brazil by forestalling her hope for Oriental supremacy on the basis of the Dutch East Indies, and by our retaining the Philippines, from whose base the battle can be won bloodlessly by us in advance.

Admiral Dewey has already taught Germany that it may not be safe for her to override the Monroe Doctrine by and by, as was purposed. America little comprehends the bearing of the ownership of the Philippines on our own and on the international future. The excitement of the Orient and the apprehension of Europe should suggest that there is more involved than either crossroads politicians, on the one hand, or mere theorists, on the other, imagine.

I have attempted no exhaustive discussion of the Philippine problem. It has many phases; and there may be considerations averse to retention sufficient to overbalance the foregoing. I have simply sought to determine whether the Address has an indirect bearing on our problems. If Europe really covets South America (her own testimony must be admitted); if our occupation of the Philippines would halt the system of European equivalence (the witness of Europe's fears and Germany's deeds applies); then there can be little doubt that Washington's Farewell Address indirectly favors our retention of the Philippines.

NOTES

1. Genêt arrived in the United States in 1793 and proceeded to violate American neutrality by such actions as commissioning American ships as French privateers. As a result, Washington demanded his recall.—ED.

2. Randolph replaced Jefferson as Secretary of State in 1794. He was forced to resign from office in 1795 after being accused of handing over state secrets to the French minister, Jean Fauchet.—ED.

3. The French attempted to establish a puppet empire in Mexico under Austrian Archduke Maximilian. As a result of pressure by Secretary of State William Henry Seward, the French withdrew their troops in 1867. Maximilian was later executed by the Mexicans.—ED.

4. Jones is referring to a boundary dispute between British Guiana and Venezuela which the British agreed reluctantly in 1895 to arbitrate as a result of American pressure, including threat of war.—ED.

5. In December 1895 Dr. Jameson made a filibustering raid into the Transvaal Republic in South Africa in order to protect the rights of the British *Huitlanders* against the dominant Boers. For a brief period Jameson's action threatened to lead to war between England and Germany, who supported the Boers. The raid was generally condemned throughout the world.—ED.

Washington and Entangling Alliances
BY ROLAND G. USHER

Precisely what had Washington in mind when he incorporated in his Farewell Address the famous dictum about "entangling alliances"? Can we prove that he meant what he has been understood to mean? What circumstances led him to this conclusion; how permanent did he believe this isolation should be; how considerable a modifying influence did he assign to future exigencies? It can hardly be gainsaid that definite answers to these questions would go far to settle the doubts in the minds of many Americans concerning future foreign policy, for many feel it safer to follow what they believe to have been the counsel of Washington than to form foreign alliances in an attempt to solve present American problems.

Fortunately, the very full evidence enables us to answer

Reprinted by permission from *North American Review*, CCIV (July 1916), 29-38.

definitely all questions about the Farewell Address that are of significance. Like most important State papers, it was not composed entirely by Washington but was evolved with the assistance and collaboration of Hamilton and Madison, both of whom drafted it in full. After much discussion and correspondence with them and with others, Hamilton's final draft, with many alterations and excisions by Washington himself, was utilized. So full is our information about Hamilton's thoughts and about Washington's own ideas that we can almost trace the Address in the correspondence of the two men for the preceding years.

Washington himself has left us no doubt as to the primary purpose of this document. He says explicitly in a letter written at the moment of publication: "the principal design of it is to remove doubts at the next election" as to his candidacy for the office of President. In 1796, as his advanced age began to enfeeble his health, and the desires always strong in him for a quiet country life became more and more insistent, he felt that he could not accept a third term as President. He had, however, been so abused and vilified in the public press for several years, his character so aspersed, his motives so invariably questioned and misunderstood, that his modest and retiring nature shrank from announcing that he would not be a candidate for fear that his enemies would promptly impute to him vanity and conceit. In those days the Presidential electors were supposed to ballot in secret for candidates who had not previously announced to the people their willingness to accept election, and Washington rightly felt that, in declaring he sought no further political office, he would lay himself open to the charge of coveting what others had no intention of offering him. Such scruples seem to us, at this distance, strained and unnatural in his case, but the importance which Washington attached to them is evinced not only in his correspondence with Madison in 1792, but in the letters to Hamilton and others in the months when the Address itself was in preparation. As an expedient, he hit upon the idea of a "valedictory address," which, apparently occasioned by more general and permanent considerations, would thus make the statement of his unwillingness to become a Presidential candidate incidental to larger issues.

A second motive which played a great part in his decision was the desire to answer in some dignified and impressive manner the extraordinary campaign of vituperation which had been directed against him and his policy. For us who have been accustomed to think of the Farewell Address as delivered to a patriotic and affectionate nation, eager to receive from its most honored and revered statesman his parting words of counsel, it is a shock to learn that Washington meant it to be his justification before posterity for a policy which had been as roundly abused and more generally disapproved by contemporaries than perhaps any other ever initiated by an American statesman. Here again his own innate modesty made him hesitate to defend himself openly for fear he should reveal the depth of the wounds such hostility had caused him, and for fear lest his enemies should exult over an admission that he felt defense necessary. As he wrote Hamilton, the Address must defend him and his policy without making either him or his policy too prominent. Joined to these motives was the hope in Washington's mind that he might still possess sufficient influence—which he seems at this time to have doubted—to restrain the people from an alliance with France which he believed imminent and both unwise and inexpedient.

In the last paragraphs of the Address itself, Washington has struck for us its keynote: "With me, a predominant motive has been to gain time to [*sic*] our country to settle and mature its yet recent institutions and to progress without interruption to that degree of strength and consistency which is necessary to give it, humanly speaking, the command of its own fortunes."

Throughout the years of his Presidency the fact which had been borne in upon him by events had been the weak and defenseless condition of the country. An aggregation of struggling people organized into States, deeply jealous of each other, loaded with foreign and domestic debt, with a credit scarcely established, and with neither army or navy, it seemed to him that our greatest problems were domestic, and our greatest necessity sufficient time to solve them. He was afraid that the Constitution might not work, that the strong anti-Federalist party, hostile to it, might gain the upper hand and abolish it. A leader the malcontents had found in Thomas Jefferson, and active expression of their policies had appeared in the various newspapers which Jefferson subsidized. In Virginia and in the Mississippi Valley Washington knew an anti-national movement was being nourished by the men in his own councils. The Whiskey Rebellion against the authority of the Federal Government had, to be sure, been crushed, but the probability of other resistance was great.

And this country, weak, disorganized, and divided within itself, was, he saw, entirely dependent for its prosperity upon its foreign commerce. It produced what it could not consume and what it must sell either in the West Indies or in Europe. It had been accustomed to buy in Europe, chiefly in England, most of those commodities necessary to a civilized existence. By the sale of their own produce in the West Indies, American merchants had bought sugar and molasses which they carried to England and exchanged for manufactured goods needed in America. The dependence of the new Government and its people upon Europe was dire. What we raised could be sold only to European nations or to their colonies. What it was almost imperative for us to buy had to be obtained from them. Just at this time, too, an extremely lucrative trade with France had sprung up in American grain, the first truly American product, except tobacco, to find sale in any quantity in Europe.

In the way of this exchange, upon which the prosperity of the whole country was seen directly to depend, stood Great Britain; English manufactured goods were those most desired; the British West Indian colonies furnished the best markets for American produce. Yet the recent Revolution and the events of the subsequent years had thoroughly embittered English statesmen and led them to maintain restrictions exceedingly onerous to their former colonists. That the British statesmen had much reason for their distrust Washington was forced to admit. The Treaty of 1783 had not been executed by the Americans; the Loyalists had been maltreated and their property confiscated, despite the promises in the Treaty; nearly all the private and public debts owed by Americans in England had been repudiated during or after the war; and there was genuine doubt abroad whether the new Government under the Constitution was likely to maintain its credit and observe its promises any better than had the States and the Confederation.

Yet to the harassed President it was clear that without a navy we could not coerce Great Britain's fleet; that such access as we had to the West Indies and to Europe in general we must obtain with her consent. As Hamilton wrote to Washington in 1794: " 'Tis our error to overrate ourselves and underrate Great Britain;

we forget how little we can annoy; how much we may be annoyed." Washington therefore concluded that the United States must preserve peace at all costs and was urged thereto "by motives of policy, interest, and every other consideration, that ought to actuate a people situated and circumstanced as we are, already deeply in debt, and in a convalescent state from the struggle we had been engaged in ourselves."

This period of probation, when America's weakness thrust upon her a policy of circumspection and political isolation, was estimated by Washington and Hamilton at not less than twelve nor probably more than twenty years. In the Farewell Address Washington thus phrased this notion: "The period is not far off when we may defy material injury from external annoyance . . . when we may choose peace or war as our interests guided by justice shall counsel." Shortly before he had written: "If this country is preserved in tranquillity twenty years longer, it may bid defiance in a just cause to any Power whatever; such in that time will be its population, wealth, and resources."

The idea of no entangling alliances seems to have originated in negative conclusions. It was not that Washington felt that no alliance could be beneficial. The strength of the British sea power, the probable continuance of its supremacy, and the extent of American dependence upon Europe, made cordial relations with Great Britain essential; an alliance with that country was therefore *prima facie* expedient and desirable. The closer our contact (always assuming that we retained our political independence), the more advantageous the relation would be for both countries. But he saw that this alliance was one which the state of the public mind both in England and in the United States made impossible; the Revolution almost prevented the conclusion of any favorable understanding between the Governments.

At the same time, both he and Hamilton felt—and their idea descended as a tradition—that England's own interests would compel her in the long run to sanction practically that extent of intercourse with Europe and the British dominions which was imperative for America. Nor were they blind to the fact that England's own interests were a better foundation for American privileges than any paper alliance. To develop more cordial relations, to make possible for Great Britain concessions without loss of self-respect, to facilitate, where possible by diplomatic methods, arrangements and concessions: such must be the policy of the United States. A reconquest by England Washington scouted, not only as impossible of success, but as a move which the British themselves would not attempt. The one European Power which could reach America, which in fact held America in her hands, he believed was already convinced that conquest was unwise. Eminently desirable for the rapid promotion of American commerce, an alliance with Great Britain's sea power was fortunately neither imperative for defense nor essential to ensure the continuance of that minimum of economic privilege upon which the prosperity of the country depended. In her own interests Great Britain must perforce concede in practice that minimum which we could not dispense with, and in time the growth of the United States might make possible the exaction of more, or an alteration of sentiment in both countries might result in an amicable adjustment.

But at all costs, Washington felt, the United States must not further antagonize the sea power and thus risk the loss of that minimum of privilege. Under the stress of war or urged by resentment and passion, Great Britain might rescind that, and from its loss calamity must ensue. A commercial crisis at that precise juncture Washington felt would overturn the Constitution and put into an overwhelming majority the anti-national forces, already hostile to his own policies and the great measures of Hamilton for the funding of the debt and the establishment of the public credit at home and abroad. Yet such an alliance the great majority of the American people, led by Jefferson, seemed firmly determined to make. France, who had aided us during the Revolution and with whom we had signed a defensive treaty, was now at war in Europe with Great Britain, Austria, and the majority of the smaller states. For America, demonstrations in favor of France were common; Jefferson and his partisans declared that the existing treaty and the honor of the nation alike counseled assistance to those who had before helped us. So great was the popular enthusiasm and so vigorous were the expressions of hostility to Great Britain, so determined were the attempts to force Washington's hand and compel an alliance with France or a war with England, that the President was hard pressed to resist.

Both he and Hamilton felt, however, that to ally with France was suicide. The prosperity of the United States depended upon an access to the West Indies and to Europe which the British fleet could interdict completely. The consequences of a restriction of privilege had already demonstrated how terrible would be the result of its complete loss. Alliance with England was out of the question, but favorable commercial terms and at least a certain tolerance were essential. Nor did there seem to be a remote possibility of assisting France while the British fleet ruled the sea. Hamilton even contended that France had aided us during the Revolution solely to advance her own interests, and that we therefore owed her no debt of gratitude. In the end, Washington issued a proclamation of neutrality; snubbed Genêt and replied in a friendly but reserved tone to the fervid letters from Paris; and sent Jay to England to negotiate as favorable and extensive a commercial treaty as could be had. The President was not optimistic as to the extent of privilege likely to be achieved, but felt with Hamilton that under the circumstances the United States must be satisfied with what could be had, and hoped that a change of conditions and perhaps of public feeling in both countries would in the future make the extension of commercial privileges possible. As he wrote to Lee, the proclamation of neutrality was intended to restrain, "as far as a proclamation would do it, our citizens from taking part in the contest."

In the Farewell Address he attempted to defend this policy by means of general propositions of advice which were really intended to convey to the men of the time some such ideas as these: Beware of alienating unnecessarily the sea power upon which you are dependent. Do not, under present circumstances, think of an alliance with France which must be based upon theory and sentiment rather than upon mutual interest. Beware of all foreign alliances which pledge the country to more assistance than it is capable of rendering or expose it to dangers which it has no means of resisting. Remember that time must elapse before the United States can become strong enough to take its place in the world and develop an independent foreign policy suited to its needs and its prospects. Until then beware of all entanglements, and even then beware of permanent alliances which the very growth of the country may itself render inexpedient in a few years. Like a weak country, a rapidly growing country must frequently revise its policies in accordance with the exigencies of times and occasions. For years to come temporary alliances will serve even extraordinary emergencies.

The following sentences include those portions of the Farewell Address which are significant in this connection, and they seem to bear, without straining or unnecessary twisting, the interpretation just sketched:

> Nothing is more essential, than that permanent, inveterate antipathies against particular Nations [Great Britain] and passionate attachments for others [France] should be excluded; and that, in place of them, just and amicable feelings towards all should be cultivated. . . . Sympathy for the favorite Nation, facilitating the illusion of an imaginary common interest, in cases where no real common interest exists, and infusing into one the enmities of the other, betrays the former into a participation in the quarrels and wars of the latter, without adequate inducement or justification. . . . And it gives to ambitious, corrupted, or deluded citizens (who devote themselves to the favorite nation) [the Anti-Federalists] facility to betray or sacrifice the interests of their own country, without odium, sometimes even with popularity. . . . Such an attachment of a small or weak, towards a great and powerful nation, dooms the former to be the satellite of the latter. . . . Against the insidious wiles of foreign influence (I conjure you to believe me, fellow-citizens), the jealousy of a free people ought to be constantly awake. . . . Real patriots [Federalists] who may resist the intrigues of the favorite [France] are liable to become suspected and odious; while its tools and dupes [Jefferson et al.] usurp the applause and confidences of the people, to surrender their interests. . . .
>
> The great rule of conduct for us, in regard to foreign nations, is in extending our commercial relations, to have with them as little *political* connection as possible. So far as we have already formed engagements, let them be fulfilled with perfect good faith. Here let us stop. Europe has a set of primary interests, which to us have none, or a very remote relation. Hence she must be engaged in frequent controversies, the causes of which are essentially foreign to our concerns. Hence, therefore, it must be unwise in us to implicate ourselves, by *artificial ties,* in the *ordinary* vicissitudes of her politics, or the *ordinary* combinations and collisions of her friendships or enmities. Our detached and distant situation invites and enables us to pursue a different course. If we remain one people, under an efficient government, the period is not far off, when we may defy material injury from external annoyance;

when we may take such an attitude as will cause the neutrality we may at any time resolve upon, to be scrupulously respected; when belligerent nations, under the impossibility of making acquisitions upon us, will not lightly hazard the giving us provocation; when we may choose peace or war, as our interest, guided by justice, shall counsel. . . . It is our true policy to steer clear of permanent alliances with any portions of the foreign world; so far, I mean as we are now at liberty to do it. . . . Taking care always to keep ourselves, by suitable establishments, on a respectable defensive posture, we may safely trust to temporary alliances for extraordinary emergencies. . . . Harmony, liberal intercourse with all nations, are recommended by policy, humanity, and interest.

From the earlier portions of the Address comes corroboration of this view that the document was primarily intended as a defense of Washington's policies and opinions rather than as a permanent statement of future policy. At the same time, everyone who reads that remarkable paper must be struck by the prescience displayed by Washington in formulating his original policy upon those subjects permanently significant and vital to the welfare of the American people. Whatever his intentions may have been, he certainly mentioned no subject of purely transient interest and did group those permanent features of policy which the development of the country was to affirm. The necessity of union, the dangers of sectionalism, the importance of a prompt obedience to the Federal Government, the dangers of factional conflict between political parties, the encroachment of the various departments of the Government upon each other, the imperative necessity of the maintenance of public credit—such advice was the result of particular events and controversies upon which he himself had taken the unpopular side; but later events demonstrated the farseeing wisdom of his choice and the accuracy of his analysis of conditions. The Farewell Address did not itself create a policy for the country: it formulated definitively those policies which Washington had already decided were expedient so long as the country's economic weakness remained pronounced, so long as the European situation made any alliance suicidal except that with the sea power, and while the Revolution made impossible and undesirable any close political connection with the late mother-country.

The Address, however, stresses with persistence three points. The situation which made such policies expedient Washington believed would disappear within twenty years, and then a more definite, more permanent, and less negative policy might be formulated. He further gave personal directions to the printer that the word "political" was to be italicized in the phrases concerning relations with Europe. The distinction he wished to draw was between political and economic relations, the former of which he felt should be as slight as possible with all nations, including Great Britain, and the latter of which he was clear should be as extended as possible with all nations, and in particular with Great Britain. Finally, he constantly distinguished between permanent political alliances, which he believed inexpedient for the United States because we had no interest in the "ordinary" friendships or enmities in Europe, and temporary political alliances, which he felt would be under extraordinary emergencies essential. His warning against European alliances emphasized again and again all engagements which were not rooted in American interests, adding that until the country had attained greater development America could have no political (not economic) interests which a European alliance would be necessary to defend.

It should, therefore, be clear that Washington himself explicitly implied in the Farewell Address that the growth of the country would probably invalidate his counsel regarding entangling alliances within twenty years. Would he not be the last to hold that the American people are today to feel themselves bound to follow under present conditions a counsel regarding alliances explicitly based upon the fundamental problems of a small, weak, disorganized, debt-ridden country in which firm constitutional government, the public credit, and nationality, had yet to be established beyond the possibility of change?

Part II
The Farewell Address
Between Two Wars

THE VIEW THAT Washington in the Farewell Address had advocated a policy of nonentanglement in world affairs survived the entry of the United States into World War I. During the debate following the war's end in 1918 over joining the League of Nations, during the similar controversy in the 1920's over joining the World Court, and again during the 1930's when the threat of war loomed once more, this position was championed by the opponents of increased American international commitments. Their argument followed generally one of two lines: some repeated the long-held view that Washington had opposed any form of world involvement; others held that he had merely opposed entangling alliances. The latter were not against America playing a major role in world affairs; but they wanted the country to pursue a unilateral course and not obligate itself to other nations. One of those who took this position was Senator

Henry Cabot Lodge. As an expansionist in the 1890's, Lodge
had emphasized Washington's own interest in expansion. During
the fight over the League of Nations he stressed the first President's appeal to American nationalism:

> The principles of the Farewell Address in regard to our foreign
> relations have been sustained and acted upon by the American
> people down to the present moment. Washington declared against
> permanent alliances. He did not close the door on temporary
> alliances for particular purposes. Our entry in the great war just
> closed was entirely in accord with and violated in no respect the
> policy laid down by Washington. When we went to war with
> Germany we made no treaties with the nations engaged in the war
> against the German Government. The President was so careful in
> this direction that he did not permit himself ever to refer to the
> nations by whose side we fought as "allies," but always as "nations
> associated with us in the war." The attitude recommended by
> Washington was scrupulously maintained even under the pressure
> of the great conflict. Now, in the twinkling of an eye, while
> passions and emotions reign, the Washington policy is to be en-
> tirely laid aside and we are to enter upon a permanent and indis-
> soluble alliance. That which we refuse to do in war we are to do
> in peace, deliberately, coolly, and with no war exigency. Let us
> not overlook the profound gravity of this step.[1]

Advocates of the League and World Court challenged Lodge's
interpretation of the Farewell Address, one which was essentially
the same as that of the strict isolationists. In 1923 St. George
Leakin Sioussat of the University of Pennsylvania argued against
the notion that in seeking common action with other nations for
peace and justice, America was disregarding Washington's counsel. Nine years later the Lincoln scholar James G. Randall even
maintained that the phrase "entangling alliances" against which
the first President was supposed to have spoken had actually first
been stated publicly by Thomas Jefferson.

In their writings, Sioussat and Randall share basically the same
view. Before their time, both proponents and opponents of increased American commitments in the world had attempted to
relate their position to Washington's counsel. While Sioussat and
Randall note that the first President did endorse agreements aimed
at establishing international peace, they emphasize the fact that
the Farewell Address has little relevance for the present age. Wash-

ington, they state, was concerned in his message not with formulating guidelines for the future but with handling the situation in 1796. Disturbed by the rift in the country over the struggle between England and France and fearful of the ramifications of American participation, he advised his fellow citizens to follow a policy of noninvolvement.

In 1934 Samuel Flagg Bemis, then of George Washington University, gave classic expression to this view. Undoubtedly one of the most influential diplomatic historians of the last forty years, Bemis has had a lasting influence on students of the Federalist era. His study of the Revolution, his works on the Jay and Pinckney treaties, and his prize-winning volumes on John Quincy Adams,[2] are still the standard works on the diplomacy of the new nation.

In general, Bemis regards the Founding Fathers as extremely skillfull diplomats. He is not, however, unmindful of domestic influences on the nation's foreign policy. But the theme he stresses throughout his works is the advantages which the United States gained as a result of European rivalry and struggle. During the Revolution, France's desire for revenge against England led to her active support of the rebellious colonies.[3] Again in 1795 the United States obtained the highly favorable Pinckney Treaty from Spain because the Madrid government feared an Anglo-American alliance against her New World possessions.[4]

Despite her success in international affairs, the United States never escaped from the complications of European war, which in 1796 threatened to lead to American involvement. It is in the context of this European factor that Bemis views the Farewell Address. He regards the address as a milestone in American diplomacy and the most affirmative statement to that time that the United States was a sovereign nation which was not to be used as a tool of foreign intrigue.

NOTES

1. Speech made before the United States Senate, February 28, 1919, and reprinted in Henry Cabot Lodge, *The Senate and the League of Nations* (New York, 1925), pp. 227-61.

2. *The Diplomacy of the American Revolution* (paperback ed., Bloomington, Ind., 1957); *Jay's Treaty: A Study in Commerce and Politics* (paperback ed., New Haven, 1962); *Pinckney's Treaty: America's Ad-*

vantages from Europe's Distresses, 1783-1800 (paperback ed., New Haven, 1960); *John Quincy Adams and the Foundations of American Foreign Policy* (New York, 1949); and *John Quincy Adams and the Union* (New York, 1956).

   3. Bemis, *Diplomacy of the American Revolution,* pp. 255-56.
   4. Bemis, *Pinckney's Treaty,* pp. 294-314.

The Farewell Address in the Twentieth Century

BY ST. GEORGE LEAKIN SIOUSSAT

One hundred years ago today, on the twenty-second of February, 1832, Daniel Webster made an address in celebration of the first centennial commemoration of the birth of George Washington. In that speech, made in the city which bears Washington's name, the great Massachusetts orator said:

> A hundred years hence, other disciples of Washington will celebrate his birth, with no less of sincere admiration than we now commemorate it. When they shall meet, as we now meet, to do themselves and him that honor, so surely as they shall see the blue summits of his native mountains rise in the horizon, so surely as they shall behold the river on whose banks he lived, and on whose banks he rest, still flowing toward the sea, so surely may they see, as we now see, the flag of the Union floating on the top of the Capitol;

Reprinted by permission from *The General Magazine and Historical Chronicle of the University of Pennsylvania*, XXXIV, (1934), 319-30.

and then, as now, may the sun in his course visit no land more free, more happy, more lovely, than this our own country!

The hundred years envisioned by Mr. Webster are at an end; and today, all over "this our own country," by a multitude that ranges from the children in the schools to the President of the United States, tributes of loving respect are being tendered to him who, long ago, was called "the best of great men and the greatest of good men."

On this Commemoration Day I have the honor to represent the Trustees and the Faculty of the University of Pennsylvania and those who by their presence join with these in tribute to Washington. At any time a high calling, this is one which, on this Bicentenary, evokes an humble spirit. In the brief period of this address, I shall forego any attempt to recount the whole life of George Washington: and I shall leave to those in whose power I have greater confidence the appeals of eulogistic oratory. Instead, I wish to bring to your attention but one fact of the first President, but one of the state papers which bear his name. It is my purpose to consider very briefly Washington's Farewell Address and, in particular, that part of it which has to do with the external relations of the United States. In this endeavor I have in view two principal ends: first, to show that the issuing of the Farewell Address, like most matters of History, was a more complicated and involved incident than we sometimes imagine; and secondly, to make clear to you the necessity of avoiding what to my mind is a dangerous misinterpretation of Washington's advice.

Nearly every one of us, I am sure, when in a reflective mood, must sometimes have been inclined to doubt whether we of the twentieth century can understand the life of a man born two hundred years ago. George Washington grew up in a colonial atmosphere; in a world run by hand, horse and water power; in a society of patriarchal slavery; at a time when, as to business, the corporate form of enterprise was still in its infancy. How can he be understood by an age which is tending to be collectivistic and mechanical?

Such an understanding can be attained only by an intellectual effort. One has constantly to guard himself against the greatest of fallacies—the fallacy of simplicity. Nothing is easier than to have some one idea, some catchword, which fixes itself upon one's mind, often to the exclusion of further interest. . . .

This "catchword" propensity of ours no doubt accounts in part for the continued vogue of the cherry-tree story of Parson Weems. There is nothing hard about it.

Speaking a bit more seriously, there is to be noted also a very general inclination to demand and be satisfied with very simple explanations of phenomena by referring them to single causes. . . .

In considering the question, then, as to how we know about a distant century, we have first to be on our guard against the fallacy of simplicity. But there presses a second thought. None of us has ever seen or heard George Washington. How he looked, indeed, we pretty well know, by reason of the multitude of portraits and busts that have survived from his time to ours. As to what he thought and what he did, however, we have to depend on the materials, the documents, written or printed, which remain from his time to ours. But in transferring into your mind or my mind the thoughts embodied in those documents there are two psychological factors that must not be overlooked: the mental equipment, the significance of the individual of the eighteenth century who speaks to us in the document; and the mental equipment and interpretation of the twentieth-century individual who reads the document. For the individual furthermore, we may write in, with increasing complication, the age, the country, the race, the religious body, the political party. . . .

In the thought of anyone who has not devoted to the matter some special study, it would no doubt be assumed that Washington's Farewell Address was given to the world at the time when he retired from the Presidency. But that was not the case. General Jackson, indeed, when he laid down his Executive duties, on March 4, 1837, did issue a valedictory address; as did President Andrew Johnson at the end of his term, 1869. But the Farewell Address of Washington was given to a Philadelphia newspaper and published on September 19, 1796, several months before the end of Washington's second term as President. The reason for this early publication of what was intended as a valedictory address is perfectly well known. After considering the matter, the President decided to combine in one pronouncement his intended utterance of farewell and a notice to the American people that he would not accept a third term: in other, later and more succinct words, a declaration that he did not choose to run.

But, as is also well known, the idea of such an address had been in the President's mind long before. In 1783 at the end of the Revolutionary War an early precedent had been afforded by the address to the Governors of the States on disbanding the Army. But the real basis appeared in 1792 as Washington's first term was drawing to a close. Strongly averse to a reelection, he considered the propriety of withdrawing his name, and asked James Madison for advice as to this course and as to the preparation of an address of farewell. He then submitted to Madison the following paragraph which reveals so fully how far it was the President's own thoughts which appeared in the later Address.

That to impress these things it might, among other things be observed, that we are *all* the children of the same country—a country great and rich in itself—capable and promising to be, as prosperous and as happy as any the annals of history have ever brought to our view—That our interest, however diversified in local and smaller matters, is the same in all the great and essential concerns of the Nation.—That the extent of our Country—the diversity of our climate and soil—and the various productions of the States consequent of both, are such as to make one part not only convenient, but perhaps indispensably necessary to the other part;—and may render the whole (at no distant period) one of the most independent in the world.—That the established government being the work of our own hands, with the seeds of amendment engrafted in the Constitution, may by wisdom, good dispositions, and mutual allowances; aided by experience, bring it as near to perfection as any human institution ever approximated; and therefore, the only strife among us ought to be, who should be foremost in facilitating and finally accomplishing such great and desirable objects; by giving every possible support, and cement to the Union.—That however necessary it may be to keep a watchful eye over public servants, and public measures, yet there ought to be limits to it; for suspicions unfounded, and jealousies too lively, are irritating to honest feeling; and oftentimes are productive of more evil than good.

In 1792 the matter was adjourned by Washington's reluctant determination to accept a second term. When, four years later—that is, in 1796—the same question again arose, Mr. Madison was no longer in the close relation to the President which he had held in 1792. Alexander Hamilton was then Washington's chief counsellor and to him the President turned, sending to Hamilton the draft of an address which Madison had drawn up, together with some suggestions of his own. He asked Hamilton first to elaborate the draft which he, Washington, had sent and secondly, if he saw fit, to prepare one of his own. When Hamilton did this, Washington, with characteristic modesty, selected the Hamilton draft, and after further correspondence and some few changes this appeared as the Farewell Address.

It is regrettable and unfortunate that the fame of great state papers often leads us to forget that they arise out of actual conditions and are the product of real men. The Emancipation Proclamation, for example, was the outcome of no closet study, but of a very real and practical political evolution in time of war. The Declaration of Independence has, indeed, its sonorous preamble, which is written, as the schoolmen used to say, "under the aspect of eternity," but the "Facts Submitted to a Candid World" were red hot partisan indictments of King George III, struck off in the glow of an actual situation and to promote a particular object. So it was with the Farewell Address. It may be easier and simpler merely to learn its words by heart and to repeat them year after year, but one cannot understand them unless he recalls the circumstances in which they were uttered. Let us briefly examine these circumstances.

When the Revolutionary struggle had entered upon the phase of rebellion and it became necessary to seek aid abroad, American agents were sent to the various European courts to plead for assistance. They had a very unhappy time. But the French court was induced, through the activities of Franklin and those who preceded him, at first to grant secret aid, and later to enter into a formal alliance. At the time welcomed with enthusiasm, this alliance brought the indispensable recognition of the United States and aid in money, goods, ships, sailors and soldiers, without which Yorktown would have been impossible. But on the other hand, this alliance tied our infant republic very closely to the French monarchy. It was a fear that the French had obligations in other quarters that might operate against the best interest of the United States which later led Jay and Adams to break their instructions and, persuading the older Franklin, to negotiate separately the treaty of peace with Great Britain in 1782. Just about the time that the government of the United States began under the Constitution, the French Revolution entered into its first phases and soon thereafter passed from these conservative beginnings into the excesses of the Terror, the regime which, to some good people brought up on Burke, Carlyle and Dickens, still constitutes the "French Revolution." In his scholarly work *The Revolutionary Spirit in France and the United States,* Bernard Faÿ, more popularly known as the biographer of Franklin and the author of one of the most recent lives of George Washington, has traced sympathetically the spiritual union which existed between Revolutionary France and a large element in the United States until the latter years of the eighteenth century, when this unity was overthrown under the Federalist regime. There is not time to tell the whole story. We need only remind ourselves of the wild enthusiasm with which the earlier phases of the Revolution in France were followed in this country, and in this very city; of the outbreak of the European war, the decision of the President and his Cabinet to maintain a policy of neutrality, and the resentment thus engendered in France, where it was felt that we were evading our treaty obligations; of the mistakes of citizen Genêt and of Washington's displeasure and Genêt's recall; of Monroe's unhappy mission to France, and of the unwisdom of Fauchet and Adet, Genêt's successors in the French legation. It may be well to remember, also, that France contributed to the unrest of the people in the Mississippi valley, and that, as the war between France and England developed, our shipping suffered from the attacks of both powers. Jefferson and Hamilton, who differed on this as on so many questions, had resigned from the Cabinet, and after the folly of Edmund Randolph, Jefferson's successor as Secretary of State, that important office, after going abegging for awhile, was, in 1796, in the hands of the useful Federalist man of all work, Timothy Pickering.

If we were tied closely to France by treaty, we were pressed physically even more closely by England with its Canada to the north, and by Spain with its great empire to the south; Spain, drifting back to the old *entente* with France, was thereby exposing her Gulf possessions to English attack and to United States filibustering. The Federalists had concluded a fairly good treaty with Spain and a very bad one with England; the indignation at Jay's

Treaty was augmented, on the part of many, by the recall of Monroe from Paris. The Whiskey Insurrection, centering in this state, was over, and Hamilton's system was more securely established. But the agitation of the Democratic Societies, so obnoxious to Washington, continued. The central figure, that of Washington, was soon to be lost; for the first time a real election was to test the political stability of our young government. These were the conditions in which the Farewell Address was formed. Only a few weeks apart from the date of its appearance, Hamilton, somewhat forgetful of its injunctions against parties, and desiring to secure the substitution of Pinckney for Adams as the Federalist choice for the Presidency, wrote:

> But it is far less important who of many men that may be named shall be the person, than that it shall not be Jefferson. We have every thing to fear if this man comes in and from what I believe to be an accurate view of our political map I conclude that he has too good a chance of success, and that good calculation, prudence, and exertion were never more necessary to the Federal cause than at this very critical junction. All personal and partial considerations must be discarded, and every thing must give way to the great object of excluding Jefferson.

It is with this background in view—and only with this background in view—that we can really interpret the Farewell Address. But with regard to those paragraphs which relate specifically to our foreign affairs, another word of comment is necessary. Washington's draft of 1792, sent to Madison, had dealt chiefly with the need of the Union and had not touched on foreign affairs; but when he wrote to Hamilton in 1796, the recent events which we have already sketched, and especially the criticism of his foreign policy, led him to suggest to his spokesman:

> That we may avoid connecting ourselves with the politics of any nation, farther than shall be found necessary to regulate our own trade, in order that commerce may be based upon a stable footing, our merchants know their rights, and the government the ground on which those rights are to be supported.

In the paragraph which follows this, Washington urged pride in the name of an American and the danger that our dignity as a distinct nation would be absorbed, if not annihilated, by enlistment under the banners of any other nation and that we should "guard against the intrigues of any and every foreign nation, who shall endeavor to intermingle, however covertly and indirectly, in the internal concerns of our country, or who shall attempt to prescribe rules for our policy with any other powers," and so forth.

These were Washington's words. Hamilton made, and Washington accepted, that expansion which produced the sentences, now so familiar, of the Farewell Address. In this you will recall first the general injunctions "Observe good faith and justice toward all Nations. Cultivate peace and harmony with all.—Religion and Morality enjoin this conduct; and can it be that good policy does not equally enjoin it?" Then comes the warning against "permanent, inveterate antipathies against particular nations and passionate attachments for others." "The Nation, which indulges toward another an habitual hatred or an habitual fondness, is in some degree a slave"—either to its animosity or to its affection. Then follows a somewhat lengthy illustration of the dangers of antipathy and attachment, respectively. "Such an attachment of a small or weak, toward a great and powerful nation, dooms the former to be the satellite of the latter." Then, after warning against "the insidious wiles of foreign influence," the Address presents the better-known passages:

> The great rule of conduct for us, in regard to foreign Nations, is, in extending our commercial relations, to have with them as little *Political* connection as possible.—So far as we have already formed engagements, let them be fulfilled with perfect good faith.—Here let us stop.—
>
> Europe has a set of primary interests, which to us have none, or a very remote relation.—Hence she must be engaged in frequent controversies, the causes of which are essentially foreign to our concerns.—Hence therefore it must be unwise in us to implicate ourselves by artificial ties in the ordinary vicissitudes of her politics, or the ordinary combinations and collisions of her friendships, or enmities.
>
> Our detached and distant situation invites and enables us to pursue a different course.—If we remain one People, under an efficient government, the period is not far off, when we may defy material injury from external annoyance; when we may take such an attitude as will cause the neutrality we may at any time resolve upon to be scrupulously respected; when belligerent nations, under

the impossibility of making acquisitions upon us, will not lightly hazard the giving us provocation; when we may choose peace or war, as our interest guided by our justice shall counsel.

Why forego the advantages of so peculiar a situation?—Why quit our own to stand upon foreign ground?—Why, by interweaving our destiny with that of any part of Europe, entangle our peace and prosperity in the toils of European ambition, rivalship, interest, humour, or caprice?

These are the essential paragraphs, reenforced with the statement that " 'Tis our true policy to steer clear of permanent alliances, with any portion of the foreign world," but with the limitation that existing engagements must be observed and that temporary alliances may be trusted for extraordinary emergencies. Even with regard to commercial intercourse there should be an equal and impartial hand and temporary, rather than permanent, arrangements. For "there can be no greater error than to expect, or calculate upon real favours from Nation to Nation.—'Tis an illusion which experience must cure, which a just pride ought to discard."

In this analysis, it has been necessary to allude to the parts which Washington and Hamilton respectively had in the formation of the Address. One of the most significant and valuable contributions to the understanding of this, it may be interesting to note, came, in the year before the Civil War, from the great lawyer of this city, Horace Binney. But today it is not so important to enter into detail as to this question of phraseology—for the advice of the Farewell Address that America should avoid European control was not original with either Washington or Hamilton. On the contrary, just as Jefferson frankly said that in the Declaration of Independence he was but repeating what was in everybody's mouth, so the doctrine of the Farewell Address belonged to *all* the Fathers. To cite a single example: when John Adams was in France, in 1782, as Peace Commissioner, he recorded the following conversation with Richard Oswald, who represented Great Britain:

"You are afraid," says Mr. Oswald today, "of being made the tools of the powers of Europe." "Indeed I am," says I. "What powers?" said he. "All of them," said I. "It is obvious that all the powers of Europe will be continually manoeuvering with us, to work us into their real or imaginary balances of power. They will all wish to make us a make-weight candle, when they are weighing out their pounds. Indeed it is not surprising; for we shall very often, if not always, be able to turn the scale. But I think it ought to be our rule not to meddle. . . ."

The isolation doctrine of the Farewell Address was, then, the expression of a natural desire, in the infancy of this nation, to be let alone by a Europe that threatened our very life.

In the early years of the nineteenth century the aspiration to the attainment of isolation reached its greatest disappointment, and the need for securing real independence had its greatest demonstration, when Europe plunged once more into war, and Jefferson and Madison, trying to pursue Washington's policy of neutrality and peace, had to revert first to the Revolutionary idea of commercial boycott and then to war with England. . . . It will be enough for us to realize that not until the end of the Napoleonic wars in Europe, and of our second war with England did the United States arrive at real independence and equality.

And what we then attained was independence and equality and peace—not *isolation*.

We have now to turn to the study of the other factor in the historical transmission from the past to the present—the circumstances and the psychology of today. What shall we say of the Farewell Address in the light of our present circumstances and as a guide in the perplexities of the twentieth century?

I forbear to press upon you the obvious,—to stress, for example, the significance of the vast changes which have come through the successive steps in the application of steam, electricity and other discoveries of science, or to do more than mention the shrinkage of the world in the light of these devices of man's ingenuity. One reason why I do not lay chief emphasis on these mechanical contrivances of man is the patent fact that they can be used, like one's own hand, for ill purposes, as well as for good. All the great means by which man has learned to chain the forces of nature may be used, unfortunately, as our ancestors once used spears and bows and arrows: to guard and perpetuate a narrow parochialism, or an imperialistic nationalism. After all, it is the spirit of man that remains the important thing.

I would rather remind you how men's need of each other's

products has brought not only keen rivalry for markets, but the economic interdependence of nations. These forces have been long at work. One can hardly picture anything more American, farther removed from the rest of the world, than the farmer of the 1830's, plowing with his team a wheat field in Indiana or Illinois. But the keen-minded English woman, Harriet Martineau, when she wrote: "Every British settler who ploughs a furrow in the prairie, helps to plough up the foundations of the British Corn Law," was a good prophet: for the inter-relation of the food supply of Great Britain and America had a vast deal to do with the revolutionary changes in British tariff policy under Sir Robert Peel.[1] The Negro slave hoeing cotton in Georgia or Arkansas seemed to be a purely American institution. Yet slavery in the United States was really affected by British policy in the West Indies, by what went on in the coffee plantations of Brazil and in the sugar plantations of Cuba, while all had to consider the cheap labor of India. In the great struggle of 1861-65, cotton played a major role in the efforts of the Confederacy to secure aid in England and in France.

Earlier depressions than that of our day have operated in both hemispheres. That bad finances in one country affect the relations of that country with other lands was realized in the forties when many American states, including Pennsylvania and Maryland, were for awhile unable to pay interest on their bonds. In recent years, American capital, whether public or private, has not observed a policy of isolation. The world of finance, at least, has become definitely an international world, with the United States of America in first place.

But into recent history, whether of debts and reparations, of American soldiers fighting in Europe, of peace and disarmament plans from the Hague Conventions to the present conference,[2] I am not going to enter. I should like, however, to make the point that all these movements and events have merely carried out the logic of what went before, have only demonstrated the unreality of American isolation. In 1901, just after the Spanish-American War, and long before it had ever entered our heads that American soldiers would be on the Marne, the American historian Albert Bushnell Hart, bringing to an end his valuable little book on *The Foundations of American Foreign Policy,* wrote:

If there is to be in the coming century a great battle of Armageddon—once more Europe against the Huns—we can no more help taking our part with the hosts of freedom than we can help educating our children, building our churches, or maintaining the rights of the individual. There is no proper and permanent doctrine of foreign policy which does not recognize the United States as the great leader in all American affairs, and one of the great leaders in the affairs of mankind. There is no safe or permanent doctrine which does not recognize our sisterhood with other nations under international law. The "doctrine of permanent interest," therefore, is a doctrine of peace in America, international fellowship in the Eastern hemisphere, and civilization everywhere.

Let us now frankly face the question: is this all a defiance of the Farewell Address? Have we departed from the principles of Washington? More particularly, are they correct who cite the Farewell Address against all participation by the United States in common action for peace and international justice?

In the first place such an interpretation is not justified by the phrases of the Address itself. Whenever it is proposed to subordinate the liberty of the United States to any foreign power through a permanent alliance, as did the French treaty for which we were so thankful in 1778, but which we found so irksome in 1796, the injunction of Washington will be as forceful as the day it was uttered. Those passionate attachments to foreign powers or hatreds of foreign powers, of which the Address warned us, have not always been restrained in recent years by some who are most vociferous in their conservatism. But the participation of the United States in international cooperation for the improvement of the world is a very different matter, which is not forbidden by any part of the Farewell Address, properly understood and interpreted. Nor is it a true filial loyalty to Washington so to argue.

Looking back today at his commanding figure, let us inform ourselves a little as to his usual attitude of mind. Was he bound by tradition and circumstance, or did he meet new conditions as they arose?

We sometimes forget that Washington, conservative as he was by nature, marched a long way with the reformers of the eighteenth century. Like Cotton Mather, Franklin and Jefferson, he, too, stood for inoculation against smallpox. Though not as aggressive as Jefferson, he, too, hoped for the ending of negro slavery. He, too, was willing to accept religious toleration. He, too, had education at heart. He was the most progressive of farmers. He had that vision which has marked our captains of industry, of which he has the rightful claim to be called one. He was the patron of Rumsey's first experiments. And in the establishment of a better connection between the Ohio Valley and Virginia he saw the political consequences which would follow economic improvement. In his youth he wore the uniform of a British militia officer; dressed, as a civilian, in British clothes; and was in friendly association with British noblemen. As one of this group in Virginia, he engaged in the traditional warfare with the historic enemy, France. Yet, in devotion to a principle, he took arms against the government which had held his allegiance and, later, with very mixed feelings, sought and accepted the cooperation of that French kingdom against which he had fought in earlier days. When the government which the states had framed in the Articles of Confederation to take the place of that of Great Britain proved ineffective, he came forth from his retirement to take part in a second Revolution—a peaceful one, the setting aside of the legal authority which held the states together and the substitution for it of the Constitution of the United States. He did not believe in the immutability of the Constitution, but on the contrary held that it was "not free from imperfections" and advised its acceptance on the ground that "a Constitutional door is open for future amendments and alterations." "There are some things in the new form, I will readily acknowledge," he wrote to Edmund Randolph, "which never did, and I am persuaded never will, obtain my cordial approbation; but I did then conceive, and do now most firmly believe, that in the aggregate, it is the best constitution that can be obtained at this epoch; and that this, or a dissolution of the Union, awaits our choice, and are the only alternatives before us. Thus believing, I had not, nor have I now, any hesitation in deciding on which to lean."

And, trustful of the future, he wrote: "I do not think we are more inspired, have more wisdom, or possess more virtue, than those who will come after us."

Can it be that the first American, the Father of his Country, would refuse, if he were now in our midst, to devote that which, next to his character, was his nearest approach to genius, his capacity for organization, to those efforts, tentative and clumsy and failing though they may be in the beginning, which look to organizing a better world of international relations?

With the inescapable conviction that Washington was always ready to accept that which was new if he believed the acceptance of it for the common good, it is wrong, it seems to me, to distort a warning against the interference by the great and powerful nations of Europe in the politics of the feeble United States of 1796 into a prohibition of the assumption by a great world power of the twentieth century of the responsibilities which attach to its fortunate position. And, as to this larger view, we do not have to argue either *a priori* or from analogy. For, in the words which he sent across the sea in 1786 to Lafayette, we have a clear expression of Washington's sympathy towards the establishment of world peace and towards the more liberal ideas of international law, which were coming to the front at the end of the eighteenth century, and of which the United States furnished so many able advocates.

> Although I pretend to no peculiar information respecting commercial affairs, nor any foresight into the scenes of futurity, yet, as the member of an infant empire, as a philanthropist by character, and (if I may be allowed the expression,) as a citizen of the great republic of humanity at large, I cannot help turning my attention sometimes to this subject. I would be understood to mean, I cannot avoid reflecting with pleasure on the probable influence, that commerce may hereafter have on human manners and society in general. On these occasions I consider how mankind may be connected like one great family in fraternal ties. I indulge a fond, perhaps an enthusiastic idea, that, as the world is evidently less barbarous than it has been, its melioration must still be progressive; that nations are becoming more humanized in their policy, that the subjects of ambition and causes for hostility are daily diminishing; and, in fine, that the period is not very remote, when the benefits of a liberal and free commerce will pretty generally succeed to the devastations and horrors of war.

It is true, alas, that before Washington had gone to his rest, humanity, "that tireless traveller," had walked once again in the valley of the shadow of death. It is true that the years of the twentieth century, like the years of the eighteenth and the nineteenth century, find him still footsore and weary and tempted to disillusionment. The good causes of the world all have their Valley Forges, their "times that try men's souls," and their failures and disappointments which recall poignantly Washington's cry, "The game is pretty near up." But on this day when especially we commemorate him, and with the most enduring of the inheritances left by him—his indomitable resolution—in mind, will anyone refuse to stand up with him who was our Captain in war, our great Patriot, and, with him be counted "a philanthropist by character . . . a citizen of the great republic of humanity at large"?

NOTES

1. In 1846 the British prime minister, Sir Robert Peel, succeeded in carrying through Parliament legislation which repealed the Corn Laws, as the tariff acts protecting grain were called.—ED.

2. Sioussat is referring to the Temporary Mixed Commission of Experts which was appointed by the League of Nations in 1921 and which during the next years studied the question of arms traffic without making any definite recommendations.—ED.

George Washington and "Entangling Alliances"

BY J. G. RANDALL

The effect of historical inaccuracies or of deliberate forgeries upon international relations has been brought forcibly to mind by events of recent years. . . .[1]

There are certain historical notions that are well-nigh universal. They constitute part of the mental furniture of the average citizen. An excellent example is the belief that it was Washington who used the phrase "entangling alliances" in laying down fundamental principles as to our relations with European countries. In the writings of publicists, in the speeches of politicians, in newspaper editorials and cartoons, there are continual references to this famous phrase which is usually put into the mouth of Washington by bare reference as if on the assumption that Washington's words

Reprinted by permission from *The South Atlantic Quarterly*, XXX (July 1931), 222-29.

are so well known that the original of the supposed "quotation" need not be presented. It would seem, therefore, to be high time for a sober historical inquiry into the matter.

Briefly, the fact is that the famous phrase "entangling alliances" came not from Washington at all but from Thomas Jefferson. In his first inaugural address, March 4, 1801—in every way a notable state paper—Jefferson announced his political confession of faith, and gave his countrymen a statement of what he deemed the "essential principles of our Government." As to foreign affairs he advised "peace, commerce, and honest friendship with all nations, entangling alliances with none."[2]

It is true, of course, that Washington did deal with the matter of alliances in his Farewell Address of 1796. His actual words as revised for delivery to Congress were as follows:

> Europe has a set of primary interests, which to us have none or a very remote relation.—Hence she must be engaged in frequent controversies, the causes of which are essentially foreign to our concerns.—Hence therefore it must be unwise in us to implicate ourselves, by artificial ties in the ordinary vicissitudes of her politics, or the ordinary combinations and collisions of her friendships, or enmities.
>
> Our detached and distant situation invites and enables us to pursue a different course.—If we remain one People, under an efficient government, the period is not far off, when we may defy material injury from external annoyance; when we may take such an attitude as will cause the neutrality we may at any time resolve upon to be scrupulously respected; [when] belligerent nations, under the impossibility of making acquisitions upon us, will not lightly hazard the giving us provocation; when we may choose peace or war, as our interest guided by . . . justice shall counsel. . . .
>
> 'Tis our true policy to steer clear of permanent alliances, with any portion of the foreign world;—so far, I mean, as we are now at liberty to do it—for let me not be understood as capable of patronizing infidelity to existing engagements. . . .
>
> Taking care always to keep ourselves, by suitable establishments, on a respectably defensive posture, we may safely trust to temporary alliances for extraordinary emergencies.—[3]

One might ask: What is the point of this exact quotation of Washington's words and of setting them off against the words of Jefferson? Was not Jefferson himself a great leader whose words are worth quoting? And did not Washington advise against extending our political connection with Europe? An affirmative answer to both these questions may be readily given. And incidentally it may be added that no responsible American statesman of the present day, whether in discussing the Kellogg peace pact[4] or in considering the merits of the World Court or similar matters, has any serious intention of departing from the wise and salutary counsel of both Washington and Jefferson, whose ideal, by the way, was not isolation, which even in that day was impossible, but independence, neutrality in matters that did not concern us, and harmonious relations with other countries.

The nub of the matter is not to deny that the avoidance of "entangling alliances" is sound policy, nor to refute the claim that such avoidance is in line with the principles of the "fathers," but to note the fact that loose quotations from Washington without looking up Washington's actual words constitute a pernicious practice which is commonly accompanied by irrational inferences from the words cited; and to make the plea that, if straight thinking is worth anything, then historical quotations intended to affect present-day policies should not be vaguely or irrationally employed. In making any historical quotation, it is fair to demand at least three things: that the words of the original be looked up and quoted precisely; that the quotation be given in such a way as not to do violence to the meaning and intention of the original as shown by a study of the context; and that any applications of the quotation to present-day affairs be made with an intelligent understanding of the extent of the analogy between the historical circumstance at the time the statement was made and the present event with which it is linked. Furthermore, a historical citation should be offered merely for what it is worth. It should not serve as a substitute for sound discussion of the merits of the main question treated.

The usual reference to Washington's words on the subject is hardly more than a vague groping for a passage which cannot be exactly recalled from memory, but there is a well-known chain of newspapers in this country which carries the following motto: " 'Honest Friendship With All Nations—Entangling Alliances With None.'—George Washington." In other words, here is a case where Jefferson's words are quoted exactly, indicating that the source has been consulted, but the words are ascribed to

Washington! The reader may draw his own conclusions as to the fairness of this type of historical juggling.

Since Jefferson's words are quoted, and since they are attributed to Washington, an inquiry as to the policies of both Washington and Jefferson is in order.[5] Washington wrote in a day of European struggle and intrigue and in an age of violence growing out of the French revolutionary wars. He had been a beneficiary of the French alliance of 1778 which was a powerful factor in the attainment of American independence from England. This, by the way, is the only alliance ever made by the United States.[6] When the French government had assumed that the alliance was still in force in 1793 and had attempted to enlist troops on American soil, bring captures into American ports, and set up French prize courts within American territory, Washington had wisely demanded the recall of the French diplomatic agent Genêt and had issued his proclamation of neutrality, pledging that we would maintain a conduct "friendly and impartial" toward both belligerent groups and that American citizens would be punished for infringement of this neutrality. According to his interpretation the alliance of 1778 was not applicable to the existing war because, among other reasons, it was not a defensive war on the part of France, nor a war which had any relation to the purpose of the original alliance. In the furious contest of Federalists and Anti-Federalists under Washington the international situation had been used by both sides for party purposes; and the bitter conflicts between pro-French and anti-French interests had come near to disrupting the American body politic. Furthermore, for centuries it had been traditional that a general war in Europe inevitably involved America, not because of world questions being involved, but merely because the American continent had been a kind of pawn of European diplomacy and European rivalries. Bearing these things in mind, Washington advised not that we should have nothing to do with Europe, not that we should not coöperate with European countries on matters of general international concern or of American concern, not even that we should avoid all alliances whatsoever, but that it would be "unwise . . . to implicate ourselves . . . in the ordinary vicissitudes of her [i.e., Europe's] politics, or the ordinary combinations or collisions of her friendships, or enmities." This advice to avoid questions that are essentially or primarily European is by no means a counsel of complete isolation or a warning that we should not deal with European countries on matters that are common to Europe and ourselves. As to alliances, Washington advised that we "steer clear of permanent alliances," adding that "we may safely trust to temporary alliances for extraordinary emergencies." This reference to temporary alliances as well as the qualification of the warning against permanent alliances (to the effect that existing engagements be scrupulously kept), shows how far Washington was from any notion of absolute isolation. Besides the warnings thus far mentioned, Washington also warned against acts of our citizens which might give just offense to other nations. In his fourth annual address to Congress, November 6, 1792, he said:

> Observations on the value of peace with other nations are unnecessary. It would be wise, however, by timely provisions, to guard against those acts of our own citizens which might tend to disturb it, and to put ourselves in a condition to give that satisfaction to foreign nations, which we may sometimes have occasion to require from them.[7]

The admonition that Americans be mindful of the rights of other nations indicates that Washington's other remarks as to avoiding matters of European politics should not be given a truculent interpretation; for the reciprocal nature of international relations was ever in Washington's mind. Efforts toward the peaceful and judicial settlement of international disputes had received powerful endorsement under Washington in connection with the Jay treaty of 1794 in which various questions in dispute with England were referred to joint commissions of arbitration.

As to Jefferson, the true author of the phrase "entangling alliances," the pacific nature of his policies is well known. During the Napoleonic wars he was ready to go to great lengths to avoid involvement in the European conflict, even to the point of shutting off American commerce by the embargo. Jefferson continued and further clarified the policy of "non-participation" in European affairs, sometimes miscalled the policy of isolation. His words along this line in his third annual message to Congress, October 17, 1803, are very pertinent:

> Separated by a wide ocean from the nations of Europe, and from the political interests which entangle them together, with productions and wants which render our commerce and friendship useful to them and theirs to us, it cannot be the interest of any to assail us, nor ours to disturb them. We should be most unwise,

indeed, were we to cast away the singular blessings of the position in which nature has placed us, the opportunity she has endowed us with of pursuing, at a distance from foreign contentions, the paths of industry, peace, and happiness; of cultivating general friendship, and of bringing collisions of interest to the umpirage of reason rather than of force.[8]

One may well ask whether the effect of the widespread quotation of Jefferson's words "entangling alliances," with all the implications as to present international policies that are made to attach to these words, is not precisely the opposite of the true intention of his mind. At any rate, one may be justified in taking the last words of the above passage and pointing out their appositeness to present-day international affairs: ". . . bringing collisions of interest to the umpirage of reason rather than of force."

Both Washington and Jefferson, in the passages quoted, were addressing not Europe, but their own countrymen. They were counseling restraint and international reasonableness on the part of American citizens. Both stressed the advantages of the separating ocean and of our natural location not as a justification for a policy of isolation, but rather as an insurance that, so long as we made good as an independent power fulfilling international obligations, we need fear no attack from Europe. As we of today look back upon that period, one of the most significant factors to bear in mind is that foreign questions constantly engendered internal partisanship. The first three of our presidents, because of efforts made in the direction of peaceful relations with European countries, were subjected to the severest partisan attacks at home: Washington because of the Jay treaty; Adams for his efforts toward peace with France in 1800; and Jefferson because of his resolute refusal to permit the United States to be dragged into the maelstrom of the Napoleonic struggle.

When President Hoover laid the revised World Court protocols before the Senate, we saw in cartoons and editorials renewed references to Washington and "entangling alliances." The phrase has become once more a tool of anti-World-Court propaganda. What one finds here is a misapplication of a misquotation. A misquoted passage is taken; and inferences are drawn from it which would not even be justified if the quotation were genuine. Both Jefferson, in advising that appeal be made to the "umpirage of reason," and Washington, in the various instances of peaceful international adjustment that arose in connection with the Jay treaty, favored principles which are essentially those of the World Court today. . . .

In all these discussions of international policy, when great leaders of the past are quoted, much may be gained if the careful historian's attitude of fidelity to fact be preserved. No harm can come from an honest and genuine quotation of Washington's or Jefferson's words; but as to the implications or conclusions to be derived from them, individuals must necessarily differ. As to the particular words "entangling alliances," which have been singled out for special treatment in this article, a proper and honest quotation can never be objectionable, though it might indeed be said that the truth which the words contain is so universally acepted that it partakes somewhat of the nature of a platitude. We do not need to be continually told that two and two make four. So with "entangling alliances." We all oppose them; and on this matter there is no really vital difference of opinion. As to the propagandist use that is made of the phrase by cartoonists and editors, however, there is need for a great deal of clarifying discussion.

NOTES

1. P. W. Wilson, "Forgeries That Have Made History," *Current History,* XXXIII (November 1930), 187-94.

2. James D. Richardson, *Messages and Papers of the Presidents,* I, 323.

3. There were ghost writers even in Washington's day. The Farewell Address was written by Hamilton and copied by Washington. The text as found in W. C. Ford, ed., *Writings of Washington,* XIII, 316-18, is followed above, except that certain deleted words are not reproduced.

4. This was an agreement in 1928 between Secretary of State Frank B. Kellogg and French Foreign Minister Aristide Briand denouncing war as an instrument of national policy. It was eventually signed by sixty-four nations.—ED.

5. For illuminating discussions of important phases of early American diplomacy, see the following articles by C. A. Berdahl: "The Early Attitude of the United States Towards the Peaceful Settlement of International Disputes," *League of Nations Chronicle,* III, No. 2, 2; "The Early Attitude of the United States Towards the Principle of International Organization," *ibid.,* III, No. 3, 2.

6. During the World War the United States was not allied with the other enemies of Germany. The official documents of the period always refer to the "Allied and Associated Powers."

7. W. C. Ford, *Writings of Washington,* XII, 209.

8. P. L. Ford, ed., *Writings of Thomas Jefferson,* VIII, 273.

Washington's Farewell Address:
A Foreign Policy of Independence
BY SAMUEL FLAGG BEMIS

The Farewell Address is often thought of as an expression of abstract ideas of policy looking toward the future, but with little reference to the events of 1796. Its fundamental ideas were, on the contrary, suggested by experience, and very recent and painful experience. To comprehend Washington's point of view and feel the weight of his advice, it is necessary to consider the historical setting, and, for that, to go back to the outbreak of a general European war in February and March, 1793.

In the desperate conflict with the allied monarchies of the First Coalition the French Republic expected to find a valuable counterweight in the independent United States, separated from Great Britain by French diplomacy and arms in the previous war. Thoroughly conscious of the naval impotence of the new Amer-

Reprinted by permission from the *American Historical Review*, XXXIX (January 1934), 250-68.

ican nation, France had preferred not to invoke the *casus foederis* of the treaty of alliance of 1778—the defense of the French West India Islands. A neutral United States promised greater advantages: (1) as a possible transatlantic base of operations against enemy colonies and commerce, (2) as the largest remaining neutral supply of provisions and naval stores, commodities that perhaps might be passed through the British navy under cover of the neutral flag. To finance both of these objects there was the gradually maturing American debt.

President Washington's proclamation of neutrality and the refusal of his government to lend itself to Genêt's projects soon showed France that her ally did not intend to involve itself in the European war by becoming such a base of belligerent naval and military operations. France perforce acquiesced in that decision, being still unwilling to invoke the letter of the alliance. This was because the actual belligerency of the United States which had no navy was worth nothing in itself and had the really great disadvantage of making American shipping immediately liable to capture and confiscation as enemy property. The neutrality of the United States, even though it could not serve as a base for such projects as Genêt attempted, was far more serviceable than American military assistance. The principal object of France was to secure from neutral America provisions for her beleaguered homeland and colonies, imported in American ships under protection of the principles of the commercial treaty of 1778; free ships free goods; provisions and naval stores not contraband; neutral right to trade in non-contraband goods to and between unblockaded enemy ports.

This Franco-American treaty did not bind France's enemy, Great Britain, the principal maritime belligerent. The British had never admitted these "novel" principles. They considered them as exceptional articles in particular treaties binding only between the signatory parties. When hostilities commenced in 1793 Great Britain began seizing enemy property right and left wherever it could be found outside neutral territorial waters, whether in enemy or neutral bottoms. British prize courts under orders in council began to apply the Rule of 1756,[1] itself an innovation as late as the Seven Years' War. Secretary of State Thomas Jefferson protested in the name of the United States against this practice, which was contrary to the articles written into the Franco-

American treaty and all the other European treaties of the United States. But Great Britain was not bound by those treaties.[2] The United States was powerless to challenge the British navy. American credit, newly established, depended primarily on tariff revenue, and tariff revenue depended principally on imports from Great Britain. The collapse of credit at this time would have meant the collapse of the newly established nationality of the United States. Rather than go to war with Great Britain, President Washington took Alexander Hamilton's advice and ratified Jay's Treaty with England which acquiesced in British naval practice for the next twelve years, in effect for the duration of the war.[3] That treaty did not violate the treaties of the United States with France. It recognized a condition which already existed, namely, that the United States could not compel Great Britain to observe the terms of the Franco-American treaty. In 1793 the other maritime powers, which in the War for American Independence had followed principles similar to those of the Franco-American treaty, made treaties with Great Britain agreeing to harass the commerce of France in every possible way. These powers included the old Armed Neutrals of 1780,[4] except Sweden and Denmark. A group of ardent, hateful enemies ringed France about by land and sea to close her frontiers, to sweep her commerce from the seas, to take her colonies from her, and to deprive her of naval supplies and of foodstuffs. The neutral United States, the ally of yesteryear, which France herself had brought into the world, stood aloof and acquiesced in this British naval-diplomatic system of strangulation. Thus were frustrated the advantages of neutral carriage which France had relied on from the American treaty of amity and commerce of 1778.

This situation was aggravated in the eyes of French statesmen by Jay's Treaty. If in the face of that document and of British practice the French were still to adhere to the terms of the American treaty, they would have to stand quietly by and watch British cruisers take French property from neutral American ships, confiscate American-owned naval stores as contraband when *en route* in American vessels to France, and preëmpt (as was the British practice) foodstuffs under similar conditions. Deprived thus by belligerent action of naval stores, foodstuffs, and of the advantages of neutral carriage, they would find themselves obliged to abstain from following the British practice; they would have to watch these same goods go unchallenged by French warships into British harbors to feed and strengthen the might of the enemy.

It is not difficult to understand that this seemed unfair to France, and that Jay's Treaty seemed an outrageous, even a treacherous document, made by an ungrateful nation. But one would be more ready to sympathize with France if her own hands were clean. We must remember that when John Jay signed his famous treaty with Lord Grenville on November 19, 1794, France herself was pursuing and had been pursuing, off and on, since May 9, 1793, a maritime policy of retaliation in practice identical with that of Great Britain in the treatment of neutral shipping, and had been applying it to American ships and cargoes,[5] and that notwithstanding her obligations under her treaty with the United States. As in later European wars (1803-1812, and 1914-1917) the force of these belligerent retaliations fell heavily on the neutral United States and developed grave diplomatic problems. Unlike the later wars, in this case the United States was protected by the paper and ink of a treaty against such practice on the part of one belligerent. Nevertheless, French spoliations on American shipping rivaled those of Great Britain. French privateers and naval vessels also vied with the British in violence and outrages against neutral crews and passengers.[6]

The French diplomatic commission, headed by Joseph Fauchet, which in 1794 had succeeded the ruined Genêt in Philadelphia, did not even pretend to reconcile French maritime policy with the obligations of the treaty of commerce of 1778. Nevertheless it claimed for France all the articles of the treaty which were of advantage to her, and requested benevolent interpretations of them. The Committee of Public Safety, in drawing up instructions for these commissioners, anticipated that there would be objections in the United States to the retaliatory French decrees. Admitting deviations from the treaty it became the task of the commissioners to extenuate French policy on the ground of altered circumstances.[7]

Washington and his advisers had foreseen the possible further effect on France of the intended treaty between the United States and Great Britain when John Jay, the Federalist, pro-British diplomatist departed on his famous mission to London. To mask this mission they sent to France the pro-French Republican senator from Virginia James Monroe, an old opponent of Jay's diplomacy since 1786, who considered Jay's mission as mischievous and in the Senate voted against his confirmation. Monroe never saw Jay's instructions, possibly was not aware of their real scope.

Like an apostle of the rights of man, Monroe set to work to persuade the French government to observe the treaty of amity and commerce of 1778. The restrictions on private trade in French harbors, the embargoes, the delays in payment for purchased cargoes, had already so jeopardized the American provision supply that the Convention admitted the force of the American remonstrances on every point except free ships free goods.[8] The envoy now argued for the full and entire enforcement of the articles of the treaty. He appealed to old friendship and present interest. He contended that it would be good policy for France to repeal her obnoxious decree before Great Britain should repeal hers. If she did so, it would combine all America in condemnation of the conduct of the British; if she did not, any later repeal would appear merely to be forced by her enemy. At just this time news arrived[9] of the setting aside, by an order in council of August 6, 1794, of the British provision order of June 8, 1793 —this had been a means in London of easing the English negotiations with Jay. It reënforced Monroe's argument in Paris. The French law of May 9, 1793, had made the duration of the "retaliatory" maritime measures contingent upon the repeal by the enemy of his illegal procedure. The Convention now (January 2, 1795) availed itself of this provision to yield to the importunities of the ingratiating James Monroe. "As a grand act of honesty and justice," it wiped out at one stroke all of the offensive decrees and enjoined the strict observance of the provisions of the treaty of 1778.[10] Orders were immediately given for the adjudication of all claims arising out of violations of that treaty.

Monroe's triumph was short-lived. Before anything very effective could actually be done about the relief of the claimants, the significance of Jay's Treaty[11] began to be suspected in Paris. In August, 1795, the text arrived from Philadelphia. It completely undid Monroe's successes. In 1796 Washington recalled the unhappy minister for not having defended with sufficient vigor the new English treaty.[12] In truth Monroe had repeated to the French government the arguments and defenses sent to him by Secretaries

of State Randolph and Pickering. They read well, but one may
doubt that his heart was in his words. He thought Jay's Treaty a
shameful document.[13] There is evidence suggesting that he had
confidential conversations with the French Revolutionary leaders
about "the real dispositions of his countrymen," conversations
which he did not reveal to his own government.[14] He kept up
an intimate correspondence with Madison,[15] and other friends of
Jefferson, who opposed Jay's Treaty and favored a pro-French
policy. He certainly led the French government to believe that
any treaty of amity between the United States and Great Britain
would never be ratified.[16] When it was known that a treaty had
been signed, Monroe repeated this assurance.[17] When Jay's Treaty
went through Congress he tried rather lamely to explain its
success, and still argued that it would be good policy for the
French Republic to observe loyally the terms of its American
treaties; the example of that loyalty and the contrasting attitude
of the British government would win the good will of the American *people,* from whose eyes the scales of British deception must
eventually fall.[18] He led them in Paris to believe that the people
would overthrow the administration of President Washington as
a result of the treaty, that better things might be expected after
the election of 1796.[19] This supposition was reënforced by advice
from the French diplomatic representative in the United States,
Fauchet, and his successor Adet, and by Americans in Paris like
Monroe's friend, Tom Paine.

After Jay's departure from New York Fauchet had become
increasingly nervous about the object of the new mission. He
sent one of his colleagues to Paris to warn the Committee of Public
Safety that something was in the air, and to say that the other
two members of the commission, La Forest and Petry, could not
be trusted because they hobnobbed with Alexander Hamilton and
other Federalists.[20] When the news of the signature of the treaty
and rumors of its contents began to leak out, the French minister
became very much exasperated. His notes of protest against
fancied violations of neutral obligations under the treaty of 1778
took on a more rasping tone, full of intimations of American
disloyalty. Fauchet tried by fair means and foul, but in vain, to
block the ratification of the treaty by the Senate. He hoped with
Secretary Randolph that the President might not sign the ratification, even though the Senate had so advised and consented. His

successor Adet, encouraged by the widespread popular protests, labored with the House of Representatives to refuse the appropriations necessary to carry it into effect. When the treaty passed unscathed through the House, Adet's last hope was that the people would overthrow the administration of President Washington in the forthcoming election of 1796.[21] Through the agency of organs of the Republican press which he manipulated and inspired to the extent of his limited financial resources, and by means of the democratic societies which had arisen at the wave of Genêt's wand to applaud the French Revolution, the French minister was working with might and main to that end.[22] He did not know, of course, of the President's determination, long since fixed and presently to be announced, to refuse a third term.

In Paris, American affairs had received less attention than they merited. Before the reorganization of the French government under the constitution of the Year III (1795) the rapidly changing administration of the foreign office failed to give them methodical attention. French diplomatists at Philadelphia complained bitterly that their dispatches went unanswered. For months they waited without instructions. None of them had been told what to do about Jay's Treaty. Fauchet, and his successor Adet, had acted on their own responsibility in their protests against that instrument. The new Directory put the conduct of foreign affairs on a more businesslike basis, under a single minister, Charles Delacroix. He straightway brought in a report concerning the United States. Washington must go, he said. "A friend of France must succeed him in that eminent office." He continued:

> We must raise up the people and at the same time conceal the lever by which we do so. . . . I propose to the Executive Directory to authorize me to send orders and instructions to our minister plenipotentiary at Philadelphia to use all the means in his power in the United States to bring about the right kind of revolution [*l'heureuse Révolution*] and Washington's replacement, which, assuring to the Americans their independence, will break off treaties [*sic*] made with England and maintain those which unite them to the French Republic.

As in the case of the Netherlands at that time, France and French agents regarded that political party in the United States which was most useful to their purposes as the "patriot" party. Jefferson, Madison, Monroe, Robert R. Livingston, Senator Taze-

well of Virginia, Governor Clinton of New York, and Governor
Mifflin of Pennsylvania were patriots. Washington, Hamilton, Jay,
Rufus King, and John Adams were aristocrats unfriendly to real
liberty. The French foreign office looked on the United States
as "the Holland of the New World." It hoped for and expected
a popular revolution there, on French models, such as did take
place in Holland in 1795, to overturn the existing régime of
ordered liberty, to cast off the formidable ascendency of President
Washington and his Federalist advisers who themselves were es-
teemed to be beyond the reach of French influence and purpose.[23]

At first the Directory decided on a more positive step to offset
Jay's Treaty: to send a special envoy extraordinary to Philadelphia to recall Adet and to announce the end of the Franco-
American treaties and then himself to withdraw.[24] Monroe con-
fidentially urged Delacroix against such action: it would please
the enemies of both countries. "Left to ourselves," he hinted,
"everything will I think be satisfactorily arranged and *perhaps
in the course of the present year*: and it is always more grateful
to make such arrangements ourselves than to be pressed to it."[25]

Delacroix[26] and the Directory took the advice of President
Washington's minister to await the President's overthrow. They
blamed Washington, Hamilton, and the Federalist Senate, in short
the elected government of the people of the United States, against
which, according to French agents and correspondents (including
Americans in Paris), the people were now in an uproar, from
Boston to Savannah. Well they knew that Monroe's hint referred
to the approaching presidential election of 1796.[27] They decided
to temporize, to protest, to argue (Monroe had advised them not
to abandon their claims for redress), pending the new presidential
election, to work up "patriot" sentiment against Washington's
administration. To this effect they approved instructions to a
new minister.[28] Later came news of the success of Jay's Treaty
in the House of Representatives. They then decided not to send
any new minister after all, but keep Adet in Philadelphia for a
short while at least, and to follow his advice, and that of the
returned Fauchet, to hearten the pro-French "patriots" in America
by an unmistakable denunciation of the policy of the executive
of the United States, lest by French silence the election should
go in Washington's favor.

The inveterate tendency of French policy to stir up the American people against their government had gradually steeled the sympathies of President Washington against the old ally. Though Washington could not know the inner counsels of the French Directory—least of all when he had a minister like Monroe in Paris—the policy of France had been made abundantly apparent by the French diplomatists in Philadelphia. Since Genêt's time they had been openly or covertly attempting to join forces with the anti-Federalist opposition. They had been able to promise themselves much from such strategy because of radical political affinities and because of the memory of French help in the American Revolution. But the French alliance, indispensable as it was to American independence, had always been a great embarrassment to American diplomatists. It was so even during the diplomacy of the Revolution itself, when Vergennes had wavered under the threats of a separate Spanish peace (though his wavering has become known only to scholars in our own day). It was so during the peace negotiations of 1782 in Paris. Experience with it showed the Fathers the danger to independence and sovereignty of any other alliance. Toward the close of the war Congress shrank from committing itself to the Dutch proposal to join the Armed Neutrality. In 1786 John Jay's initialed alliance with Spain (never revealed fully until the twentieth century) collapsed before the opposition of the Southern states who feared for the Mississippi. Soon after, the South united with New England (anxious about its fisheries)[29] and wrote into the Constitution that potent provision that no future treaty could be ratified except by the vote of two-thirds of the senators present in the upper chamber of the national legislature, that Senate in which there must always be exactly two senators from each state. To a certain degree this fixed a constitutional obstacle against European entanglements. More than one delegate supported it for that reason.[30]

The French alliance had become increasingly embarrassing after the French declaration of war on England, February 1, 1793. The proclamation of neutrality was a tangible expression of a sane American policy not of isolation but of diplomatic independence. Washington refused all new foreign alliances. As Hamilton so indiscreetly told the British minister, Hammond, in 1794, he rejected the Swedish invitation to join the second, abortive, armed neutrality of 1794. He also turned down Godoy's famous "propositions for the President," of that same year, for a Spanish alliance, as Pinckney too later repelled them in Madrid. In short, the very life-saving French alliance had long since cured the United States of any hankering for more allies.

The first twenty years of American independence had in fact made American statesmen shy of Europe, and they have remained so ever since. Their writings (with the possible exception of James Monroe, whose name after 1823 was to become so inseparably associated with abstention from European politics and wars!) are full of affirmations that it was the true policy of the United States to steer clear of European politics.[31]

Tom Paine had been the first to express this, in 1776. "'Tis the true interest of America, to steer clear of European contentions, which she never can do, while by her dependance on Britain, she is made the make-weight in the scale of British politics."[32] "I do not love to be entangled in the politics of Europe," wrote John Adams in 1777.[33] In the Virginia ratifying convention in 1788, Madison speaking for the adoption of the new Federal Constitution asked: "What is the situation of America?" and answered, "She is remote from Europe, and ought not to engage in her politics or wars."[34] Jefferson in France had written in 1787: "I know too that it is a maxim with us, and I think it a wise one, not to entangle ourselves with the affairs of Europe."[35] Again, in 1790: "At such a distance from Europe, and with such an ocean between us, we hope to meddle little in its quarrels or combinations. Its peace and its commerce are what we shall court. . . ."[36] Hamilton repeatedly had used words almost identical with essential portions of the text of Washington's Farewell Address of 1796.[37] So had the President, particularly in 1795.[38]

If George Washington had retired from the presidency in the spring of 1793,[39] as he originally intended when he first consulted James Madison about the draft of a valedictory, we may presume that he would never have said anything about foreign affairs. There would have been no Farewell Address of the kind that has become so familiar to us—though we cannot say that the policy itself would not soon have been formulated. Certainly Washington's suggestions, and Madison's draft, for a possible valedictory in 1792, did not touch foreign affairs. In the summer of 1796, however, foreign affairs were uppermost in the mind of the Father of His Country. Then unalterably resolved not to serve another term, he prepared to indite a final message to the American people at large.

It was to remove foreign interference in our domestic affairs, to preserve the nation and the people from Europe's distresses, that the retiring first President, with a particular eye to relations with France, marked out for his now private adviser, Alexander Hamilton, the subjects which he would like to include in his final address. In characteristically familiar and felicitous phrases —many of which we may find already expressed in the *Federalist* and other products of his pen—Hamilton wrote out the President's ideas.[40] Of Washington were the trunk and branches of the sturdy tree. The shimmering foliage dancing and shining in the sunlight was Hamilton's. The President edited several drafts before the address was finished. He cast out at least one extraneous thought which Hamilton tried gratuitously to slip in. Despite Hamilton's principal part in the phrasing of the document, and his previous expression of some of the ideas, we may be sure that in the final text the two men were thinking together in absolute unison. The Address was as directly pointed to the diplomatic problems of the time of the French Revolution as were Woodrow Wilson's Fourteen Points to the intricate diplomacy of the World War. President Wilson and Colonel House worked no more intimately together on that document in 1918, drafting and redrafting its clauses, than did President Washington and Colonel Hamilton in 1796, composing and recomposing the paragraphs of the Farewell Address.

The immortal document, ever since a polestar of American foreign policy, represented the crystallization of the experience of remarkably clear-headed men with foreign affairs since the Declaration of Independence. It was given forthwith to the public in a newspaper.[41] It spoke directly to the great and simple audience of the American people. "The name of AMERICAN," it said to them, putting the word into bold type, "which belongs to you in your national capacity, must always exalt the just pride of Patriotism, more than any appellation derived from local discriminations." We must keep in mind the involvement of the French alliance in American diplomacy and domestic politics as we read the Farewell Address, even as the authors of the document had that constantly before them.

It began thus with an appeal to support the *National Union*.
The orthodox phrase Federal Union does not occur in the document, a very significant omission. It continued with a counsel
against the practice of party politics, lest the new nation be un-
dermined by internal dissension assisted by foreign intrigue. The
first President and his adviser Alexander Hamilton believed that,
with the system of checks and balances in the new government,
party politics was unnecessary for the preservation of ordered
liberty. The rise of an opposition they identified with a faction
opposed not only to the policies of the administration but to the
new national government itself. They connected this faction with
the French government and its agents.

Turning to the subject of foreign affairs, the Address admonished his fellow citizens to steer clear of European alliances and
wars. It justified American neutrality whilst the nation, assisted
by the advantages of so peculiar a situation, might grow strong
enough to command its own fortune. In these words and these
counsels the authors of the Address had continually before them
the apparition of the life-giving, but the entangling, French alliance, and the distant scene of the great wars engulfing Europe.
They had behind them the problems solved by Jay's Treaty and
by Pinckney's Treaty, thanks to the occupation of Britain and
Spain with those troubles in Europe.

The immediate purpose of the Address was to strike a powerful
blow against French intermeddling in American affairs.[42] After
the victory of Jay's Treaty in the House of Representatives it had
been Adet's advice, and this was also recommended by the returned Fauchet,[43] that some strong and positive action ought to
be taken to make the American ally more amenable to French
interests. The people, both of those agents had reported—and
reported most voluminously—were in favor of France and opposed to their government, but if France did not call Washington's government to terms, and thus support the action of the
"good" people to overthrow it, nothing could be hoped from
them. Adet advocated[44] that the French Republic proceed to
treat American ships precisely as the United States government
allowed its flag to be treated by Great Britain, that is, according
to the principles of Jay's Treaty. This was, indeed, what France
had been doing up to January 3, 1795, when Monroe secured
from the Convention the full and entire recognition of the treaty

60951

of 1778. But that "grand act of honesty and justice" had not been enforced since the nature of Jay's Treaty had become suspect in France. Nor was it ever to be. It was to be the United States government itself which was finally to pay—throughout a century of litigation—most of the damages to its citizens wrought by the French spoliations in this war.

Jay's Treaty at last having gone into effect, the French Directory prepared its denunciation of the treachery of Washington's government. As a warning to the American people of worse things to follow if President Washington were continued in office, it decided to suspend Adet's functions, and with them formal diplomatic relations with the United States. Characterizing Jay's Treaty as equivalent to an alliance between France's principal enemy and her old ungrateful ally, it proceeded to invoke against American shipping, as a reprisal for that perfidious treaty, the maritime principles of that document itself.[45] If Jefferson should be elected, the plan was to restore relations on the old basis, hoping that a new treaty with France might undo Jay's.[46]

To his great satisfaction Adet was able to communicate to the United States government, on October 27, 1796, the text of a decree of the Directory announcing that "All neutral or allied Powers shall, without delay, be notified that the flag of the French republic will treat neutral vessels, either as to confiscation, as to searches, or capture, in the same manner as they shall suffer the English to treat them."[47]

A few weeks later (November 15) he announced the definite suspension of his functions, not, indeed, to indicate a formal rupture between the United States and France, "but as a mark of just discontent, which is to last until the government of the United States returns to sentiments, and to measures, more conformable to the interests of the alliance, and the sworn friendship of the two nations."

It was now the eve of the presidential election of 1796. The several states were choosing their electors. They still had to meet and cast their votes. The precedent had not yet become set which allows the electors no canvass or deliberation among themselves. The French move was studiously calculated to influence the electors to choose Jefferson instead of John Adams.[48] With this in mind, according to his instructions, Adet accompanied his announcement of suspension of his functions with a long and *ex-*

parte review (with documents) of the whole quarrel between France and the United States over American neutrality. He included a passionate indictment of Jay's Treaty, all under cover of a fervid manifesto to the American people. A summary in English of the contents of this note appeared in the newspapers before the translation of the French original could be prepared in the Department of State. "Let your Government return to itself," wrote Adet, addressing the people rather than the government to which his note was delivered, "and you will still find in Frenchmen faithful friends and generous allies."[49]

To that uncompromising Federalist, Timothy Pickering, old soldier, negotiator of Indian treaties, professional and capable officeholder, and general utility man in Washington's cabinet, now fell the task of defending the foreign policy laid down in the Farewell Address. Four others had declined the proffered appointment of Secretary of State, with its meager emolument, before he took it. Though Pickering had no special training for the office, he was a facile penman and a sharp-minded debater. These were the qualifications principally in demand from 1795 to 1800.

Space only forbids us to describe and to analyze Pickering's defense of American neutrality, of Jay's Treaty with England, in short of the foreign policy of George Washington. We may be sure that it was inspired by Alexander Hamilton,[50] the man who inspired Jay's Treaty and who phrased the Farewell Address. The remarkable public disputations took the form of instructions to Charles C. Pinckney dated January 16, 1797, who had already sailed to France as successor to the recalled Monroe; but their real purpose, as shown by their immediate release to the press on January 19, 1797,[51] was to serve as a counter-manifesto to Adet's passionate attacks on the administration and his undercover efforts to secure the election of Thomas Jefferson rather than John Adams, the champion of Washington's policies. The historian today who is privileged to read the archives of France and the United States can have no serious quarrel with Pickering's eloquent rebuttal of French charges of American ingratitude directed against Washington's government, nor with his blunt conclusion after a long review that France owed fully as much to the United States as the United States owed to France in the way of services rendered. The day for finesse had passed. It was time that someone put the truth in this way to the American people, at a moment when foreign diplomacy was again trying to reach over the heads of their government to whip them into European complications. Even then in 1795 and 1796 while French diplomatists were accusing the United States of ingratitude and treachery, they themselves were plotting to reestablish control and tutelage over the American republic by getting Louisiana and West Florida back from Spain, allying France with the southwestern Indians, and tempting the allegiance to the Union of the new western states, to build up thereby a new colonial empire that would be the preponderant power in the New World.[52]

The instructions to C. C. Pinckney,[53] embodying these arguments, rank . . . as one of the greatest defensive documents in the diplomatic history of the United States. Pickering's paper clinched the case of President Washington's foreign policy.

Before the document was printed the presidential electors had elected John Adams President by a majority of one vote and a margin of three votes over Thomas Jefferson, who became Vice President according to the original constitutional provision. Washington's successor fully recognized that the significance of his election lay in the question whether the American people were to govern themselves or be governed by foreign nations.[54] As President he took over Washington's policies, and, to his later vexation, his entire cabinet.

We cannot conclude that Pickering's instructions to Pinckney decided the election. It had been won already. The dispatch was published after the votes of the electors had been announced on the first Wednesday in January, but before they were formally counted on the first Wednesday in February. The document was rather an appeal to the people to support the foreign policy of Washington—and of Hamilton—and an argument to open the door to an escape from the French alliance, by proving, as Hamilton suggested, that the United States had maintained good faith with its engagements; that if the conduct of the other party released it, the release should not be refused, so far as possible without compromising peace. "This idea is very important," Hamilton wrote to Wolcott, of course for Pickering's benefit.[55]

Despite the high hopes which France had placed on Jefferson's election, both John Adams and his close contestant, the new Vice President, Thomas Jefferson, were equally good Americans (albeit of different political philosophy), and, incidentally, almost equally good friends of France. Nor were they unfriendly to each other. Jefferson had gone so far as to authorize his friend Madison to advise electors, in case of a tie, to vote for Adams as a statesman of senior claims to the presidency.[56] Adet came to sense this relationship before he left. He wrote:

> Mr. Jefferson likes us because he detests England; he seeks to draw near to us because he fears us less than England; but tomorrow he might change his opinion about us if England should cease to inspire his fear. Although Jefferson is the friend of liberty and of science, although he is an admirer of the efforts we have made to cast off our shackles and to clear away the cloud of ignorance which weighs down the human race, Jefferson, I say, is an American, and as such, he cannot sincerely be our friend. An American is the born enemy of all the peoples of Europe.[57]

Such was the historical setting of the famous Farewell Address. Such were the reasons for its pronouncement in 1796, so different a pronouncement from what it would have been if given to the people in 1792. Such was its victory over foreign intrigue within our own country. It did not disown the French alliance, but it taught a patronizing ally that we were an independent and a sovereign nation, and that the French Republic could not use in America the tool that had been so successful with the border satellite states in Europe, the lever of a political opposition to overthrow any government that stood in the way of French policy, purpose, and interest. In Washington's time avoidance of foreign alliances and of foreign entanglement was a question of independence and national sovereignty. What we have generally construed as a policy of "isolation" we ought really to interpret as a policy of vigilant defense and maintenance of sovereign national independence against foreign meddling in our own intimate domestic concerns.

NOTES

1. Trade which was closed in peacetime could not be opened in wartime.—ED.

2. Great Britain had accepted these principles in the treaty of commerce in 1786 with France, but of course that treaty had ceased to exist with the outbreak of war.

3. I have dwelt in detail upon the significance of this in my *Jay's Treaty* (New York, 1923).

4. A league of neutral nations organized during the Revolution to prevent British violations of their maritime rights.—ED.

5. The various French laws and decrees affecting neutral commerce were:

May 9, 1793. Law of the National Convention decreeing orders to naval officers and commanders of privateers to bring in "neutral ships laden in whole or part either with foodstuffs belonging to neutrals and destined to enemy ports, or with goods belonging to the enemy," the former to be purchased at the price they would have commanded at the port of their intended destination, the latter to be confiscated, and an allowance to be fixed by the prize court for freight and detention.

This act was professedly in retaliation for specified British spoliations on neutral ships and was retroactive to all prizes brought in since the beginning of the war [which implies that some had been brought in before the occasion for "retaliation"]. Compare it with similar provisions of Article 1 of the British order in council of June 8, 1793. The law of May 9 was to cease to have effect when the enemy powers should declare free and non-seizable foodstuffs which were neutral property and destined to the ports of the French Republic, as well as merchandise belonging to the French government or French citizens on board neutral ships. *Lois et artes du gouvernement* (Paris, Imprimerie Royale, 1834), VII, 51-2. The laws and decrees referred to here may also be found in the convenient *Collection complète des lois*, etc., of J. B. Duvergier, under each date. *American State Papers, Foreign Relations* (Washington, 1833), I, 377 [hereinafter cited as A.S.P., F.R., I].

May 23, 1793. Law of the National Convention exempting American ships from the operation of the law of May 9, 1793, "conformably to Article XVI [sic] of the treaty of February 6, 1778" [Article XVI deals with the irrelevent matter of restoration of captures made by pirates. Presumably Article XXIII was meant]. *Lois et actes,* VII. 82; A.S.P., F.R., I, 365.

May 28, 1793. Law of the National Convention repealing the law of May 23, 1793, which exempted American ships. *Lois et actes,* VII, 82-3.

July 1, 1793. Law restoring the exemption of American ships, in phraseology identical with that of May 23, 1793. *Ibid.,* VII, 174.

July 27, 1793. Law decreeing the full execution of the law of May 9, 1793, relative to neutral ships loaded with foodstuffs owned by neutrals or with enemy property. *Ibid.,* VII, 241-42.

March 24, 1794. Law decreeing: "The treaties of navigation and of commerce existing between France and nations with whom she is at peace shall be executed according to their form and tenure." *Ibid.,* VIII, 414-15.

November 18, 1794. Decree of the Committee of Public Safety enjoining French naval officers and commanders of privateers to enforce the law of nations and the stipulations of treaties, "conformably to the terms of the decree of the National Convention of July 27, 1793." A.S.P., F.R., I, 689, 752. This decree does not appear in the *Recueil des actes du Comité de salut public,* edited by Alphonse A. Aulard. Jay's Treaty was signed on November 19, 1794.

6. In addition to an undetermined number of captures at sea, Fulwar

Skipwith, American claims agent at Paris in October, 1794, stated that there were nearly 300 vessels in the ports of France suffering from embargoes (a later list showed that the Bordeaux embargo accounted for 103 cases), spoliations, delays, breaches of contract, non-payment of purchased cargoes, etc. The United States Court of Claims, which completed adjudication of the French Spoliation Claims for 1793-1800 (responsibility having been assumed by the convention with France of 1800) awarded a total of $7,149,306.10 for 1853 authentic cases of spoliation. Each case did not however represent a particular ship. Congress has appropriated to date only $3,910,860.61, to pay part of these claims. To this may be added $5,000,000 for claims of a special character, assumed by the United States in 1803, in part payment for Louisiana—to wit: embargoes, detention and appropriation of goods in French harbors, money due from the French government for purchases, etc.

7. *Correspondence of the French Ministers to the United States, 1791-1797*, Frederick J. Turner, ed., in Annual Report of the American Historical Association, II (1903), 291.

8. A.S.P., F.R., I, 677.

9. See report of Merlin de Douai, brumaire, an III, *Archives du ministère des Affaires étrangères, Correspondance politique, États-Unis*, Vol. 42, 186-204.

10. Law of 13 nivôse, an III, *Bulletin des lois de la République française, 1° sér.*, III, No. 107; decree of the committee of public safety, 14 nivôse, an III (Jan. 3, 1795), A.S.P., F.R., I, 624 [in English translation; not in Aulard].

11. Before the repeal of the retaliatory decrees the committee had asked Monroe about the treaty; and he had conveyed to them information from Jay, to the effect that it contained nothing contrary to the existing treaties of the United States; and had promised that as soon as he might be informed of its contents he would inform the committee. This promise impelled Monroe to refuse to accept from Jay a *confidential* statement of the contents of the treaty. Monroe's *View of the Conduct of the Executive on the Foreign Affairs of the United States, connected with the Mission of the French Republic during the Years 1794, 5 and 6* (Philadelphia, 1797), pp. xvii-xxviii.

12. Monroe's instructions and dispatches are printed in A.S.P., F.R., I, and in his exculpatory *View*. Washington's studied comments on the *View*, written at Mount Vernon on the margin of its pages, are printed in appendix II to Daniel C. Gilman's *James Monroe* (Boston, 1883, 1898). Beverley W. Bond, Jr.'s "The Monroe Mission to France, 1794-1796," in The Johns Hopkins *Studies in Historical and Political Science*, XXV (1907), 9-103, did not have available the valuable sources in the French ministry of foreign affairs. The various deliberations of committees on Monroe's notes, and relevant reports, quite voluminous, are in Arch. Aff. Étr., Etats-Unis, Vol. 42, particularly 17, 141, 186-204.

13. Monroe to Joseph Jones, Sept. 15, 1795. Calendar, in Division of MSS. of the Library of Congress, of the Gouverneur Collection of Monroe

Papers, now privately owned. Gilman, *James Monroe,* p. 62, printed a portion of this letter.

14. Monroe wrote to the committee of public safety a "non-official letter," December 27, 1794, asking that a member of the Committee be deputed to have frank conversations with him concerning any propositions "about to be made to the American government on this subject [i.e., possible propositions] or any other (if you desire) tending to acquaint you [the committees] with the situation and the *real* dispositions of my *countrymen* [italics inserted]." Arch. Aff. Étr., États-Unis, Vol. 42, 445.

15. Stanislaus Murray Hamilton, ed., *Writings of James Monroe* (New York, 1898-1903), II, *passim.*

16. Adet to the committee of public safety, 14 thermidor, an III (Aug. 1, 1795) *Corr. Fr. Min.,* p. 762.

17. "I assured them, generally, as I had done before, that I was satisfied the treaty contained in it nothing which could give them uneasiness; but if it did, and especially if it weakened our connexion with France, it would certainly be disapproved in America." Monroe to the Secretary of State, Apr. 14, 1795, A.S.P., F.R., I, 702. He did convey to the Committee of Public Safety Jay's only statement to him about the treaty, that it contained nothing contrary to the treaty stipulations of the United States with other countries.

18. "Exposé sommaire," etc., dated 1796, in the Monroe Collection of MSS, Library of Congress. Internal evidence proves Monroe to be the writer, and one presumes from the same evidence that it was directed to the French government, although I have not found it in the French archives.

19. Monroe to the minister of foreign affairs, Paris, 28 pluviôse, an IV (Feb. 17, 1796), Arch. Aff. Étr., États-Unis, Vol. 45, 146.

20. *Corr. Fr. Min.,* pp. 373, 380, 410, 419; Arch. Aff. Étr., États-Unis, Vol. 41, 291, 377, 408.

21. *Corr. Fr. Min.,* p. 894. Neither Fauchet and the commissioners, nor their successor Adet, had any actual instructions concerning Jay's Treaty. Once they left Paris, they received scant attention from the Committee of Public Safety.

22. Bernard Faÿ, *L'esprit révolutionnaire en France et aux-États-Unis à la fin du XVIIIᵉ siècle* (Paris, 1925), pp. 254-60. "All these intrigues are sad and displeasing to study when one remembers the sincere enthusiasm which the masses of the American people then testified for France," *ibid.,* p. 255. John Bach McMaster, *History of the People of the United States* (New York, 1883-1913), II, Ch. IX, is in effect a digest of opposing press and pamphlet comment. The arguments of the Republican press against Jay's Treaty, against Washington, against the Farewell Address, and finally against the candidacy of John Adams, reflect the paragraphs of the political correspondence of the French foreign office with its American legation.

23. To this point there is a remarkable analysis of American politics in relation to French policy, by the undersecretary of the sixth division of

the foreign office; "Memoir on the United States, Florida and Louisiana," 12 frimaire, an IV (Dec. 3, 1795). Arch. Aff. Étr., États-Unis, Vol. 44, 407-17.

24. Report on the minister of foreign affairs to the Executive Directory, 27 nivôse, an IV (Jan. 17, 1796), *ibid.*, Vol. 45, 41-53.

25. Monroe to the minister of foreign affairs, Paris, 28 pluviôse, an IV (Feb. 17, 1796), *ibid.*, Vol. 45, 147 [italics inserted]. This highly significant note was not revealed to his own government and is enough to justify Washington's removal of Monroe. Monroe summarized the arguments he had made to Delacroix in a letter to the Secretary of State on February 20, 1796, but made no reference to any written note of his and said nothing about the hint he had given.

26. Delacroix to Monroe, Paris, 1 ventôse, an IV (Feb. 20, 1796), *ibid.*, Vol. 45, 160.

27. Observations on Mr. Monroe's letter to the minister of foreign affairs, not dated, *ibid.*, Vol. 45, 148.

28. "Memoir of Political Instructions to the Citizen Vincent, to be sent as Minister Plenipotentiary of the Republic to the United States," *Recuil des actes du Directoire exécutif,* A. Debidour, ed. (Paris, 1910), I, 748; II, 621. Some charges against Vincent's integrity apparently stopped his departure. Later Monroe's protest against the appointment of Mangourit, the former French consul at Charleston during Genêt's obnoxious operations, was effective.

29. R. Earl McClendon published a useful note on the "Origin of the Two-Thirds Rule in Senate Action upon Treaties," *American Historical Review,* XXXVI, 768-72.

30. J. Fred Rippy and Angie Debo, "The Historical Background of the American Policy of Isolation," *Smith College Studies in History,* IX, Nos. 3 and 4 (Apr.-July, 1924), 140.

31. Rippy and Debo, "American Policy of Isolation," have collected numerous expressions of abstention from European politics.

32. *Common Sense* (Philadelphia, 1776, 1st ed.), p. 38.

33. Rippy and Debo, "American Policy of Isolation," p. 90.

34. Gaillard Hunt, ed., *The Writings of James Madison* (New York, 1900-1910), V, 151.

35. Paul Leicester Ford, ed., *The Writings of Thomas Jefferson* (New York, 1892-1899), IV, 483.

36. To Monsieur de Pinto, New York, August 7, 1790, *The Writings of Thomas Jefferson,* Memorial ed. (Washington, 1903-1904), VIII, 74.

37. Over the signature of *Horatius,* arguing for the ratification of Jay's Treaty, Hamilton wrote in 1795: "If you consult your true interest your motto cannot fail to be: 'PEACE AND TRADE WITH ALL NATIONS; beyond our present engagements, POLITICAL CONNECTION WITH NONE.' You ought to spurn from you as the box of Pandora, the fatal heresy of a close alliance, or in the language of *Genêt,* a true *family compact* with France. This would at once make you a mere satellite of France, and entangle you in all the contests, broils, and wars

of Europe." The text continues: "'Tis evident that the controversies of Europe must often grow out of causes and interests foreign to this country. Why then should we, by a close political connection with any power of Europe, expose our peace and interest, as a matter of course, to all the shocks with which their mad rivalship and wicked ambition so frequently convulse the earth? 'Twere insanity to embrace such a system." Henry Cabot Lodge, ed., *The Works of Alexander Hamilton* (New York, 1885-1886), IV, 366-67.

38. To Patrick Henry, Oct. 9, 1795; to Gouverneur Morris, Dec. 22, 1795; Worthington Chauncey Ford, ed., *The Writings of George Washington* (New York, 1889-1893), XIII, 119, 151. Washington refused to lend his official intercession to assist the release from Austrian and Prussian prisons of his dearest friend, Lafayette, for fear of involving the United States in Europe's wars. See my article in *Daughters of the American Revolution Magazine,* LVIII, Nos. 6, 7, and 8 (June, July, August 1924).

39. I have profited from discussions of President Washington's policies with Mr. Frank Louraine of Washington, D.C., particularly on the significance of the Farewell Address in 1796, instead of 1792.

40. Horace Binney in one of the first critical essays in American historiography analyzed the authorship of the document. *An Inquiry into the Formation of Washington's Farewell Address* (Philadelphia, 1859).

41. Claypoole's *American Daily Advertiser* (Philadelphia, Sept. 19, 1796).

42. Enclosing the document, Adet reported: "It would be useless to speak to you about it. You will have noticed the lies it contains, the insolent tone that governs it, the immorality which characterizes it. You will have no difficulty in recognizing the author of a piece extolling ingratitude, showing it as a virtue necessary to the happiness of States, presenting interest as the only counsel which governments ought to follow in the course of their negotiations, putting aside honor and glory. You will have recognized immediately the doctrine of the former Secretary of the Treasury, Hamilton, and the principles of loyalty that have always directed the Philadelphia Government." *Corr. Fr. Min.* p. 954.

43. See Fauchet's long Memoir on the United States of America, 24 frimaire, an IV (Dec. 15, 1795), Arch. Aff. Étr., États-Unis, Vol. 44, 457-529.

44. *Corr. Fr. Min.,* pp. 900-6.

45. The minister of foreign affairs to Adet, 7 fructidor, an IV (Aug. 24, 1796), Arch. Aff. Étr., États-Unis, Vol. 46, 144-45. See also drafts and reports associated with these instructions, *ibid.,* 133-40.

46. Same to same, 12 brumaire, an V (Nov. 2, 1796), *ibid.,* 355-58.

47. Translation of an extract from the resolves of the Directory, of the 14th messidor, an IV (July 2, 1796). A.S.P., F.R., I, 577. This extract is not printed in the proceedings for that date of the Actes du Directoire exécutif.

48. *Corr. Fr. Min.,* p. 972.

49. A.S.P., F.R., I, 583.

50. See Hamilton to Wolcott, Nov. 22, 1796. George Gibbs, *Memoirs of the Administrations of Washington and John Adams, edited from the papers of Oliver Wolcott* (New York, 1846), I, 398.

51. It was transmitted to Congress on January 19, 1797, and immediately ordered to be printed. It appeared in the *Aurora* in installments between January 24 and February 3, 1797.

52. Arch. Aff. Étr., États-Unis, Vols. 39-42.

53. A.S.P., F.R., I, 559-76.

54. In his Inaugural Address he said: "If the control of an election can be obtained by foreign nations by flattery or menaces, by fraud or violence, by terror, intrigue, or venality, the Government may not be the choice of the American people, but of foreign nations. It may be foreign nations who govern us, and not we, the people, who govern ourselves."

55. Gibbs, Nov. 22, 1796, I, 400.

56. Edward Channing, *A History of the United States*, IV, 173.

57. *Corr. Fr. Min.*, p. 983.

Part III
The Farewell Address: Post-World War II Interpretations

T HAT WASHINGTON'S Farewell Address was a statement of independence rather than isolationism remains the accepted interpretation in most works on the Federalist era. The same holds true for the view that the conduct of American diplomacy revolved largely around taking advantage of European distresses.[1] Certain works published since the end of World War II, however, have suggested that more was involved in policy-making than a reaction to international affairs and that the Farewell Address was not merely a statement of independence.

In his study of foreign policy during Washington's administration, Alexander DeConde has emphasized the importance of the political struggle between Federalists and Anti-Federalists. Referring to the President's valedictory, he notes that most of it was concerned with the need for political unity rather than nonentanglement in European affairs. It was primarily a piece of Federalist political propaganda, he maintains, one designed to rally the high public esteem for Washington against the growing strength of the Anti-Federalists. Support for the Federalist party had waned after the signing of Jay's Treaty in 1794. While it seemed probable that Washington could be reelected, Alexander Hamilton, whom DeConde regards as the real author of the Farewell Address, was concerned for both the future of his party and the relations he had cultivated between England and the United States. He therefore advised the President to deliver his address in such a way that noninvolvement in European affairs, and support for both Washington and the Federalist party, would be synonymous in the eyes of the electorate.

Nathan Schachner has also interpreted the Farewell Address within the context of the domestic political situation. Instead of regarding it as a propaganda tract, he emphasizes Washington's concern with the growing sectional split created by party passions. Schachner therefore interprets the address primarily as a plea for national unity.

In contrast, Felix Gilbert notes how colonial experience, English political ideas, and the views of the French *philosophes* (especially the Physiocrats) influenced the Founding Fathers. From an awareness of their country's geographic isolation and from arguments then prevalent in England, Gilbert points out, American leaders early developed the idea they could benefit materially by remaining aloof from European affairs. The ideas of the Physiocrats further determined the Americans against foreign entanglements. To these French thinkers, a policy structured on both political and military connections and Machiavellian concepts of power politics was corrupt. Such a policy was to be replaced by one based on reason and noninvolvement, except for those areas of commercial relations and mutual cooperation among nations where involvement (if not reason) was called for. These views infused a lasting idealism into America's attitude toward foreign affairs. They also resulted in apparently contradictory tendencies in its foreign policy. That is, while remaining aloof from European affairs betokened a policy of isolationism, mutual cooperation among nations implied a program of participation in world affairs. "American foreign policy," Gilbert notes, "was idealistic and internationalist no less than isolationist."

Events after the Revolution forced the United States both to follow more traditional methods and concepts of diplomacy and to become involved in European affairs. Yet the dichotomies between idealism and realism, internationalism and isolationism, remained; in fact, they were echoed in Washington's Farewell Address. According to Gilbert, herein lies the real significance of the first President's message. While Gilbert admits the relation of party politics and sectional division to the Farewell Address, one which both DeConde and Schachner suggest, he feels that the Address had far more significance: it fused divergent views on foreign affairs into a single comprehensive statement of policy.

Like Gilbert, a number of other scholars have suggested the existence of continuing threads in the foreign policy of the early republic. But they maintain that enlightenment ideas had little influence on its leaders. Much more important to their interpretation is the new nation's thrust westward which American diplomats used in order to gain favorable terms from European countries.

Recognition of the relationship between frontier expansion and foreign policy is not a new historical development. Numerous historians have cited the Mississippi Valley as a factor in the diplomacy of the Federalist era.[2] More recently a number of historians have suggested that the urge to expand, commercially as well as politically, has been the determining factor behind the country's foreign policy, not only during the early republic, but throughout its history.[3]

One of those most responsible for this renewed emphasis on the importance of expansion in American foreign policy has been William Appleman Williams, formerly of the University of Wisconsin; his writings have received wide, and sometimes critical, attention. America was settled, Williams notes, at a time when mercantilism was the dominant political-economic force in England. Central to the mercantilist viewpoint was the idea that the government had the obligation to promote the general welfare and common good of corporate society; this was to be achieved by delegating authority to individuals or groups whom the state would aid and protect. Important also to mercantilism was the belief that the world was finite and its resources limited. Therefore, the only way for a nation to be certain of providing for the corporate good was self-sufficiently to control the world's wealth—even to the point of taking it away from someone else. As part of the British mercantilist empire, the American colonists were greatly influenced by such thought; a sense of corporate responsibility inspired their leaders. Because they were mercantilists, they viewed expansion as necessary to assure fulfillment of the nation's needs. Having broken from the British empire, Williams states, they sought to establish a mercantilist empire of their own in the New World. Commenting on the Farewell Address, he thus remarks, "it was a mercantilist manifesto for an unchallengeable empire."[4]

While Williams makes only passing reference to the first President's valedictory, and scarcely analyzes its contents, this writer has reached conclusions about Washington's message which support Williams' interpretation. Noting a similarity between ideas expressed in the Farewell Address and ideas long held by Washington, I view the Address in terms of the vision which the first President early maintained of the new nation's future. Washington had developed the concept of an expanding nation ("a rising empire," as he called it) which would someday take its place among the world's great powers. The President's concern for national unity and noninvolvement in European affairs—the two ideas in his parting message which historians have most strongly emphasized—were ones which he frequently expressed, usually in relation to his concept of America's destiny. In my view, the Farewell Address expresses Washington's concept of American empire, one which he made his legacy to the new nation.

Historiography of the Farewell Address has thus come almost full circle, with recent interpretations of the valedictory bearing a remarkable similarity to those written at the turn of the century. No longer, however, does the first President's message have the impact on foreign policy issues that it had sixty or even twenty-five years ago. While references to the Address are still occasionally made,[5] historians have all but destroyed the myth that Washington intended the United States perpetually to pursue an isolationist foreign policy. At the same time, the dominance of the United States in world affairs for most of this century has made Americans realize the futility of trying to base the country's policy on supposed doctrines promulgated at a time when even the most sanguine of the Founding Fathers realized that America was still a fledgling power. As a result, Washington's Farewell Address is now important only for the insights it affords into the policies and leaders of the Federalist era. In this respect, however, it does remain a classic document in American history.

NOTES

1. See, for example, Esmond Wright, *Fabric of Freedom, 1763-1800* (New York, 1961), pp. 202-13, and John C. Miller, *The Federalist Era, 1789-1801* (New York, 1960), pp. 192-202. See also the concluding volume of Douglas Southall Freeman's *George Washington* (7 vols., New York, 1945-1957), written after his death by John Carroll and Mary Wells Ashworth, pp. 403-7.

2. See, for example, Arthur P. Whitaker, *The Mississippi Question, 1795-1830: A Study in Trade, Politics and Diplomacy* (New York, 1934), and *The Spanish-American Frontier, 1783-1795: The Westward Movement and the Spanish Retreat in the Mississippi Valley* (Boston, 1927); Arthur Burr Darling, *Our Rising Empire* (New Haven, 1940); Richard Van Alstyne, "The Significance of the Mississippi Valley in American Diplomatic History," *Mississippi Valley Historical Review*, XXVI (September 1949), 215-38.

3. Most of the recent work on expansion in American foreign policy is concerned with the period after 1890. But Richard Van Alstyne has reviewed the importance of this factor throughout the nation's history in his incisive *The Rising American Empire* (New York, 1960). See also his *Empire and Independence: The International History of the American Revolution* (New York, 1965), which regards the coming of the Revolution in terms of a quest by Americans to establish their own empire in the New World.

4. *The Contours of American History* (paperback ed., Chicago, 1966), pp. 28-174. See also his "The Age of Mercantilism: An Interpretation of the American Political Economy, 1763 to 1828," *William and Mary Quarterly*, XV, 3rd ser. (1958), 419-37.

5. In 1965, for example, James J. Wadsworth, author and former United States representative to the United Nations, noted five guidelines in Washington's valedictory by which he felt the United States should conduct its relations with other nations. These included a recognition of the uniqueness of the United States and an awareness that "It is in a nation's best interest to act with good faith and justice toward all other nations." Wadsworth concluded, "Ours should be a quiet, confident sort of faith, calculated to convince others, as it has ourselves, that we can help make this the best of all possible worlds." See his "Some Timely Advice from President Washington," *Saturday Review*, XLVIII (February 20, 1965), 18, 97.

Washington's Farewell, the French Alliance, and the Election of 1796
BY ALEXANDER DeCONDE

When in 1789 George Washington became the nation's first president the French alliance was the cornerstone of American foreign policy. It largely had made possible American independence and had established American foreign policy orientation. At the end of Washington's second term, in fact as he prepared his farewell to public life, the life-giving alliance was practically dead and the United States was virtually at war with France. Why, in eight formative years, did such a drastic reversal in foreign policy take place?[1] A full answer to this question would be long and complex; yet by looking closely at the election of 1796 and by reviewing the Farewell Address in its political context we may find a partial answer as to how the alliance received its mortal wound. We may also find additional reason for revising the traditional interpreta-

Reprinted by permission from the *Mississippi Valley Historical Review,* XLIII (March 1957), 641-58.

tion of the Farewell Address as a wise, timeless, and unbiased warning to the nation.

The blow from which the alliance never recovered was the Jay Treaty of 1794.[2] While this Federalist-negotiated treaty averted a war with England, a war which Federalists feared, the major objectives which John Jay had been expected to win were not realized. Because it failed to obtain specific concessions on impressment, ship seizures, and Indian raids on the frontier, the treaty infuriated Republicans and others who still nutured a Revolution-bred hatred of England.[3] At the same time it blighted Franco-American relations. Successive French revolutionary governments were convinced that the Jay Treaty violated the Franco-American treaties of 1778 and that the American government had accepted it against the will of an overwhelming public sentiment. Believing that the bulk of the American people were pro-French even though Washington's Federalist government was pro-English, the French sought to arouse their allies, the American people, to their true interest. This true interest was alliance with France and disassociation with England, America's natural enemy and France's major antagonist in war since February, 1793.[4]

To arouse the American people in defense of the 1778 alliance the French Directory in June, 1795, sent to the United States a new minister, a young man in his early thirties, Pierre Auguste Adet. To the French the Jay Treaty created an intimate alliance between the United States and France's worst enemy. In Adet's instructions, therefore, the idea that the treaty violated the French alliance stood out as the foremost grievance against the Washington administration.[5]

Despite French anger, and despite Adet's attempts to prevent ratification, the Senate approved the Jay Treaty eleven days after Adet had landed in Philadelphia. Two months later, while Adet continued his efforts to kill it, Washington ratified the treaty.[6] England accepted the ratified treaty and in April, 1796, after a long, last-ditch battle in which Adet used all the influence he could muster against the treaty, the House of Representatives voted funds to implement it. To Adet as to other Frenchmen this meant the end of the 1778 alliance and another triumph for England and English gold.

Not knowing that Washington already had decided to retire from the presidency, Adet now saw the overthrow of Washington and his Federalist administration as the only salvation for the 1778 alliance. Adet and the French Directory viewed the Washington administration as the captive of English policy; to save the alliance it had to be replaced by a pro-French Republican administration.[7] Charles Delacroix, French foreign minister, advocated inciting an uprising against Washington to break the Jay Treaty and to invigorate the alliance. Thomas Jefferson, he believed, would replace Washington and thus France would command the influence in the United States which she deserved. Prospects for the defeat of Washington were good, he believed, since the President, once the idol of the American people, had become to some an object of scorn and even hatred as the result of the Jay Treaty; already the journals attacked him, his principles, and his conduct.[8]

Taking into account what it conceived to be the temper of American popular opinion, and with the objective of destroying English influence in the United States and salvaging the 1778 alliance, the French government intervened actively in the presidential election of 1796. Through Adet and other French officials in the United States the Directory openly supported the Republican party and wherever possible attacked the Federalist party.[9] French intervention in the election became, therefore, one of the main issues in the campaign of 1796. The fate of the alliance hung on the outcome of the election.

The decision of the Directory to intervene in the 1796 election, while a decisive factor, contributed but one element to the complex politics of the election. Domestic issues and the Jay Treaty itself contributed others. Final acceptance of the treaty plunged Franco-American relations to their lowest depths since independence and marked a great political triumph for Federalists. Yet to Republicans all hope of ultimately defeating the treaty did not appear lost. Seeing the extent of the Jay Treaty's unpopularity, Republican leaders believed that it would make an excellent campaign issue in the 1796 election as an unrivaled party rallying point for national sentiment. Thomas Jefferson, James Madison, and other party leaders believed that popular opinion remained still largely pro-French and anti-British. Being politicians they reacted logically. Their party had ready-made national issues; they had only to exploit them properly and victory would be theirs. Republicans, consequently, carried over into the election of 1796 their campaign against the Jay Treaty and the pro-British "system" of Alexander Hamilton.[10]

Granted the logic and appeal of the Republican campaign plan, a towering obstacle—the person and prestige of George Washington—stood in the way of success, as was clear to the French. So deep was the impression Washington had made on fellow Americans that to attack him would be to risk injuring the attacker. Twice he had been chosen president without a dissenting vote. Had he so desired he could undoubtedly have held office for a third term, for, as a foreign observer remarked, "there is a Magic in his name more powerful in this Country than the Abilities of any other man."[11] No man, moreover, was better aware of this than Jefferson. "Republicanism," he advised, "must live on it's [*sic*] oars, resign the vessel to it's pilot [Washington], and themselves to the course he thinks best for them."[12]

Despite Washington's great political strength the situation in 1796 was far different from 1789 and 1792; Washington probably could have had a third term, but not by unanimous choice. In political battles over neutrality, the Jay Treaty, and other issues, he had divested himself of nonpartisanship. To Republicans and Francophiles the guise of being above party and of working for the welfare of the nation as a whole, in view of his intimate connections with his Federalist subordinates and his consistent practice of acting in accord with their principles, appeared the sheerest hypocrisy.[13] In town and country some men now spat at the mention of his name, denounced him as a monocrat and an Anglomaniac, and prayed for his removal from office. Washington in 1796 had become a central figure in emerging party politics; he was a principal target for the violent personal politics of the time; and to the French he was the main barrier to reactivation of the 1778 alliance.[14]

So bitter was feeling between English and French partisans that domestic issues drifted into relative insignificance. In their conviction that the Federalist administration did not truly represent the American people, the French were encouraged by pro-French partisans among Republicans who indicated that the Federalist government would topple if only France were to take a strong stand.[15] As the election year of 1796 opened, Republicans intensified their attacks against the Federalist administration. The Jay

Treaty and the loud cry of aristocracy, monarchy, and plutocracy aroused deep popular emotions. Mutual hatred characterized the two large political segments of the American public.

With his government under fire on both domestic and foreign policy and with himself the target of unrestrained scurrility, Washington found the demands of his office increasingly difficult to endure. Publicly he maintained a dignified silence, but privately he revealed the strain.[16] Even he had come to see that the myth of nonpartisanship was shattered, and that his concept of an administration above party and the tumult of politics had been illusory. Foreign relations had exploded the myth while serving as a catalyst in the formation of national political parties. This was an issue capable of transforming the opposing local alliances of Federalist and anti-Federalist into integrated national parties—an emotional foreign policy issue capable of capturing public imagination in a way which abstruse problems of finance could not.[17]

Despite his increasing distaste for the office and the increasing speculation about his not wishing to be a candidate for a third term, the President remained silent as to future plans. Leaders of both political parties, however, had little doubt that he would not run. "He gave me intimations enough," asserted John Adams, "that his reign would be very short." Early in 1796, and even before, both parties had laid tentative plans which did not include Washington as a candidate.[18]

The attacks on Washington grew increasingly bitter during the year. Opponents charged that he had betrayed a solemn pledge to France by destroying the French alliance. Personal attacks accused him of taking more salary than was allotted him. His mail was tampered with for political advantage, and forged letters of 1777 were refurbished and printed as genuine. Particularly cutting was Tom Paine's bitter attack from Paris, which city was the source, Federalists were convinced, of the anti-Washington campaign.[19] Jefferson, too, had lost patience with the exalted role of Washington. The President, he wrote, like Samson had had his head "shorn by the harlot England."[20]

Despite pressures to stay and ride out the storm, Washington disclosed in May, 1796, that he intended definitely to retire.[21] If he had nurtured at all the desire to seek a third term it was killed by the acid criticism to which he had been subjected. The President decided not to seek a third term not only because he sought retirement in his old age but also because he was disgusted with the abuse from political opponents. "The true cause of the general's retiring," declared one of his staunchest supporters, "was . . . the *loss of popularity* which he had experienced, and the further loss which he apprehended from the rupture with France, which he looked upon as inevitable."[22]

Once the decision to retire was made, Washington turned to Hamilton, as usual, for advice. When, he asked, would be the best time for publication of his farewell to the nation? Hamilton, with his eye on the coming election, advised that the public announcement be held off as long as possible. "The proper period now for your declaration," wrote Hamilton, "seems to be *Two Months* before the time for the Meeting of the Electors. This will be sufficient. The parties will in the meantime electioneer conditionally, that is to say, *if you decline*; for a serious opposition to you will I think hardly be risked."[23]

Three months before the gathering of electors Washington announced to the nation his intention to retire. Although in 1792 he had planned a valedictory to the nation and James Madison had drafted one, the September, 1796, version, in which Hamilton's hand was prominent, became a piece of partisan politics directed specifically against Republicans and Francophiles who had made Washington's last years miserable. At the time, it was recognized for what it was: a political manifesto, a campaign document. The 1792 version, drawn up before popular passions had been stirred by war in Europe, did not, for example, stress politics nor did it touch on foreign affairs. In the 1796 version partisan politics and foreign affairs were central.[24]

Washington's specific target in foreign affairs, heartily seconded by Hamilton, was the alliance with France. He struck at Adet's partisan activities, at French meddling in American politics (while passing over British meddling), and at the allegedly dangerous implications of the French alliance. Washington told Hamilton that had it not been for the status of "party disputes" and of foreign affairs he would not have considered it necessary to revise his valedictory. He was convinced that a warning to the nation was necessary to combat foreign (French) intrigue "in the internal concerns of our country." It is indeed easy "to foresee," he warned, "that it may involve us in disputes and finally in War, to fulfill political alliances." This was the crux of the matter; Washington believed that the French alliance was no longer an asset to the country.[25]

Washington's valedictory trumpeted the Federalist answer to Republican accusations that the administration had sold the country to the British; it countered the anti-administration furor over the Jay Treaty; it was a justification and defense of his policies. As such it was designed and as such it became the opening blast in the presidential campaign, contrived to prevent the election of Thomas Jefferson. The Farewell laid the basis for Federalist strategy of using Washington's great prestige to appeal to patriotism, as against the evil of foreign machinations, to make "Federalist" and "patriot" synonyms in the minds of the electorate. Under the banner of patriotism the Farewell spearheaded the attack on the opposition party and on French diplomacy.[26]

In the address Washington opened with the announcement that he would not be a candidate for a third term and then stressed the advantages of union and the evils of political parties. Having in mind, undoubtedly, the French Republic, he advised against "a passionate attachment of one Nation for another." Such "sympathy for the favourite nation," he warned, leads to wars and quarrels "without adequate inducement or justification." Then followed the oft-quoted "Great rule of conduct" that with foreign nations we should have "as little *political* connection as possible." While stressing fidelity to "already formed engagements," he announced that " 'tis our true policy to steer clear of permanent Alliances with any portion of the foreign world." Washington deplored the growth of political opposition, chastised the public for its attachment to France, and concluded with a defense of his foreign policy, particularly his much criticized policy of neutrality which was based on the Proclamation of April 22, 1793. He called this the "index" to his plan or policy.[27]

Although cloaked in phrases of universal or timeless application, the objectives of the address were practical, immediate, and partisan. Men often attempt to rationalize their partisan political views in pronouncements studded with timeless patriotic appeals; so it was with Washington and Hamilton. The valedictory bore directly on the coming election, on the French alliance, and on the status of Franco-American relations in general.

While expressed cogently and linked forever with Washington's name, the main ideas and foreign policy principles of the Farewell were not unique with either Hamilton or Washington. They were prevalent Federalist ideas on current foreign policy and politics, and can be found expressed in various ways in the polemical literature of the time. The concept of no entanglement with Europe, for instance, was a common one among Federalists and others. More often than not it was a universalized reaction against a specific annoyance—the French alliance. Stated as non-involvement with Europe, an attack against the alliance had great psychological appeal. In time this specific meaning was lost and only the generalization remained.[28]

As partisans had expected, Washington's words stoked an already hot political situation. "It will serve as a signal," exclaimed New England Federalist Fisher Ames, "like dropping a hat, for the party racers to start."[29] The Farewell was indeed soon under partisan attack. Washington's advice for the future, taunted William Duane, "is but a defence for the past." Referring to the warning against "permanent alliances," he exclaimed, "this extraordinary advice is fully exemplified in your departure from the spirit and principle of the treaty with France, which was declared to be permanent, and exhibits this very infidelity you reprobate in a most striking and lamentable light." The President had not, Duane continued, "adhered to that rigid and neutral justice which you profess—every concession to Britain in prejudice of France was a deviation from neutrality." Much of the evil which Washington attributed to faction, he claimed, came from the Federalist party. "Your examples of party influence are uniformly drawn from occasions wherein your personal opinions, your pride and passions, have been involved."[30] As to Washington's advice to steer clear of permanent alliances, why, critics asked, was it unwise to extend the nation's political engagements? Was not the Jay Treaty a political connection, practically an alliance with England?[31]

To James Madison—who earlier had feared that under Hamilton's influence the address would become a campaign document— the valedictory confirmed his assumptions; it was all politics. Under the complete influence of the British faction, Madison wrote, Washington obviously sought to destroy the French alliance. "It has been known," he continued, "that every channel has been latterly opened that could convey to his mind a rancor against that country [France] and suspicion of all who are thought to sympathize with its revolution and who support the policy of extending our commerce and in general of standing well with it. But it was not easy to suppose his mind wrought up to the tone that could dictate or rather adopt some parts of the performance."[32]

Minister Adet believed wrongly that the address would arouse the indignation of pro-French "patriots" and would not have the effect on the people that the British faction hoped it would. He consequently plunged into the campaign to see to it that the address would not have its intended effect.[33] Looking upon John Adams as an enemy of France and a friend of England, he electioneered brazenly for Jefferson. The future conduct of France toward America, he made clear to Americans, would be governed by the election's outcome.[34]

Beginning at the end of October and timing himself carefully, Adet began publication of a series of public manifestoes designed to influence the electorate. He conjured up the prospect of war with France, stressing that Jefferson's election would eliminate such a possibility. With the Quakers of Pennsylvania, Federalists lamented, Adet's strategy of fear worked. Fearing a Federalist-sponsored war against France, Quakers cast their votes for Republicans.[35] "French influence never appeared so open and unmasked as at this city [Philadelphia] election," cried William Loughton Smith, Hamilton's congressional mouthpiece. "French flags, French cockades were displayed by the Jefferson party and there is no doubt that French money was not spared. . . . In short there never was so barefaced and disgraceful an interference of a foreign power in any free country."[36]

Adet's procedure was to write an official note to the Secretary of State and then to send a copy for publication to Benjamin Bache's Philadelphia *Aurora*. In his note of October 27, for example, he protested against American foreign policy and appealed to the people to renew their friendship with France by disavowing the Jay Treaty and honoring the French alliance.[37] A few days later (November 5) the pages of the *Aurora* carried Adet's second manifesto, dubbed by Federalists the "cockade proclamation." In the name of the Directory it called on all Frenchmen in the United States—in the land of an ally—to mount the tricolored cockade, symbol of liberty. Those who did not so give public evidence of their support of the French Republic were to be denied the services of French consuls and the protection of the French flag. Immediately the tricolored cockade blossomed in the streets.

Americans as well as Frenchmen wore it as a badge of devotion to the French cause. It became, in short, a symbol of republicanism.[38]

Ten days later Adet followed the "cockade proclamation" with his last and most florid note, which he again sent simultaneously to the Secretary of State and to Bache's *Aurora*. In it he announced that as a result of the Jay Treaty his function as minister had been suspended and that he was returning to France.[39] Adet had timed his announcement so that it might have a maximum political influence, particularly on the electors who were soon to meet to choose Washington's successor.[40]

Adet's notes and Secretary of State Timothy Pickering's replies were used as campaign ammunition by both sides. Federalists, of course, were furious. They denounced Adet's pronouncements for what they were—brazen electioneering maneuvers by a foreign agent. John Adams, against whom the last note was directed, found "it an instrument well calculated to reconcile me to private life. It will purify me from all envy of Mr. Jefferson, or Mr.Pinckney, or Mr. Burr, or Mr. any body who may be chosen President or Vice President."[41] William Cobbett, violent Francophobe and anti-Jeffersonian, published Adet's note under the title of *The Gros Mousqueton Diplomatique; or Diplomatic Blunderbuss*. He ran with it, of course, an adverse commentary.[42]

Friends of France, according to Adet, were delighted. Republican leaders were willing and even eager to use the issue of the French alliance to gain votes. But, contrary to Adet's opinion, they were not happy with the French minister's personal interference. Madison, for instance, maintained that Adet's note announcing his return to France worked "all the evil with which it is pregnant." Its indiscretions, he added, gave comfort to Federalists who had the "impudence" to point out that it was "an electioneering maneuver," and that "the French government had been led into it by the opponents of the British treaty."[43]

Adet did not realize that his activities worked mainly to injure the cause he sought to aid. French popularity, according to competent observers, decreased as a result.[44] Disgusted by Adet's conduct, Washington drew even closer to the British. One piqued New England writer went so far as to declare that since Adet's electioneering on behalf of Jefferson "there is not an elector on this side of the Delaware that would not be sooner shot than vote for him." And Philip Key maintained that Adet's meddling "irretrievably diminished that good will felt for his Government & the people of France by most people here."[45]

Unaware of any adverse reaction, Adet and his intimates believed that his actions and the Directory's measures would influence the presidential electors decisively in favor of Jefferson.[46] What Adet and the Directory had not taken into account was that invariably when a foreign diplomat takes sides openly in the domestic politics of the nation to which he is accredited he makes the party leader he seeks to aid appear to be the pawn of a foreign government. Such a charge, whether or not true, gives the opposition the opportunity of patriotically denouncing foreign interference and of posing as the defender of national honor against foreign subversives. So it was with the Adet case. His activities seemed to confirm the very warnings of foreign interference that were stressed in Washington's Farewell Address.

Sensing the opportunity, Federalists attacked the French alliance, denounced French domestic interference, and pitted the patriotism of Washington and Adams against the Jacobin-tainted Republican campaign. Voters were importuned to beware of foreign influence; to "decide between the address of the President and the [French]"; to follow Washington's counsel. Adet and the Directory, they were told, wished to draw the nation into war and to sever the western from the Atlantic states. No doubt clouded the Federalist mind; the Union was in danger.[47]

Federalist warnings, persistent though they were, did not stop French interference in American politics; nor did the interference end with the choosing of electors in November. Few of the electors were pledged to a specific candidate, so the campaign continued with increasing tumult until December 7, when the electors cast their ballots. Adet, having suspended his diplomatic functions, remained in Philadelphia to continue his anti-administration campaign. He and the Republicans hammered at similar themes, stressing that if Adams were elected, the errors of the Washington administration would be continued, since Adams was committed to Washington's tragic policies; and that such policies would lead to war with France.

Candidate Adams, on the other hand, believed that only time would tell whether "the French Directory have only been drawn in to favor the election of a favorite, or whether in their trances and delirium of victory they think to terrify America, or whether in their sallies they may not venture on hostilities." He advised that under the circumstances "Americans must be cool and steady if they can."[48]

But Americans were not cool and steady. In newspapers and elsewhere they debated the French alliance, the mounting crisis with France, and the possibility of war.[49] Hamilton, as was his practice in time of crisis, wrote articles for the press to reply to Adet's manifestoes, to defend administration foreign policy, and to attack the French alliance.[50] Another prominent Federalist, Noah Webster, editor of the *American Minerva,* wrote a series of articles in which he also attacked the alliance. His articles were reprinted and widely circulated. In the Federalist press, in fact, attacks on the alliance now became common. Webster in his articles stressed that France had equated the term ally with that of vassal; "an *open* enemy," he declared, "is less dangerous than an *insidious friend.*" Although the British, too, had injured the United States, Webster maintained that the American connection with Great Britain was stronger than the French alliance because "our connection with her is solely *an alliance of interest.* This is the true basis of all national connections. We are therefore in no danger from Great Britain."[51]

In the first week of February, 1797, the American people finally learned the results of the election. Although the Federalist victory was narrow, it was enough to sink French hopes for a revived alliance. By "three votes" John Adams, who wisely had perceived that he was "not enough of an Englishman, nor little enough of a Frenchman, for some people," was elected second president of the United States.[52]

Jefferson, however, captured the second highest electoral total and became vice-president.[53] America's first contested presidential election therefore, although a clear-cut Federalist victory, gave some comfort to Republicans and struck fear into Federalist ranks. But Republican strength had not been sufficient to overturn the government and hence to reverse the course of Franco-American relations. To staunch Hamiltonian Federalists this aspect of the election was indeed sweet. In various election post-mortems, in New England in particular, such Federalists rejoiced that the "French party is fallen," and that the French alliance was at last valueless. Even Adet, one of them pointed out, "avows, and it is rather a tough point to avow, that our treaty is disadvantageous."

Now he might inform the Directory that it has "been deceived by the revolutionary Americans in Paris; that we (at least the Yankees) have not been traitors, and have ceased to be dupes."[54]

With the Federalist victory, narrow though it was, the Farewell Address had done its work. The French alliance which had been drawn to last "forever" and which had been the core of American foreign policy when Washington launched the federal government was practically dead as he prepared to leave office. Despite French and Republican efforts to the contrary, and in large part because of the impact of Washington's Farewell, the basic foreign policy orientation of the United States remained pro-British.[55] The Farewell Address now belonged to posterity and posterity had given it meanings to fit its own problems.

NOTES

1. A few months after Washington had left office, the French, in taking stock of the defunct alliance of 1778 and the serious state of American relations, asked the same question. Louis-Guillaume Otto, "Considerations sur la Conduite du gouvernment des États-Unis envers la France, depuis 1789 jusqu'en 1797" [Paris, June 17, 1797], Archives des Affaires Étrangères, Correspondance Politique, États-Unis (Reproductions in the Library of Congress), XLVII, 401-18.

2. For background on the Jay Treaty see Samuel F. Bemis, *Jay's Treaty: A Study in Commerce and Diplomacy* (New York, 1923); Frank Monaghan, *John Jay: Defender of Liberty* (New York, 1935), pp. 361-404; Joseph Charles, "The Jay Treaty: The Origins of the American Party System," *William and Mary Quarterly,* XII, Ser. III (October 1955), 581-630; and Bradford Perkins, *The First Reapprochement: England and the United States* (Philadelphia, 1955), pp. 1-6.

3. That the treaty violated the "rights of friendship, gratitude, and alliance which the republic of France may justly claim from the United States" was a foremost criticism of Jay's work, a criticism which had great popular appeal. See the memorial emanating from a mass meeting of citizens in Philadelphia, July 25, 1795, cited in Margaret Woodbury, "Public Opinion in Philadelphia, 1789-1801," *Smith College Studies in History,* V, Nos. 1-2 (Northampton, Mass., 1919-1920), 88. "Junius Americanus," in *New York Herald,* reprinted in *Virginia Herald and Fredericksburg Advertiser* (June 26, 1795), attacked the administration for neglecting France and surrendering to Great Britain's tyranny. For a French commentary on American public opinion in regard to the Jay Treaty see François de la Rochefoucauld-Liancourt, *Travels through the United States of North America in the Years 1795, 1796, and 1797* (2 vols. London, 1799), I, 381-82.

4. See, for example, Joseph Fauchet to Committee of Public Safety,

April 19, 25, 1795, Frederick J. Turner, ed., *Correspondence of the French Ministers to the United States, 1791-1797* (American Historical Association Annual Report, 1903, II (Washington, 1904), 649-50, 662-63. For an astute French analysis of the status of the alliance at the time of the Jay negotiations, see Philippe A. J. Létombe to Commission of Foreign Relations, Archives des Affaires Étrangères, Correspondance Politique, États-Units, XL (1794), 241-47.

5. Adet's instructions, dated October 23, 1794, are in Turner, ed., *Correspondence of French Ministers*, pp. 721-30. For biographical details on Adet, see *Nouvelle Biographic Generale* (Paris, 1852), I, 278; Jean Kaulek, ed., *Papiers de Barthelemy: Ambassadeur de France en Suisse, 1792-1797* (6 vols., Paris, 1886-1910), VI, 151n. Adet was second choice for the American mission. Alphonse Betrand, "Les États-Unis et la Revolution Française," *Revue des Deux Mondes*, XXXIII (Paris, May 15, 1906), 422n.

6. Adet wrote that "the President has just countersigned the dishonor of his old age and the shame of the United States." Adet to Committee of Public Safety, September 2, 1795, Turner, ed., *Correspondence of French Ministers*, pp. 776-77. The despatch is printed in translation in Gilbert Chinard, ed., *George Washington as the French Knew Him* (Princeton, 1940), pp. 106-9. In France, of course, Washington's support of the Jay Treaty was considered a tragic mistake and inimical to the 1778 alliance. See George Duruy, ed., *Memoirs of Barras: Member of the Directorate*, trans. by Charles E. Roche (4 vols., London, 1895-1896), II, 103 (entry of March 22, 1795); Michele de Mangourit to ———, December 23, 1795, Archives des Affaires Étrangères, Correspondance Politique, États-Unis, XLIV, 554. In the United States, Washington's signing of the treaty infuriated Republicans; Republican newspaper editors embarked on a concerted effort to make public life so unpalatable that Washington would virtually be driven from office. See the diary of Dr. Nathaniel Ames, August 14, 1795, in Charles Warren, *Jacobin and Junto* (Cambridge, Mass., 1931), XII, 63; Donald H. Stewart, "The Press and Political Corruption during the Federalist Administrations," *Political Science Quarterly*, LXVII (September 1952), 436. William Vans Murray, a moderate Federalist, believed that Washington ran the "risk of the most alarming discontent if he ratifies & war if he does not." William Vans Murray Papers, Commonplace Book, August 15, 1795 (Princeton University Library, microfilm copies).

7. Adet to Minister of Foreign Relations, May 3, 1796, Turner, ed., *Correspondence of French Ministers*, pp. 900-6.

8. "Rapport au Directoire Exécutif par le Ministre des Relations Exterieures," January 16, 1796, Archives des Affaires Étrangères, Correspondance Politique, États-Unis, XLV, 41-51. Part of the document is printed in Samuel F. Bemis, "Washington's Farewell Address: A Foreign Policy of Independence," *American Historical Review*, XXXIX (January 1934), 257-58.

9. "Mémoire sur les effets du dernier traité des États-Unis et de l'Angleterre, et les remèdes à employer" [May 1796], Archives des Affaires

Étrangères, Correspondance Politique, États-Unis, XLV, 323-51; Adet to Minister of Foreign Relations, May 3, 1796, Turner, ed., *Correspondence of French Ministers,* pp. 900-6.

10. Phineas Bond, British consul in Philadelphia, for example, maintained that it was pretty well understood that Republican opposition to the Jay Treaty was planned by Jefferson "for the double purpose of promoting the interests of France and of advancing" his candidacy for president. Bond to Lord Grenville, May 4, 1796, British Foreign Correspondence: America (Henry Adams Transcripts, Library of Congress). See also Harry Ammon, "The Formation of the Republican Party in Virginia, 1789-1796," *Journal of Southern History,* XIX (August 1953), 309-10.

11. Robert Liston, British minister in Philadelphia, to Grenville, October 13, 1796, Henry Adams Transcripts. The quotation is from Henrietta Liston to James Jackson, October 16, 1796, Bradford Perkins, ed., "A Diplomat's Wife in Philadelphia: Letters of Henrietta Liston, 1796-1800," *William and Mary Quarterly,* XI, Ser. III (October 1954), 604.

12. Jefferson to James Monroe, June 12, 1796, Paul L. Ford, ed., *The Writings of Thomas Jefferson* (10 vols., New York, 1892-1899), VII, 80. James Madison, too, complained of Washington's prestige. Madison to Jefferson, May 22, 1796, Madison Papers (Library of Congress), XIX, 68, cited in Nathan Schachner, *Thomas Jefferson: A Biography* (2 vols., New York, 1951), II, 581.

13. John Quincy Adams believed that Republican efforts to associate Washington with "an English party" was "a party manoeuvre," a trick "to make their adversaries unpopular by fixing upon them odious imputations." Adams to Joseph Pitcairn, March 9, 1797, Worthington C. Ford, ed., *Writings of John Quincy Adams* (7 vols., New York, 1913-1917), II, 140.

14. See, for example, Lexington *Kentucky Gazette,* September 26, 1795; John B. McMaster, *A History of the People of the United States* (8 vols., New York, 1883-1913), II, 289. While opposing him, many of Washington's critics still recognized his virtues. One, for instance, remarked that "the best man that ever lived possessing the influence of the P [resident], is a dangerous man; the more so if guided in any of his measures by others who may not be so virtuous. God grant we may never have cause to say 'curse on his virtues; they have undone his country.'" Joseph Jones to James Madison, February 17, 1796, Worthington C. Ford, ed., "Letters from Joseph Jones to Madison, 1788-1802," Massachusetts Historical Society *Proceedings,* XV, Ser. II (1902), 155.

15. At this time La Rochefoucauld-Liancourt, for example, reported that the common people in the United States were overwhelmingly pro-French and anti-British. *Travels,* II, 64-5, 139.

16. See, for example, Washington to Jefferson, July 6, 1796, and to Charles C. Pinckney, July 8, 1796, John C. Fitzpatrick, ed., *The Writings of George Washington, 1745-1799* (39 vols., Washington, 1931-1944), XXXV, 120, 130.

17. Ammon, "Formation of the Republican Party in Virginia," *Journal of Southern History,* XIX (August 1953), 300.

18. The quotation is from John Adams to Abigail Adams, March 25, 1796, Charles F. Adams, ed., *Letters of John Adams Addressed to His Wife* (2 vols., Boston, 1841), II, 214. Republicans shared the same rumors. Madison to Monroe, February 26, 1796, *Letters and other Writings of James Madison* (4 vols., Philadelphia, 1865), II, 83; Madison to Monroe, May 14, 1796, Gaillard Hunt, ed., *The Writings of James Madison* (9 vols., New York, 1900-1910), VI, 301n. For about a year George Hammond, the British minister, had heard rumors that Washington would retire in 1797. Hammond to Grenville, January 5, 1796, Henry Adams Transcripts.

19. John Quincy Adams to John Adams, August 13, 1796, Ford, ed., *Writings of John Quincy Adams*, II, 21; Paine to Washington, July 30, 1796, Philip S. Foner, ed., *The Complete Writings of Thomas Paine* (2 vols., New York, 1945), II, 691-723. For other details see Nathaniel W. Stephenson and Waldo H. Dunn, *George Washington* (2 vols., New York, 1940), II, 409; McMaster, *History of the People of the United States,* II, 249-50.

20. Jefferson to Philip Mazzei, April 24, 1796. See Howard R. Marraro, "The Four Versions of Jefferson's Letter to Mazzei," *William and Mary Quarterly,* XXII, Ser. II (January 1942), 24-5; Schachner, *Jefferson,* II, 578-79.

21. Washington to John Jay, May 8, 1796, Fitzpatrick, ed., *Writings of Washington,* XXXV, 36-7.

22. William Cobbett, *Porcupine's Works* (12 vols., London, 1801), IV, 444n. The italics are in the original.

23. Washington to Hamilton, June 26, 1796, Fitzpatrick, ed., *Writings of Washington,* XXXV, 103-4. See also Washington's letter to Hamilton, May 15, 1796, *ibid.,* p. 50; Hamilton to Washington, July 5, 1796, *ibid.,* p. 104n., and Henry Cabot Lodge, ed., *The Works of Alexander Hamilton* (9 vols., New York, 1885-1886), VIII, 408-9. Republicans recognized that Washington's delayed announcement of retirement was a political scheme emanating from Hamilton. Noble E. Cunningham, "The Jeffersonian Party to 1801: A Study of the Formation of a Party Organization" (doctoral dissertation, Duke University, 1952), p. 142.

24. A copy of Madison's suggestions for the 1792 version of the Farewell Address is incorporated in Washington to Hamilton, May 15, 1796, Fitzpatrick, ed., *Writings of Washington,* XXXV, 51-61; the September 19, 1796, version is on pp. 214-38. For a detailed analysis of the address and its various contributors, see Victor H. Paltsits, ed., *Washington's Farewell Address* (New York, 1935). Usually Washington's advice on foreign policy is taken as the substance of the Farewell. See Albert K. Weinberg, "Washington's 'Great Rule' in Its Historical Evolution," in Eric F. Goldman, ed., *Historiography and Urbanization* (Baltimore, 1941), p. 113. Marshall Smelser, in "George Washington and the Alien and Sedition Acts," *American Historical Review,* LIX (January 1954), 326, and in "The Jacobin Phrenzy: Federalism and Liberty, Equality, and Fraternity," *Review of Politics,* XIII (October 1951), 476, and Joseph Charles, in "Hamilton and Washington: The Origins of the American Party System," *William and Mary Quarterly,*

XII, Ser. III (April 1955), 262, have placed the Farewell in its context as a political document.

25. Bemis, "Washington's Farewell Address," *American Historical Review,* XXXIX (January 1934), 262-63. Washington understood that basic in any nation's foreign policy was self-interest, and that at this stage of American development it was to the nation's advantage, particularly from his Federalist viewpoint, not to be bound by the French alliance. Sound though this view may be in the perspective of mid-twentieth century, in 1796 it appeared to political opponents to be a partisan political view. To Republicans, loyalty to the alliance and hostility to England appeared the best means of promoting national self-interest. Roland G. Usher, "Washington and Entangling Alliances," *North American Review,* CCIV (July 1916), 29-38; James G. Randall, "George Washington and 'Entangling Alliances,' " *South Atlantic Quarterly,* XXX (July 1931), 221-29.

26. Wilfred E. Binkley, *American Political Parties: Their Natural Histories* (New York, 1943), p. 51. For a stimulating discussion of the Farewell Address which vigorously attacks the persistent myth that Washington's words constituted an inspired charter for a permanent foreign policy based on isolationism, see Louis B. Wright, "The Founding Fathers and 'Splendid Isolation,' " *Huntington Library Quarterly,* VI (February 1943), 173-78.

27. The quotations follow the text printed in Fitzpatrick, ed., *Writings of Washington,* XXXV, 214-38.

28. For a discussion of this point see Weinberg, "Washington's 'Great Rule' in Its Historical Evolution," pp. 109-38. The foreign policy ideas reflected in the Farewell were not even unique American principles; they can be found in the writings of certain eighteenth-century *philosophes.* See Felix Gilbert, "The 'New Diplomacy' of the Eighteenth Century," *World Politics,* IV (October 1951), 13-4, 28. For earlier expressions of the idea of non-entanglement with Europe, see the discussions relative to the congressional resolution of June 12, 1783, in Samuel F. Bemis, *The Diplomacy of the American Revolution* (New York, 1935), pp. 166-67, and Alexander DeConde, "William Vans Murray's *Political Sketches*: A Defense of the American Experiment," *Mississippi Valley Historical Review,* XLI (March 1955), 637-38.

29. Fisher Ames to Oliver Wolcott, September 26, 1796, George Gibbs, ed., *Memoirs of the Administrations of Washington and John Adams, edited from the Papers of Oliver Wolcott, Secretary of the Treasury* (2 vols., New York, 1846), I, 384-85.

30. [William Duane], *A Letter to George Washington, President of the United States: Containing Strictures on His Address of the Seventeenth of September, 1796, Notifying His Relinquishment of the Presidential Office,* by Jasper Dwight of Vermont [pseud.] (Philadelphia, 1796), Vol. 31, 40-5. In later years politicians and others referred to Washington's advice as an enduring guide to policy. See, for example, Henry Cabot Lodge's address of February 16, 1916, at Morristown, New Jersey, entitled "Washington's Policies of Neutrality and National Defense," in his *War Addresses* (Boston, 1917), pp. 117-36.

31. John C. Hamilton, *History of the Republic of the United States of America, as Traced in the Writings of Alexander Hamilton and of His Contemporaries* (7 vols., New York, 1857-1864), VI, 536-37. Although Americans viewed the Farewell in many instances as purely a political document, this is not to deny that some men wanted a genuine neutrality which would save the United States "from the exactions and solence of both" England and France. See, for example, James Kent to Moss Kent, September 19, 1796, William Kent, ed., *Memoirs and Letters of James Kent* (Boston, 1898), p. 174.

32. Madison to Monroe, September 29, 1796, quoted in Irving Brant, *James Madison: Father of the Constitution, 1787-1800* (Indianapolis, 1950), p. 442. As Washington had anticipated, opponents claimed that the motive behind the Farewell was his knowledge that if he ran he would not be re-elected. McMaster, *History of the People of the United States,* II, 290-91. Federalists were convinced that Republicans created French animosity against Washington for political reasons. See Timothy Pickering to John Quincy Adams, December 9, 1796, Pickering Papers (Massachusetts Historical Society, Boston); John Quincy Adams to John Adams, April 4, 1796, Ford, ed., *Writings of John Quincy Adams,* I, 484. Young Adams praised the address. He wrote Washington that he hoped "it may serve as the foundation" for future American policy. Letter of February 11, 1797, *ibid.,* II, 119-20. Samuel F. Bemis, "John Quincy Adams and George Washington," Massachusetts Historical Society *Proceedings,* LXVII (1945), 365-84, maintains that young Adams' ideas influenced Washington and the Farewell.

33. Adet to Minister of Foreign Relations, October 12, 1796, Turner, cd., *Correspondence of French Ministers,* p. 954; Bemis, "Washington's Farewell Address," *American Historical Review,* XXXIX (January 1934), 263.

34. Adet to Minister of Foreign Relations, September 24, 1796, Turner, ed., *Correspondence of French Ministers,* pp. 947-49. The Directory, of course, approved of Adet's meddling and counted on Jefferson's election. Delacroix wrote to Adet on November 2, 1796, that his dispatches confirmed what the Directory had expected would result from its measures directed against Washington's government. Archives des Affaires Étrangeres, Correspondance Politique, États-Unis, XLVI, 355-57. The British, too, had a vital stake in the election. Bond to Grenville, May 4, 1796, Henry Adams Transcripts. For a discussion of the 1796 election with emphasis on John Adams and domestic politics, see Manning J. Dauer, *The Adams Federalists* (Baltimore, 1953), pp. 92-111.

35. Fisher Ames to Christopher Gore, December 3, 1796, Seth Ames, ed., *Works of Fisher Ames* (2 vols., Boston, 1854), II, 206; John Adams to Abigail Adams, December 4, 1796, Adams, ed., *Letters of John Adams to Wife,* II, 231; Oliver Wolcott to Oliver Wolcott, Sr., November 27, 1796, Gibbs, ed., *Wolcott Papers,* I, 400-1.

36. William Loughton Smith to Ralph Izard, November 8, 1796, in Ulrich B. Phillips, ed., "South Carolina Federalist Correspondence, 1789-

1797," *American Historical Review,* XIV (July 1909), 785.

37. Adet to Pickering, October 27, 1796, *American State Papers, Foreign Relations* (6 vols., Washington, 1832-1859), I, 576-77. For Pickering's response of November 1, 1796, see *ibid.,* p. 578; see also Pickering to Rufus King, November 14, 1796, Charles R. King, ed., *The Life and Correspondence of Rufus King* (6 vols., New York, 1894-1900), II, 108-9.

38. The proclamation is in Archives des Affaires Étrangères, Correspondance Politique, États-Unis, XLVI, 352, and is reprinted in Cobbett, *Porcupine's Works,* IV, 154-55. Adet's promulgation of the "cockade proclamation" was under orders from his home government. Adet to Minister of Foreign Relations, November 12, 1796, Turner, ed., *Correspondence of French Ministers,* p. 967.

39. Adet to Pickering, November 15, 1796, *American State Papers, Foreign Relations,* I, 579-83.

40. Adet to Minister of Foreign Relations [November, 1796], Turner, ed., *Correspondence of French Ministers,* pp. 969-70.

41. Adams to Abigail Adams, November 27, 1796, Adams, ed., *Letters of John Adams to Wife,* II, 229.

42. Reprinted in Cobbett, *Porcupine's Works,* IV, 137-206.

43. Madison to Jefferson, December 5, 1796, Madison Papers, quoted in Brant, *Madison: Father of the Constitution,* p. 445. See also Fisher Ames to Christopher Gore, December 13, 1796, cited in Harry M. Tinkcom, *The Republicans and Federalists in Pennsylvania, 1790-1801: A Study of National Stimulus and Local Response* (Harrisburg, 1950), p. 173.

44. Liston to Grenville, November 15 and December 9, 1796, Henry Adams Transcripts. Liston complained that Republicans charged that British gold was being used in the election and confessed "that a persevering repetition of such accusations has at last the effect of procuring them a degree of credit." A prominent Republican Unitarian clergyman was surprised at how people cursed the French at this time. *The Diary of William Bentley* (4 vols., Salem, Mass., 1905-1914), II, 207 (entry of November 8, 1796).

45. For the observation on Washington, Henrietta Liston to James Jackson, 1796, Perkins, ed., "Diplomat's Wife in Philadelphia," *William and Mary Quarterly,* XI, Ser. III (October 1954), 605. The quotations are from "The People," Hartford *Connecticut Courant,* reprinted in *New Hampshire and Vermont Journal: or, The Farmer's Weekly Museum* (Walpole, N.H.), November 22, 1796, and Philip Key to James McHenry, November 28, 1796, in Bernard C. Steiner, *The Life and Correspondence of James McHenry* (Cleveland, 1907), p. 202. Congressman Robert Goodloe Harper wrote to his constituents that if there had been no other objection to Jefferson than French exertions on his behalf it would have been sufficient to oppose him. Letter of January 5, 1797, Elizabeth Donnan, ed., *Papers of James A. Bayard, 1796-1815,* American Historical Association, *Annual Report, 1913,* II (Washington, 1915), 25. Later, certain French officials came to believe that the activity of Adet coupled with that of his predecessors plus the seeming duplicity of the French government brought victory to the Federalists in 1796. Even Jefferson, it was pointed out, came to

believe that the French sought to destroy the American constitution. See James A. James, "French Opinion as a Factor in Preventing War between France and the United States, 1795-1800," *American Historical Review,* XXX (October 1924), 46.

46. Adet to Minister of Foreign Relations [November 22, 1792], Turner, ed., *Correspondence of French Ministers,* p. 972.

47. "Americanus," in *Gazette of the United States* (Philadelphia), reprinted in *New York Herald,* December 3, 1796. William Vans Murray, commenting on a letter from James McHenry, November 19, 1796, Murray Papers, Library of Congress.

48. John Adams to Abigail Adams, December 4, 1796, Adams, ed., *Letters of John Adams to Wife,* II, 231. A basic charge directed against Adams was that he was too closely connected to the British party. "Cassius," in *Philadelphia New World,* October 28, 1796, January 18, 1797, maintained in Woodbury, "Public Opinion in Philadelphia," *Smith College Studies in History,* V, 126.

49. William Willcocks, "To the People of the United States," *The Minerva,* reprinted in *New York Herald,* December 28, 1796, maintained that France from the beginning had sought to involve the United States in war. Some Federalists saw in the difficulties with France the virtue that the nation might be cured "of extraneous attachments," that the embarrassing French alliance would be destroyed. Chauncey Goodrich to Oliver Wolcott, Gibbs, ed., *Wolcott Papers,* I, 417. Republican congressman from Virginia John Clopton warned his constituents against Federalist "efforts to foment a prejudice in the public mind against the French nation." Clopton to Isaac Youngblood, January 24, 1797, John Clopton Papers (Duke University Library).

50. Under the signature "Americanus," Hamilton on December 6, 1796, published "The Answer," his reply to Adet. Lodge, ed., *Works of Hamilton,* V, 348-62. Under the signature "Americus," he published a series of articles, beginning January 27, 1797, entitled "The Warning," in which he warned against French influence and the alliance, *ibid.,* pp. 363-92.

51. Webster's articles were entitled: "To the People of the United States," and ran from December 1796 through February 1797. Harry R. Warfel, *Noah Webster: Schoolmaster to America* (New York, 1936), p. 229. The quotations are from *The Minerva,* reprinted in *New York Herald,* December 17 and 28, 1796.

52. John Adams to Abigail Adams, December 12, 1796, in Charles F. Adams, *The Life of John Adams* (2 vols., rev. ed., Philadelphia, 1891), II, 208. The electors' ballots had been announced on the first Wednesday in January but were not counted formally until the first Wednesday in February.

53. Adet realized before the meeting of electors that Jefferson "in spite of the intrigues against him," would become vice-president. Although he rejoiced in Jefferson's election he understood that the Viriginian was drawn to France primarily because he feared England. Even Jefferson,

declared the French minister, "is an American, and as such, he cannot sincerely be our friend. An American is the born enemy of all the peoples of Europe." Adet to Minister of Foreign Relations, December 31, 1796, Turner, ed., *Correspondence of French Ministers,* pp. 982-83.

54. *New Hampshire and Vermont Journal,* March 7, 1797.

55. The son of the new president caught a glimpse of the Farewell in the future of American foreign policy. The failure of the French in their attacks against Washington in the election of 1796, he believed, should reveal to them the "temper" of the American people. "Can France possibly believe," he asked rhetorically, "that Mr. Jefferson, or any other man, would dare to start away from that system of administration which Washington has thus sanctioned, not only by his example, but by his retirement?" John Quincy Adams to Joseph Pitcairn, January 31, 1797, Ford, ed., *Writings of John Quincy Adams,* II, 95-6.

Washington's Farewell

BY NATHAN SCHACHNER

The Executive Branch of the government had emerged victorious in the bitter contest with the House of Representatives [over appropriating funds for Jay's Treaty—ED.]; but the scars remained. Jefferson attributed the victory to the fact that "one man [Washington] outweighs them all in influence over the people, who have supported his judgment against their own and that of their representatives. Republicanism," he sighed, "must lie on its oars, resign the vessel to its pilot, and themselves to the course he thinks best for them."[1]

In spite of this mournful threnody Jefferson had no intention of allowing "Republicanism" to lie on its oars. This was a presidential year, and with Washington scheduled to retire, Jefferson permitted his name to be mentioned as a candidate.

Reprinted by permission of Mrs. Nathan Schachner from *The Founding Fathers* (New York, 1954), pp. 394–405.

Nevertheless the Republicans were disheartened and dismayed over their failure to kill Jay's Treaty. Madison wrote gloomily that the "crisis which ought to have been so managed as to fortify the Republican cause, has left it in a very crippled condition." He agreed with Jefferson that they had been defeated by the prestige of the President and the threat of war if the treaty failed. Nor did the early local election returns from New York, Massachusetts and elsewhere, which disclosed sharp Federalist gains, do anything to lighten the pervading gloom.[2]

In his exasperation Jefferson sat down to write a letter to his old Virginia friend and neighbor, the Italian-born Phillip Mazzei. Since Mazzei had returned to Italy, Jefferson felt that he could safely vent his accumulated load of anger to his distant friend. In this surmise, as the event will show, he was egregiously mistaken.

"The aspect of our politics has wonderfully changed since you left us," Jefferson declared.

> In place of that noble love of liberty and republican government which carried us triumphantly through the war, an Anglican monarchical and aristocratical party had sprung up, whose avowed object is to draw over us the substance, as they have already done the forms, of the British government. The main body of our citizens, however, remain true to their republican principles; the whole landed interest is republican, and so is a great mass of talents. Against us are the Executive, the Judiciary, two out of three branches of the legislature, all of the officers of the government, all who want to be officers, all timid men who prefer the calm of despotism to the boisterous sea of liberty, British merchants and Americans trading on British capital, speculators and holders in the banks and public funds, a contrivance invented for the purposes of corruption, and for assimilating us in all things to the rotten as well as the sound parts of the British model. It would give you a fever were I to name to you the apostates who have gone over to these heresies, men who were Samsons in the field and Solomons in the council, but who have had their heads shorn by the harlot England.[3]

There is no question whom Jefferson meant by the biblical references—he had Washington primarily in mind, and perhaps also John Adams. It was an indiscreet letter to write; the more so since Mazzei, volatile and voluble, could not be trusted to keep such a juicy morsel to himself. On its receipt, Mazzei translated it enthusiastically into his native tongue and caused it to be published in a Florentine newspaper. The Paris *Moniteur* picked it up, clad the damning epistle in French dress and published it with even greater enthusiasm. As though the original contents were not sufficiently explosive, the *Moniteur* thoughtfully added to them, as coming from Jefferson, an apostrophe to France.

From then on the future of the so-called "Mazzei Letter" was predestined. A Federalist sheet, the New York *Minerva,* received the incriminating issue of the *Moniteur* in its regular packet of foreign mail. The editor pounced with joy on the peripatetic letter, retranslated it into English; and thus, on May 14, 1797, it reappeared after many vicissitudes in America to plague its original author.

Fortunately, by then the presidential election was over, or the publication might have decisively changed the course of American history. For the wave of resentment and anger that swept the country over the aspersions on the now-retired President could easily have swamped the Republican party and defeated Jefferson for the vice-presidency.

The embarrassed author thought it best to keep a discreet silence in the face of all attacks; though privately he complained that the rounds of translations had distorted the sense (which they surprisingly had not, with the exception of the forged insertion by the *Moniteur*).

The publication of the "Mazzei Letter" conclusively ended the already uneasy relations between Jefferson and Washington. For some time the latter had chafed under what he considered to be ungenerous and underhanded assaults on himself by his former friends, Jefferson and Madison. He spoke of them both as the foremost opponents of the government and "consequently to the person administering it contrary to their views."

Even prior to the final break, Washington had received reports that Jefferson was denouncing him "as a person under a dangerous influence; and that, if [Washington] would listen *more* to some *other* opinions, all would be well." The angered President sent the report along to Jefferson, adding bitterly that a year or so ago "I had no conception that Parties would, or even could go, the length I have been witness to," or that "every act of my administration would be tortured, and the grossest and most insidious misrepresentations of them be made . . . and that too in such exaggerated and indecent terms as could scarcely be applied to a Nero; a notorious defaulter; or even a common pickpocket."[5]

It is no wonder that Washington thought it time for him to quit political life and retire to the privacy of his plantations. The Founding Fathers of the Republic were remarkably thin-skinned. The slings and arrows of their political opponents inflicted festering wounds which made them seek the shelter of obscurity in which to lick their hurts. Washington, Adams, Jefferson and Hamilton—all reacted in the same way and with the same air of anguished surprise.

Once the several treaties had been ratified,[6] Congress speedily dispatched the remaining business of the session. Some of the matters, however, aroused bitter if brief debate.

Tennessee, outpost of the Union, applied for admission as a sovereign state. Since the inhabitants of the territory were predominantly Republicans, and radical ones at that, the Federalists opposed the application and the Republicans demanded immediate and favorable action.

The House voted admission largely on party lines. In the Senate the debate was longer and more violent, exacerbated by the arrival in Philadelphia of the blatant William Blount, who proclaimed himself the senator-elect "from our new sister Tennessee" and the harbinger of "the rights of man."[7]

These antics goaded the Federalists to increased resistance; and the final vote was decided only by the casting ballot of Samuel Livermore of New Hampshire, acting president in the absence of John Adams. By such a narrow margin was Tennessee admitted into the Union on June 1, 1796, as the sixteenth state.

Of far-reaching importance for the future of the country was the Act for the Sale of Lands in the Northwest Territory which went into effect on May 8th. The Act provided for the survey of the vast territory in sections of 640 acres each. Four such sections were to be reserved in every township for the public benefit; the balance was offered for sale to the highest bidder at a knockdown price of two dollars an acre.[8] With the passage of the Act the process of settling legally the public lands was placed on a sound basis, and settlers hastened to purchase the offered sections and to migrate with their families to the hitherto limitless forests and prairies.

Since Hamilton's departure from the Treasury, his successor had been struggling in vain to cope with the annual deficits. Now Wolcott confessed his failure and implored the help of his predecessor.[9]

Hamilton came up with his usual remedy—increased taxation. Thereupon Congress, over the protest of the Republicans, enacted additional duties on imports and laid a tax upon the keeping of private carriages and coaches.

Six frigates had been authorized in March 1794; but they seemed destined never to advance beyond the planning stage. Nine months later Knox was sarcastically reporting that the timber for the ships was still "standing in the forests; the iron for the cannon lying in its natural bed; and the flax and hemp, perhaps in their seed."[10]

A full year after that, there had been little change; though some timber had been cut in the piney woods of Georgia and placed on board ship for carriage to the scattered shipyards where the frigates were supposed to be constructed. A House investigating committee, seeking to discover the cause of the unaccountable delays, issued a curiously modern-type report. The trouble was, it said, that there had been such an "unexampled rise of labor, provisions, and all other articles necessary to the equipment of ships of war" since the appropriation had been made that the costs had almost doubled. It recommended therefore that at such "advanced prices" work proceed on two of the authorized frigates only.[11] Congress decided to go ahead on three. It was late in 1797 before two frigates were launched—the *Constellation* and the *Constitution*. The third—the *United States*—took still another year to complete.

Treaties had been signed with Great Britain, Spain and Algiers; but they did not bring an end to European troubles nor even to disputes with the signatory states.

Rufus King, at the expiration of his senatorial term, was sent as minister to England to replace Thomas Pinckney. King, a staunch Federalist, proved a cautious and levelheaded diplomat who performed his duties as well as could be expected in a most difficult post.

Nathan Schachner

The irritating issue of impressments had been left untouched in Jay's Treaty, and King tried hard to get England to abandon them. But this was one point on which England proved consistently adamant. It took years of peace after the Napoleonic wars before she allowed the obnoxious practice to wither.

The most that King could accomplish was to negotiate the release of impressed seamen who could prove their American birth and citizenship.[12] Citizenship by naturalization in the case of the British born was not enough; England took seriously the slogan "Once a British subject, *always* a British subject."

The situation, however, was complicated by the cavalier disregard of British naval officers for orders which they believed to be, and doubtless were, issued tongue in cheek. As one captain bluntly declared: "It is my duty to keep my Ship manned, and I will do so wherever I find men that speak the same language with me, and not a small part of them British Subjects, and that too producing Certificates as being American Citizens."[13]

When Hammond[14] quit his post in the United States the British government sent Robert Liston to replace him; but the Americans soon discovered, as in the case of successive French ministers, the change was one of person and not of attitude or arrogance.

On one point, however, and that most vital, the British yielded with obvious reluctance. In accordance with the provisions of Jay's Treaty they commenced the long-delayed evacuation of the border forts which they had held since the Revolution. When the last one was surrendered—Michilimackinac on the Great Lakes— a sigh of relief rose from all Americans. The Federalists were especially exultant. *"What think ye of the Treaty now?"* they taunted the Republicans. "Had ten thousand men been employed in besieging the Western Posts—had one half of them fallen by sickness and the sword . . . the acquisition would have excited universal joy and triumph throughout the United States. . . . Eternal praises to the God of Peace and Negotiation!"[15]

The wrath of the French mounted steadily over Jay's Treaty and the strict neutrality of the Americans. They threatened to consider their own treaties as "annihilated," and practically did so by seizing every American ship found laden with goods for England. The climax of a series of captures came with the taking of the *Mount Vernon.*

Anger bubbled over in America at the news, though the Republicans justified French behavior by putting all the blame on Jay's "traitorous" treaty. Washington wished to send a special envoy to France to demand an explanation of the seizures; but the Senate was in recess. Had he the power to dispatch a special envoy, he inquired of Hamilton and Jay, without waiting for confirmation? And what should be done about Monroe, the regular minister, with whom he was thoroughly disgusted?[16]

Hamilton had not waited for the query to demand that Monroe be dismissed. As for the French aggressions, if only the British "had been wise, they would neither have harassed our trade themselves, nor suffered their trade with us to be harassed." Perhaps, he suggested, we should hint to them to put "a clever little squadron in our ports and on our coast."[17]

In truth, Monroe was acting more unaccountably in France. When the American merchants then in Paris asked him to submit for them to the Minister of Finance a memorial "claiming payment of what is due them by the government," he added an astounding postscript of his own. This was an apology for submitting the memorial "as I know the difficulty of your situation and should be happy to accommodate with it." However, as the official representative of the United States, it was his duty to transmit the American claims. They were bona fide and acknowledged, and the creditor merchants were threatened with ruin if the payments were not met. Perhaps, he told the French Minister, he could act as an honest broker between them in such wise as to aid them and yet "not embarrass your affairs."[18] Monroe could hardly have expected that such an apologetic attitude would help the cause of the American merchants; and in fact it did not. The unfortunate creditors had to cool their heels a long time before any settlement was made.

Tom Paine added to Monroe's many difficulties by choosing this time to discharge all the venom he had accumulated against Washington while languishing in a French prison. Monroe, it is true, had tried to halt Paine; but not in order to shield the President of the United States. He openly sympathized with his semi-permanent guest; and agreed with his complaints and diatribes. He feared only that the publication Paine contemplated might compromise himself. If he were personally in the clear, or if Jefferson by that time had won the election and become President, then he would be prepared to view the assault on Washington with complete equanimity.[19]

A moment after Monroe thus disclosed the state of his own mind on the matter, the bag of venom burst. With his accustomed facility of phrase and genius for vituperation, Paine published the most unmitigated attack on Washington and his conduct that had ever been put into print. He accused the President in set phrases of having been guilty of "double politics" in the conduct of his administration, of having granted "monopolies of every kind," of having grossly favored the speculators and betrayed the poor soldiers; of being, in short, "the patron of the fraud."

This was mere preamble. Paine was manifestly warming up to the congenial task. He next accused the President of lapping up adulation and calling for more, of "a mean and servile submission to the insults" of Great Britain and "treachery and ingratitude" to France. Paine harked back to the day of the Revolution to assert that the French alone had been responsible for its success, not Washington's "cold and unmilitary conduct." He even charged that "you slept away your time in the field, till the finances of the country were completely exhausted."

He vowed that Washington had deliberately wished to see him, Paine, executed in a French prison and that only Monroe's intervention had saved him. He lashed out at John Jay, at Gouverneur Morris, at John Adams, and at "the disgusted traitors that call themselves Federalists."

He ended his open letter to Washington with an apostrophe which even for that free-speaking age was unexampled in its virulence. "As to you, Sir," he thundered, "treacherous in private friendship . . . and a hypocrite in public life, the world will be puzzled to decide whether you are an apostate or an impostor; whether you have abandoned good principles, or whether you ever had any."[20]

No wonder that Monroe feared the worst. But his fate had already been decided even before the excoriating pamphlet reached America.

Almost from the moment that Pickering took over the State Department, he had determined that Monroe must go. One of his first acts was to send a sharp reproof to him for having permitted French policy, on the basis of false reports of the contents of Jay's Treaty, to develop against us as it did.[21]

This was decidedly unfair; if anywhere, the fault lay with Jay, who had refused to furnish Monroe with a copy of his treaty. But Pickering was not concerned with evenhanded justice. The unfortunate speech which Monroe had delivered on his first arrival in Paris had convinced everyone in the administration— the President as well as his Cabinet—that Monroe was not a proper representative in France.

On July 2, 1796, the Cabinet took up the presidential queries concerning his power to dispatch a special envoy without the approval of the Senate and whether he should recall Monroe. They decided that the President had no power to send a special envoy unless Monroe was first recalled; and they decided further that Monroe's action in France had been such that he ought to be recalled.[22]

Washington took no immediate action on the advice. But each letter that arrived from Monroe only deepened his anger, and brought him closer to the deed.[23] Finally, on August 22nd, Pickering had the grim satisfaction of writing a curt notification to Monroe that he was being superseded by Charles Cotesworth Pinckney of South Carolina.[24]

Monroe was thunderstruck. He had already sent home a long defense of his conduct against the rebuke administered to him on June 13th, and he thought that the episode was closed. But he should not have been astonished. Even as the notice traversed the sea, Monroe was writing a confidential letter to Madison which, had it ever fallen into administration hands, would have convicted him out of his own mouth.

He notified Madison that France had ordered Adet, the French minister to the United States, to return home and that no successor was contemplated. The reason for this abrupt breaking off of diplomatic relations, said Monroe, was the ratification and consummation of Jay's Treaty. "I have detained them seven months from doing what they ought to have done at once," astonishingly avowed the American minister. "Poor Washington. Into what hands has he fallen!"[25]

Monroe returned to the United States furious and determined at all costs to vindicate himself. Like Edmund Randolph in a similar situation, he bombarded the administration with demands for statements, justifications and the use of confidential material. Then he devoted a full year to the writing of his apologia and defense, as well as a full assault on Washington and his advisers.

When the book finally appeared, Monroe joined the perennial tribe of authors in his disgruntlement over the poor sales and notices it received; but he consoled himself with the reflection—again quite common—that "the book will remain and will be read in the course of 50 years if not sooner, and I think the facts it contains, will settle or contribute to settle, the opinion of posterity in the character of the administration, however indifferent to it the present race may be." As for the men who made up that administration, "a gang of greater scoundrels never lived."[26]

With the third presidential election in the offing, Washington was adamant in his decision to retire. He had consented to a second term only on the insistent pleas of his colleagues, Federalist and Republican alike. Now no Republican urged him to remain.

The increasing tempo of abuse during the preceding months bewildered and angered him. He winced at every epithet and reacted to every tirade. He did not intend, he declared bitterly, "to be longer buffeted in the public prints by a set of infamous scribblers." He regretted only that he had not earlier announced his decision to withdraw.[27]

He had been thinking over the form of his announcement for a long time; as far back, indeed, as the end of his first administration. He wished to make it a valedictory, in which he could give the nation the benefit of such wisdom and experience as he had accumulated in its service.

At that time, when his relations with Madison were not yet strained, he had asked him to draft the valedictory. Madison had done so; then it had been put away when Washington assumed the presidency a second time. This time he called on Hamilton to act as his guide. The first draft of what he wished to say Washington wrote himself. Hamilton revised, polished and offered suggestions.

"My wish is," said the President, "that the whole may appear in a plain style; and be handed to the public in an honest, unaffected, simple garb."[28] He also wished, he said at another time, to address "the Yeomenry of this Country" and warn them of the "consequences which would naturally flow from such unceasing and virulent attempts to destroy all confidence in the Executive part of the Government" as evidenced by the recent invectives against himself.[29]

After considerable correspondence and constant revisions of the several drafts, Washington's Farewell Address finally emerged in a form which both men thought satisfactory. In September 1796, copies were distributed to the newspapers for publication.

The Farewell Address has become one of the classics of American political literature. Its grave, measured tones, its solemn exhortations and impressive warnings, the spirit of earnestness which pervades its entire structure, have left their deep impress on American thought and diplomacy.

In retiring from public office, Washington declared, "a solicitude for your welfare" and "the apprehension of danger" had impelled him to offer certain sentiments and reflections for the consideration of the American people.

"The Unity of Government which constitutes you one people," he wrote, ". . . is a main pillar in the edifice of your real independence; the support of your tranquillity at home; your peace abroad; of your safety; of your prosperity; of that very liberty which you so highly prize." But as it was this "point in your political fortress," which both internal and external enemies sought to breach and to weaken in your mind the conviction of its truth, it was essential that all Americans guard and cherish it to the utmost, and to resist "every attempt to alienate any portion of our Country from the rest, or to enfeeble the sacred ties which now link together the various parts."

This was the major and indeed the only theme of the valedictory—the true interrelation and interdependence of North, South and West. With all the earnestness at his command Washington warned against party passions and "designing men" who sought to create the impression that "there is a real difference of local interests and views" based on geographical dispersion.

Only a "Government for the whole," he added, can give power and permanency to the Union. The Constitution, our own choice, provides that; and until it is changed by lawful means, it must be considered as a sacred obligation.

All obstructions to the execution of the laws, all combinations and associations, under whatever plausible character, with the real design to direct, control, counteract, or awe the regular deliberation and action of the Constituted authorities are destructive of this fundamental principle and of fatal tendency. They serve to organize faction, to give it an artificial and extraordinary force; to put in the place of the delegated will of the Nation, the will of a party;. often a small but artful and enterprizing minority of the Community.

This section was an obvious denunciation of the Whiskey Rebellion, the Democratic Societies and the Republican party itself. The idea of political parties had not yet become fixed and permanent in the minds of the Founding Fathers; even the Republicans themselves hated the designation, avowing that it was the Federalists who in fact represented the party or factional spirit.

Washington kindled to this theme. "The spirit of party," he continued, is baneful and leads inevitably to despotism. "It serves always to distract the public councils and enfeeble the public administration. It agitates the community with ill founded jealousies and false alarms; kindles the animosity of one part against another; foments occasionally riot and insurrection. It opens the door to foreign influence and corruption, which finds a facilitated access to the government itself, through the channels of party passions."

Thus Washington led into his second major theme—the dangers arising from foreign entanglements. "Observe good faith and justice towards all nations," he exhorted; "cultivate peace and harmony with all." Let there be neither "permanent inveterate antipathies against particular nations" nor "passionate attachments for others."

> The great rule of conduct for us [he declared] in regard to foreign nations, is in extending our commercial relations, to have with them as little *political* connection as possible. . . . Europe has a set of primary interests, which to us have none or a very remote relation. Hence she must be engaged in frequent controversies, the causes of which are essentially foreign to our concerns. . . . Our detached and distant situation invites, and enables us to pursue, a different course. . . . Why forego the advantages of so peculiar a situation? Why quit our own, to stand upon foreign ground? Why, by interweaving our destiny with that of any part of Europe, entangle our peace and prosperity in the toils of European ambition, rivalship, interest, humor, or

caprice? 'Tis our true policy to steer clear of permanent alliances with any portion of the foreign world.

These, he concluded, were the "counsels of an old and affectionate friend."[30]

It has been this final section which has always drawn the attention of the isolationists. They fail, however, to note the peculiar context of the times in which Washington issued his solemn warning. America was torn by contending groups who, in some instances, gave their allegiance more passionately to the foreign nation of their choice than to the country of their citizenship. The distance between the two continents seemed enormous, and took many weeks or even months to span. A determined and united people at home could withstand engulfment from abroad, no matter how ruthless the power or efficient the dictator. But the times have changed; jet planes, long-range bombers, submarines, atom and hydrogen bombs, radio and ideologies can penetrate the most formidable frontier. The ocean is neither frontier nor barrier any more; the outposts of the nation have moved to far-flung places whose very names were unknown to Americans in Washington's day. Indeed, it is highly probable that he would have been the first to disavow the interpretations which have since been placed upon his doctrine of "entangling alliances."

NOTES

1. Jefferson to Monroe, June 12, 1796, Jefferson, *Works* (Fed. ed.), VIII, 243-44.
2. Madison to Jefferson, May 22, 1796, Madison Papers, L.C., XIX, 68.
3. Jefferson to Mazzei, Apr. 24, 1796, Jefferson, *Works,* VIII, 238-41.
4. Washington to Hamilton, May 15, 1796, Washington, *Writings* (John C. Fitzpatrick, ed.), XXXV, 48-51.
5. Washington to Jefferson, July 6, 1796, *ibid.,* XXXV, 118-22.
6. These were the Jay and Pinckney treaties and an agreement signed with the Dey of Algiers providing for payment of tribute in return for the release of Americans captured by the Barbary pirates. In addition, the treaty called for an annual payment of $72,000 to prevent further captures.—ED.
7. Chauncey Goodrich to Oliver Wolcott, Sr., May 13, 1796, Gibbs, *Memoirs,* I, 338-39.
8. *Annals of Congress,* 3rd Cong., 1st Sess., pp. 2905-9.
9. Wolcott to Hamilton, June 17, 1796, Hamilton, *Works* (J. C. Hamilton, ed.), VI, 132-33. [Oliver Wolcott replaced Alexander Hamilton as

Secretary of the Treasury in 1795.—ED.]

10. To House of Representatives, Dec. 29, 1794, American State Papers: *Naval Affairs,* I, 6.

11. *Ibid.,* I, 17-18, 19-21.

12. Grenville to Bond, May 19, 1796, American Historical Association *Annual Report* 1936, pp. 118-19.

13. Captain H. Mowat to Robert Liston, Mar. 27, 1797, *ibid.,* p. 119n.

14. George Hammond, who was appointed in 1791 as England's first minister to the United States.—ED.

15. *Gazette of the U.S.,* Aug. 3, 1796.

16. Washington to Hamilton, June 26, 1796, Washington, *Writings,* XXXV, 101-4.

17. Hamilton to Wolcott, June 15, 1796, Hamilton, *Works* (Lodge, ed.), X, 174-76.

18. Monroe to Minister of Finance, Apr. 7, 1796, Monroe Papers, N.Y. Pub. Lib.

19. Monroe to Madison, July 5, 1796, Monroe, *Writings,* III, 19-27.

20. Paine to Washington, July 30, 1796, Paine, *Writings* (Conway, ed.), III, 213-52.

21. Pickering to Monroe, July 13, 1796, *American State Papers: Foreign Relations,* I, 737-38.

22. "Cabinet Opinion," Washington, *Writings,* XXXV, 123-24n.

23. Washington to Pickering, July 27, 1796, *ibid.,* pp. 156-57.

24. *American State Papers: Foreign Relations,* I, 741-42.

25. Sept. 1, 1796, Monroe, *Writings,* III, 52-4. DelaCroix to Monroe, Oct. 7, 1796, *American State Papers: Foreign Relations,* I, 745. Mount-florence to Monroe, Aug. 30, 1796, Monroe Papers, N.Y. Pub. Lib.

26. Monroe to Jefferson, Mar. 26, 1798, Monroe, *Writings,* III, 106ff. Benjamin Vaughan to Monroe, Sept. 2, 1797, Monroe Papers, N.Y. Pub. Lib.

27. Washington to Hamilton, June 26, 1796, Washington, *Writings,* XXXV, 101-4.

28. Washington to Hamilton, May 15, 1796, *ibid.,* pp. 48-51.

29. Washington to Hamilton, Aug. 25, 1796; *ibid.,* pp. 190-92.

30. "Farewell Address," Sept. 19, 1796, *ibid.,* 214-18.

The Farewell Address
BY FELIX GILBERT

I

When the last year of Washington's second presidential term had come around, there were no doubts in the President's mind that "ease and retirement" were "indispensably necessary"[1] to him. He now had to decide what form the announcement of his retirement should take and what would be the most appropriate moment for it.

Four years earlier, in 1792, Washington had faced a similar situation. He had wanted to return to his beloved Mount Vernon and retire to the life of a gentleman farmer. When he had asked James Madison about the most suitable procedure for carrying out his intention, Madison had advised the President to announce

Reprinted by permission of Princeton University Press from *To the Farewell Address: Ideas of Early American Foreign Policy* (Princeton, 1961), pp. 115-36.

his decision in a valedictory address to be published in the newspapers in September, so that the people would be informed before
the balloting for the presidential electors would start. At last,
however, Washington had given in to the urgings of all his political friends who had pressed him to stay on until—and this, they
said, would happen in a short time—"public opinion, the character of the Government, and the course of its administration
should be better decided."[2]

The problems besetting Washington's second administration
were far different from those of the first; they also differed
widely from the political tasks which he and his friends had
envisaged when he had decided to remain in office for another
term. The most important tasks of Washington's first presidential
term had been the establishment of the new federal administration,
the decision on a capital for the United States, and, especially,
the determination of the course which the young republic should
follow in its financial and economic policy. When Washington's
friends had urged him to continue in office because he was
needed to give "such a tone and firmness to the Government as
would secure it against danger,"[3] they were thinking that these
domestic issues demanded further consolidation under a steady
government. In Washington's second administration, however,
foreign policy, which before 1792 had appeared on the American horizon only intermittently, came into the foreground and
dominated the political scene. War had come close to America.
The war of the German powers against France broadened into
a world conflict when, in February 1793, Great Britain, Holland,
and Spain joined the struggle against the French Revolution. The
British blockade of France impinged on the pursuit of American
trade. An attack by England and Spain against the French possessions in the West Indies might lead France to demand American assistance in accordance with the Franco-American alliance
of 1778. Yet American involvement in the war was the more
dangerous because the colonies of England and Spain on the
North American continent encircled the frontiers of the United
States; it seemed unlikely that its boundaries could be defended
against the joint operations of Britain and Spain. In the month
following his second inauguration, on April 22, 1793, Washington
issued a "Proclamation of Neutrality" announcing the decision
to "adopt and pursue a conduct friendly and impartial toward

the Belligerent Powers." The President advised the citizens of the United States to avoid all acts which might be in contradiction to this attitude and threatened them with loss of protection and, if possible, prosecution in case they should violate the laws of neutrality. Although the Proclamation of Neutrality established the course which America would try to follow throughout the European conflict, the pressure of events made it frequently questionable whether the United States could hold to this position. When the Proclamation was issued, the newly appointed minister of the French Republic, Genêt, had already reached American soil and had begun his attempt to draw the United States into the war—by one-sided interpretation of the articles of the old alliance, by inflammatory appeals to the citizens over the heads of the government, and by directly unneutral acts like the equipping of French privateers in America. Genêt overplayed his hand. In the summer of 1793, Washington's government agreed on the necessity of his recall. Although Genêt's provocative attitude cooled the passionately pro-French sentiments prevalent among wide groups of the American public, this advantage for the advocates of a neutral policy was soon counter-balanced by the irritating attitude of the British government towards America. The actions of the British navy showed a blatant disregard of the American views on the rights of neutrals in wartime. Moreover, from Canada came disquieting news which raised suspicion of a military attack from the north. If gratitude for French assistance in the War of Independence and sympathy for republicanism had not been strong enough to bring the United States into war on the French side, the old hatred against George III, reawakened by the highhandedness of the British government, might provide the spark which would start the fires of war. During the spring of 1794, Washington decided to send John Jay as a special envoy to Britain—an almost desperate attempt by direct negotiations to avoid further aggravation of British-American relations.

It took almost a year, till March 1795, for the results of Jay's negotiations to become known in America. With the exception of one significant concession—the evacuation of the northern frontier posts—the British had not yielded to American wishes. They refused to abandon interference with neutral shipping in wartime. The Jay Treaty was of little avail in changing the minds of those who believed that America's place was on the side of France or that a neutrality benevolent towards France rather than an impartial neutrality was the right course for America. When the Jay Treaty was presented to the Senate for ratification in the summer of 1795, a vehement struggle developed; but the treaty was accepted with a number of votes just equalling the constitutionally necessary two-thirds majority. Washington was able to ratify the treaty.

In the light of later developments, the value of the Jay Treaty for the preservation of a neutral course in American foreign policy must be regarded as doubtful. French resentment over the conclusion of the Jay Treaty resulted in the "undeclared war against France," and the unsolved differences in the British and American views on neutrality played their part in the origin of the Anglo-American War of 1812. But Washington regarded his second term as full of lasting achievements in foreign policy. Through the Proclamation of 1793, he had set the American course towards neutrality. Without dissolving the French alliance, he had refused to interpret it as a restriction on American freedom of action. Finally, he had diminished the danger of conflict between Britain and America by a settlement which, unsatisfactory as it might be in its details, removed the risk of sudden explosion. This was the reason for the optimism with which Washington had greeted Congress at the opening of its session in December 1795: "I have never met you at any period, when more than at present, the situation of our public affairs has afforded just cause for mutual congratulation."[4] It was true that a large percentage of the public remained hostile to the government, but even this cloud was disappearing. Washington believed he could notice that in January and February "a great change has been wrought in the public mind"[5] and that the people were beginning to recognize the merits of his foreign policy.

This was the time when Washington's thoughts turned to the problems involved in announcing his intention to retire. He thought it best, as we can deduce from indications about a conversation with Alexander Hamilton in the second half of February, to use the draft for a valedictory address which Madison had set up in 1792, but to add a further section about the experiences of his second administration.

Events intervened which must have pushed such thoughts into

the background. For in March it became clear that the struggle over the Jay Treaty had not ended with its acceptance by the Senate. When the House of Representatives was asked to approve the expenditures necessary for the implementation of the treaty, the Republicans under Madison's leadership tried to upset the whole arrangement by refusing this financial request. The outcome of this great debate was uncertain until the last moment. It is evident that the renewal of the struggle over the Jay Treaty put a new construction on Washington's plans for retirement. If the opponents of the treaty had won out, this would have been a rejection of the government; and Washington's unwillingness to stand for another term could have hardly been presented as a voluntary act. It did not come to this; on April 30, 1796, by a vote of 51 to 48, the House approved the funds necessary for the implementation of the treaty.

To Washington, the debate on the Jay Treaty was one of the most important events in the history of the young republic. This was not just because approval or rejection of his foreign policy was involved. Washington viewed the attempt of the House to influence foreign policy by means of its power over the purse as a violation of the Constitution, which had confided the treaty-making power to the President and the Senate. Interference by the House in foreign affairs could be explained only as an invasion of the rights of others and an attempt to enlarge its own power. Washington saw the entire Constitution brought "to the brink of a precipice."[6]

Although the debate in the House over the Jay Treaty in March and April 1796 had shown the strength of partisan divisions in the field of foreign policy, the result was not entirely negative. Positively, the outcome of the debate represented an approval of the foreign policy of the government, and it had also clarified the constitutional issues involved in the conduct of foreign policy. Washington could rightly consider that if his first administration had established the foundations for the internal organization of the republic, his second administration had laid out the course for the management of foreign affairs. In May, Washington was free to turn again to the problems of his valedictory address. He sent his draft of a valedictory address to Alexander Hamilton, on whom he was accustomed to rely for help in the composition of state documents. This draft represented no great change from the ideas which he had expressed in February. In the first part of the draft, Washington reproduced the valedictory address which Madison had prepared for him in 1792. Then there followed a new part which, as Washington wrote to Hamilton, had become necessary because of "considerable changes having taken place both at home and abroad."[7] The addition shows that Washington regarded the events in the field of foreign affairs as the central issues of his second administration.

II

The tone of the part which Washington had written to complement Madison's draft was very different from that of the valedictory of 1792. Taking a stand high above concrete and disputed political issues and expressing generally acceptable sentiments, Madison had woven together a justification of Washington's decision to retire, a praise of the American Constitution, and an exhortation to preserve the advantages of the Union.

In the part which Washington added in 1796, the closeness and the bitterness of the political fights of the preceding months and years were clearly noticeable. The last five paragraphs of this section mentioned the attacks against the government and the abuses to which the President had been subjected. Washington's statement that his "fortune, in a pecuniary point of view, has received no augmentation from my country"[8] showed how he had been hurt by the recent criticisms resulting from revelations according to which he had temporarily overdrawn his accounts with the government. The section which stands between Madison's draft and the last five paragraphs of personal defense, and which forms the most important of Washington's additions, is the section in which foreign policy has the most prominent role.

It consists of a number of different, only loosely connected thoughts, moulded in the form of a list of "wishes,"[9] as Washington himself called them. Of these nine wishes, only the first two and the last are not directly concerned with foreign policy. However, the first wish—an admonition to extinguish or, at least, moderate party disputes—and the last—a counsel to maintain the constitutional delimitations of powers—were inspired by developments in the area of foreign policy, by the bitterness of party differences revealed in the debate over the Jay Treaty, and by the attempt of the House to have a part in the making of treaties. The remaining six wishes, which refer to issues of foreign policy, summarized Washington's experiences in his second administration. Essentially, they were ideas which Washington had expressed at other places in the same or similar form. Washington's first three recommendations in the field of foreign affairs —scrupulously to observe treaty obligations, to refrain from political connections, and to take pride in America as a distinct nation—can be found, more briefly but in the same sequence, in a letter from Washington to Patrick Henry in October 1795. In his draft for the valedictory, Washington elaborated on the dangers of foreign interference in American politics and on the necessity of realizing that in foreign affairs, each nation is guided exclusively by egoistic motives. The following wish—that America must do everything possible to keep the peace for twenty years, until which time her position would be almost unassailable—was a revision of a paragraph in a letter from Washington to Gouverneur Morris of December 22, 1795. The last two pieces of advice—the need for maintaining a truly neutral attitude and for preserving the Union as a check against destructive intentions of foreign powers—Washington had also voiced previously.

The part of Washington's draft dealing with foreign affairs represents a collection of diverse thoughts and ideas which are neither closely integrated nor systematically organized. Yet one theme permeates the various paragraphs: a warning against the spirit of faction and against the danger of letting ideological predilections and prejudices enter considerations of foreign policy. This is the topic of the central paragraph in Washington's list of "wishes," where he admonished the citizens to take "pride in the name of an American." The same theme appears in the paragraphs on the duties of neutrals and the need for union; it is impressively stated as Washington's first "wish," in which he implored the citizens to use "charity and benevolence" towards each other in case of political differences and dissensions.

Washington did not provide an analysis of the international situation into which America had been placed. Nor did he describe the course which, as a result of such an analysis, America ought to follow in foreign policy. He touched upon these points, but only lightly and selectively, almost accidentally. Washington's fundamental concern was the attitude of American citizens towards foreign policy and the need for overcoming party spirit in decisions on foreign policy.

III

Washington's condemnation of the spirit of faction arose from a deep political conviction. Although differences in political opinions might be unavoidable, Washington believed that rational discussion would always lead to a realization of the true interest of the nation. Washington saw himself standing above the parties, forcing the contentious politicians to work together under the uniting banner of the true national interest. He had tried to keep Jefferson and Hamilton in the government even when their political differences had nearly paralyzed the functioning of the administration.

In 1796, it was an equally strange idea to bring Hamilton and Madison together in a common task. One cannot help wondering whether, in giving both Hamilton and Madison a part in the composition of his valedictory, Washintgon might have hoped that he could make this document a further demonstration of his conviction that party contrasts did not exclude cooperation in a situation of national interest and that this cooperation would lend added weight to his valedictory pronouncement, securing it against the objection of being an expression of personal or partisan views.

During the preceding years, Hamilton and Madison had emerged as the leaders of the two opposing parties, the Federalists and the Republicans. Both parties maintained that their differences were irreconcilable, because each believed the other was trying to overthrow the Constitution. To the Republicans, Washington had become an enemy, a prisoner of the Federalists. On the other hand, the Federalists, who characterized Madison as an irresponsible radical, could not look approvingly upon the possible increase in Madison's reputation resulting from his collaboration in Washington's valedictory.

When, in February 1796, Washington had told Hamilton of his plan of issuing a valedictory which would consist of two parts, the one which Madison had drafted in 1792 and the other an addition for which he asked Hamilton's assistance, Hamilton expressed his reservations immediately. Hamilton preferred an entirely new document; he seems also to have raised special objections to the contents of Madison's draft and to the mention of Madison's name in the valedictory.

But Washington stuck to his plan. On May 12, 1796, Washington invited Madison to dinner, probably to talk with him about his retirement. Washington might have thought he could hardly use Madison's draft for a valedictory, still less in a changed form, without informing him. Although Madison might have felt little enthusiasm for collaborating with Washington at a time when he was sharply opposed to the President's policy, he certainly had no valid reason for objecting. The valedictory of 1792 had been written in close adherence to Washington's instructions and placed at Washington's disposal.

Three days later, on May 15, 1796, Washington sent to Hamilton material for revision which consisted of a brief introduction, Madison's draft, and the lengthy addition necessitated by the "considerable changes having taken place at home and abroad." Washington had made a concession to Hamilton's views by omitting, contrary to his original intention, a direct mention of Madison's name and by leaving out a few passages from Madison's draft. Moreover, the President permitted Hamilton "to throw the whole into a different form."[10] But as Washington indicated, he preferred his original idea of a valedictory address which contained the draft of 1792 and his recently composed additions. Even if Hamilton should decide to give the valedictory an entirely new form, he should submit at the same time another draft which would be restricted to emendations and corrections of the papers Washington had sent him.

After the debate on the Jay Treaty in the House, which had increased party bitterness, Hamilton must have found the idea of Madison's associating with Washington in the announcement of the President's retirement more inappropriate than ever. Moreover, the high praise of Republican government contained in Madison's draft could be interpreted as favoring an attitude to which Hamilton was violently opposed, that of placing America on the side of the French Revolution.

Thus Hamilton was anxious to dissuade Washington from letting the valedictory appear in the form Washington intended. Hamilton could hardly leave this to chance; thus he deliberately

employed a method which promised a politically successful outcome. Instead of starting his work by amending and correcting
the material which Washington had sent him, he first wrote an
entirely new draft, making free use of Washington's permission
to "throw the whole into a different form." On July 30, Hamilton
was able to send this new draft to Washington with an accom-
panying letter in which he said that he was now beginning with
his work on the second part of Washington's request, namely,
with the corrections and improvements of the papers which
Washington had sent him in May. However, he added immediately that "I confess the more I have considered the matter the less
eligible this plan has appeared to me. There seems to be a certain awkwardness in the thing. . . . Besides that, I think that
there are some ideas which will not wear well in the former
address. . . ."[11] The presentation of an entirely new and carefully
worked-out draft, combined with deprecatory remarks about
Washington's original plan, did its work. When, on August 10,
Hamilton sent to Washington a "draft for incorporating," as
Hamilton called his revision of the material which Washington
had sent him in May, Washington had become accustomed to
the idea of using Hamilton's "Original Major Draft" for his
valedictory address.

IV

Hamilton was at work on the "Original Major Draft" for Washington's valedictory from the second part of May till far into
July. Hamilton's wife, in her old age, still remembered that "the
address was written, principally at such times as his Office was
seldom frequented by his clients and visitors, and during the
absence of his students to avoid interruption; at which times he
was in the habit of calling me to sit with him, that he might
read to me as he wrote, in order, as he said, to discover how it
sounded upon the ear, and making the remark, 'My dear Eliza,
you must be to me what Molière's old nurse was to him.' "[12] The
care and deliberateness with which Hamilton proceeded suggests
that he was impressed by the importance as well as by the difficulty of the task.

Among the considerations which influenced Hamilton in the
composition of the document, his eagerness to avoid inserting
Madison's valedictory of 1792 was only one, and probably not

the most important one. Despite the attacks against Washington in the last years of his second term, the President enjoyed still greater authority and reputation than any other American political leader; the thoughts which he would express when he announced his final retirement from office were bound to make a deep impact on American political thinking. Hamilton must have been well aware that participation in the drafting of Washington's valedictory gave him a unique opportunity to impress on the minds of Americans some of his favorite political ideas. But he was certainly not guided exclusively by personal ambition and party interest. For almost twenty years, Hamilton had been Washington's close collaborator, and he must have felt a selfless obligation to give a dignified form to the final political manifesto of the man whom he had served and admired. Yet Hamilton's work was made still more difficult because he knew that although Washington had little confidence in his own literary gifts, he was a man of "strong penetration" and "sound judgment."[13] Washington would not place his name under a document which he could not regard as an expression of his own mind and ideas.

Thus Hamilton's draft, although very different from the material which Washington had sent him, embodied in form and substance much of Washington's draft. A paper has been preserved which permits an insight into Hamilton's working methods: an "abstract of points to form an address."[14] It lists 23 points containing brief statements of the issues with which he wanted to deal, presenting them more or less in the sequence of the Farewell Address. Of these 23 points, 13 are brief excerpts or paraphrases of Washington's draft. In the middle, from the 10th to the 19th point, Hamilton abandoned close adherence to Washington's draft, enlarging Washington's ideas and adducing new material. Thus the list of points reveals that although Hamilton did not accept Washington's plan of inserting Madison's draft of 1792 as a whole, he had few objections to the ideas outlined by Madison and Washington; indeed, he was willing to incorporate them almost literally. However, he felt the document should be strengthened; it ought to receive more body and substance.

This view is confirmed by the form which Hamilton's draft finally took. The first eight paragraphs, announcing Washington's intention to retire from political life and expressing his wishes for the future prosperity of America under a free constitution, are closely modeled after Washington's draft. Then Hamilton let Washington say, "Here perhaps I ought to stop." But he did not do so, because solicitude for the welfare of the American people urged him "to offer some sentiments the result of mature reflection confirmed by observation and experience which appear to me essential to the permanency of your felicity as a people"; these sentiments should be received as "the disinterested advice of a parting friend."[15]

With these sentences Hamilton launched a discussion leading far beyond the thoughts contained in Washington's draft. From the point of view of contents as well as from the point of view of length, this section gave the Farewell Address its real weight.

After this, Hamilton returned to a phraseology startlingly similar to that which he had used in introducing the section; he said that "in offering to you, my countrymen, these counsels of an old and affectionate friend—counsels suggested by laborious reflection, and matured by a various experience, I dare not hope that they will make the strong and lasting impressions I wish. . . ."[16] Then there followed six paragraphs of personal justification, which in contents and phraseology were patterned after the end of Washington's draft.

Thus Hamilton's chief contribution to Washington's Farewell Address was the central section of the document, which replaced the "list of wishes" of Washington's draft. Nevertheless, the theme of Washington's list of wishes, the warning against partisanship in foreign policy, was fully expressed; however, it was set in the wider framework of a general survey of domestic and foreign policy.

Hamilton gave the greatest attention to the section on foreign policy. Whereas the reflections on domestic policy corresponded to the outline given in his "abstract of points," the statement on foreign policy was entirely remodeled.

The transition from domestic policy to foreign policy followed smoothly from a warning against party spirit which opens the door to intrigues by foreigners and may lead to attachments in which the smaller nation will revolve around the larger one "as its satellite."

At this point, Hamilton repeated Washington's advice to "avoid connecting ourselves with the politics of any Nation." Hamilton was somewhat more cautious than Washington. He recommended having "as little political connection . . . as possible." Departing from Washington's draft, Hamilton did not say anything at this point about commercial relations but rather went on to justify the advice to abstain from political connections.

The necessity for this attitude, Hamilton believed, followed from the natural situation of things. Each state has certain fundamental interests which it must follow in its policy. If states are in close proximity to each other, their interests touch upon each other and clashes are unavoidable. If America were to ally herself with one of the European powers, she would inevitably have to participate in every European conflict. Such a connection with European power politics would be "artificial"; America was so distant from Europe that she did not belong "naturally" to the European system. From this analysis, Hamilton deduced a "general principle of policy" for America. Although in particular emergencies America might be forced to make a temporary alliance, permanent alliances must be avoided. In its practical consequences, this was not very different from what Washington had said in his draft. But Washington had stressed the weakness of the United States which, within the next twenty years, would make involvement in a war extremely dangerous for the existence of the young republic. By removing the time limit from this piece of advice, by basing it on unchangeable geographical conditions, and by presenting it as a principle of policy, Hamilton made the recommendation in his draft weightier, more impressive, and more apodictic.

It is significant that Hamilton treated with commerce after he had discussed the question of alliances. To him, regulation of commercial relations remained subordinated to power politics. Although America's aim should be the widest possible liberalization of commerce, a certain flexibility in practice was necessary. Commerce was a weapon in the struggle of power politics; in the arrangement of their commercial relations, nations did not follow idealistic principles but only their interests. With the exhortation to recognize national egoism as the driving force in international relations, Hamilton concluded the "counsels of an old and affectionate friend."

In its terminology and formulations, the section on foreign

policy echoed expressions and thoughts which had dominated the discussion of foreign affairs ever since America had entered the scene of foreign policy in 1776. We are reminded of Paine's *Common Sense*. We find the word "entangle" which in America had developed into a technical term for characterizing the dangerous consequences of involvement in European politics. We see the distinction between "artificial" and "natural" connections, reflecting the Enlightenment belief in a progress from a world of power politics to an era of permanent peace and increasing prosperity. We recall the famous resolution of Congress of 1783 that "the true interest of these states requires that they should be as little as possible entangled in the politics and controversies of European nations."

This use, in the Farewell Address, of terms and concepts which had been continuously applied in the discussion of foreign affairs might have been intentional. Hamilton might have felt that these reflections would be more acceptable if they appeared as a restatement of currently held views rather than as a presentation of new ideas. But behind this facade of customary terms and concepts, there was a structure of thought which was Hamilton's own.

Whether Hamilton drafted this part of the Farewell Address with the help of documents which he had previously written, or whether the similarities to his previous works on foreign policy came from such firm and definite convictions that they always took the same expression, we cannot know. In any case, just a year before Hamilton began to work on the Farewell Address, he wrote under the name Horatius a defense of the Jay Treaty which contained a warning against entanglement "in all the contests, broils and wars of Europe" in words very similar to those used in the Farewell Address.[17] Some of the formulations which the Farewell Address and the Horatius paper have in common can also be found in the Memorandum of September 15, 1790, the first written presentation of Hamilton's opinions on foreign affairs as a member of Washington's Cabinet. In this search for ancestors of the Farewell Address among Hamilton's previous writings, we might go back still further to the *Federalist*.

There are passages in Hamilton's draft of the Farewell Address which correspond closely to ideas in the *Federalist,* making it almost certain that Hamilton had this book not only on his book-shelf—as would have been a matter of course—but also on his writing desk when he drafted the Farewell Address. The warning in the Address against wars resulting from the passions of people was a restatement of Hamilton's argument in the sixth number of the *Federalist,* that "there have been . . . almost as many popular as royal wars." Stylistic similarities also exist between the eleventh number of the *Federalist* and passages of the Farewell Address on foreign policy. Ideas which in the Address were vaguely adumbrated were more clearly expressed in the eleventh number of the *Federalist*. In the Farewell Address, emphasis was laid on Europe's possessing a special political system; the consequence of this point—that America had a political system of her own—was only suggested. The statement in the eleventh number of the *Federalist* that the United States ought "to aim at an ascendant in the system of American affairs" revealed Hamilton's full thought. Because Washington hardly would have liked this open announcement of an aggressive imperialist program, Hamilton refrained from expressing this idea explicitly in the Farewell Address.

The relationship between the Farewell Address and the *Federalist* is particularly important because it shows that although Hamilton used Washington's ideas and statements of others, he placed them in a different setting and gave them a new meaning.

The law of action propounded by Hamilton in the Farewell Address was presented as the specific application of general laws ruling in the political world. It was derived from the geographical division of the earth and from the principle which dominated the life of every state: striving to increase power in line with its fundamental interests. States situated in the same geographical area were tied together in a continuous power struggle arising from clashing interests. They were members of the same political system which extended as far as its natural geographical limits. In Hamilton's formulation, the warning against connection with European power politics was derived neither from a fear of strengthening the centrifugal forces in American political life, as it dominated Washington's thoughts, nor from utopian hopes in an imminent end of the era of power politics and national division, as the founders of American independence had hoped. To

Hamilton, sovereign states, competition among them, and power politics were necessary factors in social life; successful political action depended on proceeding according to these presuppositions. Hamilton presented his advice as the necessary consequence of political science; he conceived it as an application of the eternal laws of politics to the American situation. The separation of America from Europe's foreign policy was desirable not because it might be the beginning of a change, of a reform of diplomacy, but because it corresponded to what the political writers had discovered about the political practice of the time. The intellectual framework of the recommendations on foreign policy in the Farewell Address was that of the school of the interests of the state. This is reflected not only in the phraseology and the argumentation, but also in Hamilton's attempt to summarize these counsels in a "great rule of conduct," a "general principle."

When Hamilton sent his draft to Washington, he wrote that he had tried "to render this act importantly and lastingly useful."[18] We can now better understand what these words meant. Hamilton wanted Washington to leave to his successors an explanation of the principles which had guided his policy, just as other rulers and statesmen of the eighteenth century were accustomed to doing in their Political Testaments. In revising Washington's draft for a valedictory, Hamilton transformed it into a Political Testament.

V

The "great rule" which Washington had set down in the Farewell Address served as a guide to American foreign policy for over a century; of all the Political Testaments of the eighteenth century, the Farewell Address alone succeeded in achieving political significance.

Some part of its influence is due to the "accidents of politics," to events in which the United States had, at best, a supporting role. The conflicts of the Napoleonic era and the weakening of the Spanish power broke the ring which foreign colonial possessions had laid around the territory of the United States. As long as several European states were close neighbors, the advice to avoid alliances was an ideal to be pursued rather than a feasible proposition. It became a workable policy only when effective rule by a foreign power was restricted to the north of the continent. The political separation of America from the European power struggle was strengthened by changes which took place in Europe. Nationalism and industrialism shifted the interests of the European powers, and the competition among them, into new channels. Thus, in the nineteenth century, conditions came into existence under which America's foreign policy could become a policy of isolation.

Nevertheless, the profound impact of Washington's counsels in the Farewell Address was also created by features inherent in the document itself. It was the first statement, comprehensive and authoritative at the same time, of the principles of American foreign policy. Hamilton based the discussion of foreign affairs in the Farewell Address on a realistic evaluation of America's situation and interests. Because Hamilton was opposed to American involvement in a war, to which the emotional attachment with France might lead, he emphasized the necessity of neutrality and peace. The Farewell Address, therefore, could repeat and absorb those views and concepts which expressed the mood of a more idealistic approach to foreign policy. These elements were not like ghost cities left abandoned outside the main stream of development; they were necessary stations on the road "to the Farewell Address."

Political Testaments, in general, remained closely tied to the eighteenth-century concept of power politics. The integration of idealistic assumptions constitutes the distinguishing feature of the Farewell Address. Thus it could have an appeal in the following century of rising democracy when foreign policy demanded legitimation by clearly felt and recognized values, and needed to be conducted in accordance with the will of the people.

Because the Farewell Address comprises various aspects of American political thinking, it reaches beyond any period limited in time and reveals the basic issue of the American attitude toward foreign policy: the tension between Idealism and Realism. Settled by men who looked for gain and by men who sought freedom, born into independence in a century of enlightened thinking and of power politics, America has wavered in her foreign policy between Idealism and Realism, and her great historical moments have occurred when both were combined. Thus the history of the Farewell Address forms only part of a wider, endless, urgent problem. This study is an attempt to shed light on its beginnings. With the analysis of the diverse intellectual trends which went into the making of the Farewell Address, with the description of its genesis, our story ends.

NOTES

1. Washington to Jay, May 8, 1796, Victor Hugo Paltsits, ed., *Washington's Farewell Address* (New York, 1935), p. 239. Since most of the documents which have bearing upon the genesis and history of Washington's Farewell Address are assembled and reprinted in this book, I shall quote from it.

2. *Ibid.,* p. 215.

3. *Ibid.,* pp. 215, 216.

4. John L. Fitzpatrick, ed., *Writings of George Washington* (Washington, 1940), XXXIV, 386.

5. Washington to Gouverneur Morris, March 4, 1796, *ibid.,* p. 483.

6. Washington to Charles Carroll, May 1, 1796, *ibid.,* XXXV, 30.

7. Paltsits, *Farewell Address,* p. 168.

8. *Ibid.,* p. 173.

9. *Ibid.,* p. 168.

10. *Ibid.,* p. 241.

11. *Ibid.,* p. 249.

12. Allan McLane Hamilton, *The Intimate Life of Alexander Hamilton* (New York, 1910), p. 111.

13. Jefferson on Washington, quoted in John Alexander Carroll and Mary Wells Ashworth, *George Washington* (New York, 1957), VII, 653.

14. Paltsits, *Farewell Address,* pp. 174-78.

15. *Ibid.,* p. 182.

16. *Ibid.,* p. 198. See also the Appendix for this and the following analyses.

17. Henry Cabot Lodge, ed., *Works of Alexander Hamilton* (New York, 1904), V, 181-85.

18. Paltsits, *Farewell Address,* p. 249.

Washington's Farewell Address: A Statement of Empire

BY BURTON IRA KAUFMAN

When George Washington asked Alexander Hamilton to prepare a farewell statement for him in 1796, he enclosed the draft of a message written four years earlier by James Madison announcing the President's intention to retire at the end of his first term, praising the Constitution, and pleading for the preservation of the Union. To this Washington added his own statement urging a policy of neutrality in the struggle taking place between England and France and calling for a halt to the domestic political battles which threatened to disrupt the new nation. Hamilton incorporated Washington's ideas into the final text of the Farewell Address, which was delivered to the newspapers on September 19, 1796; these ideas have since become the focus of a historical debate over the purpose and meaning of the address.

In the appended statement forwarded to Hamilton, the President also expressed a thought which has been almost completely neglected by historians. This was his conviction that, if his immediate goals were fulfilled, America would become one of the great powers in the world. "While we are encircled in one band," Washington said, "we shall possess the strength of a Giant and there will be none who can make us afraid." This idea was then incorporated into the final address:

> If we remain one people, under an efficient government, the period is not far off when we may defy material injury from external annoyance; when we may take such an attitude as will cause the neutrality we may at any time resolve upon to be scrupulously respected; when belligerent nations, under the impossibility of making acquisitions upon us, will not lightly hazard the giving us provocation; when we may choose peace or war, as our interest guided by justice shall counsel.[1]

Although the President expected America to become an important world power, he did not indicate in his draft to Hamilton how he thought that power would be achieved. Nor were his views made any clearer in the final message; perhaps that is why this particular section has received so little attention. Yet on numerous other occasions Washington elaborated on his vision and charted the path to American greatness.

In his view, the key to the new nation's future was development of its Western lands, ones which he described in 1793 as "a tract of as rich Country for hundreds of miles as any in the world."[2] Washington expected these lands to be settled as far as the northwestern areas around the Great Lakes. To open them up, he planned a number of ambitious inland navigation projects. In combination with other internal improvements, such as bridges and turnpikes, these waterways would constitute an elaborate transportation network not only linking East and West but connecting the seaboard states from Georgia to Rhode Island.

By making possible trade between larger sections of the new nation, these internal improvements would also promote national unity, a goal that Washington considered essential if America was to grow strong. As an ardent nationalist he advocated numerous other measures on which to build a common American identity. He encouraged American contributions in science and literature, and he fostered the creation of American institutions of higher learning in which he hoped to bring together youth from all sections of the nation. He urged giving the central government increased powers at the expense of the states in order to provide for the nation's common needs.

As Washington foresaw it, the country's economy would be based on agriculture; the Western lands would be brought under cultivation and their produce shipped throughout the world. Washington was not, however, narrowly agrarian in outlook. He simply regarded agriculture of paramount importance in the United States' endeavor to become economically self-sufficient. And while he felt that America would continue to be predominantly agricultural, he still encouraged the development of manufacturing and the establishment of a balanced economy.

The President's interest in opening up the West, his promotion of national unity and stronger central government, and his emphasis on self-sufficiency were all related to his vision of the United States as an expanding nation and future world power. Concerning its status in 1796, however, he had no illusions; he realized that the country was then too weak to become involved in international imbroglios. In his farewell address he therefore reiterated his earlier position that the United States follow a policy of neutrality toward European struggles. Aware of the threat which political divisions posed to the country, he also spoke out once more against partisanship and factionalism. But it must be understood that these views were always subordinate to, and directed toward, his larger vision of America's destiny.

Historians who have discussed Washington's valedictory remarks concerning political partisanship and foreign entanglements have usually taken them out of context. Those who have not studied the address in light of ideas previously expressed by the President have failed equally to understand its real significance. That is, the Farewell Address can be properly understood only in relation to Washington's concept of his country's imperial future, a concept whose roots lie in the history of both the country and the man.

Washington was born into a society of tobacco planters whose absorbing interest was land. The number of acres owned by an individual played an important part in determining his financial and social status. By this measurement Virginia, Washington's home, was a prosperous colony. It mattered little that the single-crop system of agriculture wasted the soil and produced poor returns, for vast regions of land lay open to the West. Indeed, planters were great speculators, risking entire fortunes in the purchase of acreage whose value they always expected to rise once it was settled.

Like other planters, Washington became a speculator and real estate promoter. In 1751 he invested in the Ohio Company which, two years earlier, had been granted 500,000 acres of land in the Ohio Valley. Washington continued to purchase land, becoming by the time of the Revolution one of America's largest landowners. His motives were not, however, entirely ones of personal gain. As he traveled beyond the Allegheny Mountains and through the virgin Ohio Valley during his youth and early manhood, he had also developed a lofty sense of the region's future.

A further influence on Washington's concept of America's destiny was the fact that he had grown to maturity within the British mercantile empire whose primary goals were self-sufficiency through economic integration, increased domestic production, and a favorable balance of trade. These goals were to be achieved by careful regulation of the economy and a policy of commercial and territorial expansion under which the British Empire's colonies would both provide the mother country with raw materials and furnish markets for her production. The system was supposed to be complementary; in reality the planters found themselves increasingly in debt to British merchants.

Washington early realized that as long as Virginia remained dependent on tobacco, it would be unable to escape its financial bondage to England. He therefore urged his fellow planters to diversify their crops and engage in home manufacturing.[3] To this end he made his own plantation at Mount Vernon a model of self-sufficiency. But this plan was only part of a larger design he had formulated for the colony. Aware of the potentials of the undeveloped continent, he sought Virginia's economic salvation in the creation of its own mercantile empire in which, on the Virginia-England model, the West would serve the function of colonies, sending its raw materials to the seaboard and consuming the seaboard's domestic production. Before the resources of the West could be tapped, however, he realized it was first necessary to overcome the barrier to trade posed by the ridge of the Alleghenies. To accomplish this task Washington proposed, with Thomas Johnson of Maryland, to make the Potomac River navigable and to connect it by means of canals with the headwaters of the Ohio River. Completion of this project would provide a continuous transportation system to the Atlantic and make the Potomac "the Channel of conveyance of the extensive and valuable Trade of a rising Empire."[4]

Until the events leading to the Revolution occurred, Washington thought largely in terms of Virginia alone. Concerned with protecting his colony's title to the Ohio Valley from rival claims made by Pennsylvania,[5] he was also anxious to make the area between Alexandria and Georgetown the deposit for Western trade.[6] However, as England attempted to limit frontier development (beginning with the Proclamation Line of 1763) and prevent creation of a mercantilist state in America, Washington's mercantilist views broadened to include all thirteen colonies. After the repeal of the Stamp Act in 1767 he urged his English friends to lift all prohibitions on the colonies' economic and territorial expansion. Using mercantilist arguments, he tried to convince them that colonial prosperity would inevitably benefit England since the wealth of the colonies would remain within the British empire. "I could wish it was in my power," he remarked,

> to congratulate you with success, in having the Commercial System of the Colonies put upon a more enlarged and extensive footing than it is because I am well satisfied that it would ultimately, redound to the advantages of the Mother Country so long as the Colonies pursue trade and Agriculture, and would be an effectual Let to Manufacturing among themselves. The money therefore which they raise would centre in Great Britain, as certain as the Needle will settle to the Poles.[7]

In a real sense it was British unwillingness to allow the colonies to form their own mercantilist system which led Washington to break with the mother country. As England continued to restrict colonial development, Washington encouraged formation of an American system to replace the British imperium. In the Fairfax Resolves of 1774, which he helped George Mason to prepare, he sought an end to trade with England and the establishment of nonimportation agreements, both to be enforced by a strong union of the colonies. Further to make the colonies self-sufficient, he urged that every encouragement be given "to the improvement of arts and manufactures."[8]

During the war with England, Washington's nationalism and

vision of American empire emerged clearly. Having broken with
the mother country, he now gave more thought to the new nation's
future. This direction was evident in his military strategy in which
he weighed postwar political and economic objectives with immediate military factors. In a lengthy memorandum of 1780, for
example, he reviewed the disposition of British troops in North
America and the advantages to be gained by attacking them.
Because of the immediate situation he thought his efforts should
be directed against enemy forces in New York and the Southern
states. Nonetheless, he did not dismiss the possibility of attacking
Canada, Halifax, or Bermuda. The capture of Halifax, he remarked,

> would add much weight to the reasons given in support of an
> Expedition into [Canada]; and in case of success, would be of the
> utmost importance; as it would add much, not only to the security
> of the trade of Canada, but the United States in General. Give a
> well grounded hope of rescuing the Fisheries from Great Britain,
> which will most essentially injure her Marine, while it would lay
> a foundation, on which to build one of our own. . . . And lastly,
> another Provence (Nova Scotia) which sometime ago was very
> desirous of it, would be added to the Federal Union.[9]

Throughout much of the war, in fact, the general looked toward Canada, cherishing the hope that that huge and relatively
unsettled area would join the other former British colonies. The
failure of an expedition against the province in 1776 and the
apparent unwillingness of its inhabitants to side with the Americans discouraged him from launching a second invasion until he
was absolutely certain of victory. Still, he continued to recognize
the advantages which would result from Canada's acquisition.[10]

It was because he realized that country's importance to the
Union that he reacted strongly against a plan to launch a joint
invasion of Canada with France. His close friend, the Marquis
de Lafayette, had made the proposal to Congress in 1778, where
it met a warm reception. But when that body asked Washington
for his opinion he advised against the attack. Publicly he based
his opposition on military grounds, but in a private letter to the
president of Congress, Henry Laurens, he made it clear that he
was really afraid of its political consequences. France had strong
ties in Quebec, Washington pointed out, and might desire to

remain in the conquered territory indefinitely. "Let us realize for a moment," he continued,

> the striking advantages France would derive from the possession of Canada; the acquisition of an extensive territory abounding in supplies for the use of her Islands; the opening a vast source of the most beneficial commerce with the Indian nations, which she might then monopolize; the having ports of her own on the continent independent of the precarious good will of an ally; the engrossing of the whole trade of New found land whenever she pleased; the finest nursery of seamen in the world.

At the same time, by controlling Canada the French in alliance with Spain would be able to encircle the new nation and work with the Indians to prevent its growth.[11] On the other hand, American seizure of the province would prevent this danger, and the advantages which France might have gained would accrue to the new nation.

With the war's end the victorious general returned to Mount Vernon, where he spent most of the next five years. During this time he engaged in an enormous correspondence with leading figures of the day on a variety of issues. Of central concern to Washington was the erection of a peace establishment which would assure America's destiny in the world. While others believed the new nation could continue to prosper as a weak union of thirteen states under the Articles of Confederation, the future President held a different view. He had seen the country nearly destroyed during the war by local jealousies and petty prejudices. From Mount Vernon he witnessed additional evidence of the perils of disunion and impotent government: individual states establishing their own commercial systems and competing for trade; Europeans closing their markets to Americans without fear of retaliation; land speculators casting their eyes on the West without thought of the public welfare; the industry which had emerged during the war going into decline; and the value of paper money falling. It was clear to Washington that his vision of America's future could never be attained under these circumstances.

His whole concept of empire, moreover, rested on the assumption of a united people and an integrated economy supported by a government able to provide for the nation's needs. Only by acting together, he wrote in 1783, could the thirteen states find their place in the world. Separately they would be pawns in the hands of European powers, played off against one another as soon as Europe grew jealous of America's "rising greatness as an Empire."[12] Washington therefore urged revision or replacement of the Articles to provide for a governing body able to meet the requirements of a burgeoning—and, he hoped, united—power. "Let us flatter ourselves," he remarked to the Merchants of Philadelphia,

> that the day is not remote, when a wise and just system of policy will be adopted by every State in the Union; then will national faith be inviolably preserved, public credit durably established, the blessings of Commerce extensively diffused, and the reputation of our new-formed Empire supported with as much *Eclat* as has been acquired in laying the foundation of it.[13]

Of those problems which he expected the reconstituted government to handle, none was more important in his mind than orderly Western expansion. As a result of the Treaty of Paris, the United States had secured the entire region from the Alleghenies to the Mississippi River. Almost immediately, emigrants from both the seaboard states and across the Atlantic began to settle and cultivate the frontier. Washington was encouraged by this westward movement. Having made a trip to the area between the Great Kanawha and Ohio Rivers in 1784, he noted in his diary the fertility of the soil, the abundant harvests, and the increasing population.[14] To stimulate further migration he offered the West as an asylum for the poor and oppressed of the world. "I wish to see the sons and daughters of the world in Peace," he remarked,

> and busily employed in fulfilling the first and great commandment, *Increase* and *Multiply*; as an encouragement to which we have opened the fertile plains of the Ohio to the poor, the needy and the oppressed of the Earth; and one therefore who is heavily laden, or who wants land to cultivate, may repair to thither and abound, as in the Land of promise with milk and honey.[15]

It was precisely along the frontier, however, that national feeling was least evident and danger of disunity most threatening. The Alleghenies still posed a natural barrier to trade between the frontier and the Atlantic; to reach the seaboard states, Western settlers were forced to send their goods down the Mississippi to New Orleans. Unless communication could be established with the frontier and its produce easily transported to the coast, Washington realized its people would have no predilection to remain in the Union; they might in fact separate.

To tie these new regions with the old and open the frontier to settlement, the future President proposed his earlier scheme of making the Potomac River navigable and connecting it with the Ohio. For four years he devoted a major part of his time to this project. No longer was it merely a handy tool to tap the resources of the West for Virginia's benefit; now completion of the plan was a matter of political exigency if America were to achieve its destiny in the world. Although, in a letter of 1784, Washington noted the benefits Virginia and Maryland would receive if the Potomac were opened to navigation, he also remarked, "I consider this business in a far more extensive point of view, and the more I have resolved upon the subject, the more important it appears to me; not only as it respects our commerce, but our political interests, and the well being and strength of the union also."[16] He even supported other navigation projects, including a proposal to make the Susquehanna River navigable; the more communications that were opened to the West, the closer it would be bound to the rest of the Union and the stronger the nation would become.

For the very reason that he favored inland navigation projects, Washington was also willing at first to forego the right of free navigation of the Mississippi. Just as trade with the Atlantic States would more tightly bind the Western regions to the rest of the nation, continued commerce down the Mississippi would draw them closer to Spain. He was even willing in 1786, during the Jay-Gardoqui negotiations, to sacrifice the right to navigate the Mississippi for a period of years in return for a commercial treaty with Spain. Only after he realized how divisive an issue the Mississippi question was and how determined the Western settlers were to obtain the right to navigate the river did he change his attitude and come out in favor of their position.[17]

Washington's views on inland navigation projects and free navigation of the Mississippi became part of a long-range plan which he had early formulated for settlement of the West. This plan also called for the creation of one or two states roughly equal in size and shape to present-day Ohio and Michigan. Such an area, Washington felt, would be large enough to accommodate all settlers for the immediate future. Indians would inhabit the area west of the territory and it would be a felony to trespass on their lands. According to this plan, the central government would be able to extend its influence as the nation expanded and unite the frontier regions with the more established areas, thus eliminating the possibility of separation. At the same time speculators would be prevented from grabbing distant lands for their personal profit. Finally, the Indians, safeguarded by law, would not resort to bloodshed to protect their territory. Although obviously concerned with protecting their rights, Washington did not expect the Indians to hamper further white expansion. He hoped that they would eventually become Christians and be absorbed into white civilization. Meanwhile he was confident they could be persuaded to sell their lands as they were needed and move further westward.[18]

By the time Washington became President in 1789, he was hopeful that his vision of America's future was nearing reality—that America would become a "storehouse and granary for the world."[19] The new constitution, which had been ratified in 1788, greatly enhanced the powers of the central government, including the granting of important controls over commerce and the general economy. By the Northwest Ordinance of 1787 the old Confederation had provided for settlement of the West much along the lines suggested by Washington. Construction to make the Potomac navigable had begun, and his dream of making the area between Alexandria and Georgetown the entrepôt for Western goods seemed near fulfillment.

Developments in Europe, on the other hand, appeared particularly foreboding. France was on the eve of revolution, relations between England and Spain remained tense, and war raged between Turkey, Russia, and Austria. To Washington the new nation by comparison seemed blessed by Providence. He noted that no other country had such natural advantages for the growth of agriculture and commerce, and he pointed to the almost unlimited territory which lay open for development. He expected a realization of natural happiness never enjoyed by even the most favored nations. "The natural, political, and moral circumstances of our Nascent empire," he remarked, "justify the anticipation."[20]

He was, however, under no illusion about the current weak

internal state of his country. What was needed in his view was time for the United States to develop its natural resources. This could be achieved only by remaining aloof from international affairs. Thus he made the maintenance of peace and noninvolvement in European matters two of his cardinal principles even before he learned of the Treaty of Paris ending the struggle against England. Once he assumed the office of President, he continued to urge application of these policies.[21]

As Chief Executive it became Washington's task to make his vision of America's future reality. This goal explains the great interest he took in frontier problems, such as Indian affairs, relations with Spain and England, and land speculation. Aware of separatist movements in the West, he was anxious to convince frontiersmen that the federal government would provide for them and promote their interests, especially their right to navigate the Mississippi. He also wanted to make sure that foreign nations would not prevent what he regarded as the nation's natural growth.

He even considered a scheme to acquire Spanish territory in Florida through the peaceful infiltration of American settlers. In 1791 Juan Nepomuceno de Quesada, Spanish governor of Florida, invited foreigners to settle in his region. Washington's Secretary of State, Thomas Jefferson, himself an expansionist, advised the President to take advantage of Quesada's offer. "This is meant for our people," he wrote.

> Debtors take advantage of it, & go off with their property. Our citizens have a right to go where they please. It is the business of the states to take measures to stop them till their debts are paid. This done, I wish a hundred thousand of our inhabitants would accept the invitation. It will be the means of delivering to us peaceably what may otherwise cost us a war. In the meantime we may complain of this seduction of our inhabitants just enough to make them believe we think it a very wise policy for them, & confide them in it.[22]

Realizing the excellence of the opportunity put forth by Quesada, Washington gave his Secretary permission to respond favorably to the proposal. Soon afterward he communicated the offer and Jefferson's reply to James Seagrove, American agent among the Creek Indians, and instructed him to negotiate with Quesada.[23] American settlers were eventually let into Florida. In 1810 they seized West Florida and requested its annexation to the United States just as Jefferson and Washington had hoped.

To develop the resources of the frontier regions and unite them with the more established areas, Washington continued to urge construction of his inland navigation routes, and especially the completion of the Potomac project. Congress had decided to place the seat of government on the banks of that river. Once the navigation scheme was completed and America's commerce expanded, Washington expected the capital city to become one of the great cities in the world, surpassed in size only by London and perhaps a few other European cities.[24]

At the end of his first administration, the President appeared generally pleased with the state of the nation and hopeful that his vision of America's destiny would come true. The new government was firmly established, the possibility of Western separation seemed more unlikely, and the country itself was beginning to prosper. Even efforts—including those of Washington—to make the United States more self-sufficient through the promotion of manufacturing seemed to be having some success.[25] If only the nation could continue to develop without interruption for the next several years, the President could see no reason why Americans would not rank among the most powerful and happy people in the world.[26]

Unfortunately, the French Revolution and the Hamiltonian program unleashed forces of dissension within the nation which threatened to tear it apart and destroy its chances for greatness. Having always believed factionalism and internal division to be the greatest dangers facing the young country, Washington strongly deplored these developments. When they resulted in attacks on his administration, he decided to retire from office. In May 1792 he asked Madison to prepare a farewell statement for him, and outlined for the Virginia congressman the points he wanted stressed. In leaving office he desired to "invoke a continuation of the blessings of Providence" upon America. To impress this point, he felt Madison should point out that

> we are *all* the Children of the same country; a Country great and rich in itself; capable, & promising to be, as any the Annals of history have ever brought to our view. That our interest, however diversified in local and smaller matters, is the same in all the great & essential concerns of the Nation. That the extent of our

Country, the diversity of our climate & soil, and the various productions of the States . . . are such as to make one part not only convenient, but perhaps indispensably necessary to the other part; and may render the whole (at no distant period) one of the most independant [*sic*] in the world.[27]

Washington's farewell was premature. Madison and other statesmen convinced him to stay in office, and he was reelected without opposition. But political divisions grew worse during the early years of his second administration. They were complicated in February 1793 when England and Spain united in war against France. If Washington regarded internal divisions as the nation's greatest danger, he considered European war, which could lead to American involvement, as its second most serious peril. This was especially true in 1793 when the international struggle only embittered existing political divisions within the United States. He had already made peace and noninvolvement two of his principal objectives. Determined to pursue this policy, he issued in April a proclamation of neutrality. For the remainder of his second administration he tried to steer a strictly neutral course.

Historians have regarded Washington's proclamation of neutrality as an attempt to assert a policy of independence.[28] That it most certainly was, but the interpretation does not go deep enough. Even more than a statement of independence, it was an effort by Washington to assure that the rising empire of the New World would not fall victim to the struggles of the Old. The President was aware of the advantages which war might bring the United States if it did not become involved. As a neutral nation America could develop her commerce by carrying goods between belligerent powers and their possessions. These nations would also need American products, such as ships and naval stores, to meet the requirements of war. Such commerce would lead in turn to increased consideration and respect for the United States. Nonetheless Washington preferred peace to the menace of war. He perhaps best expressed his attitude with regard to neutrality when he remarked, "The present flourishing situation of our affairs, and the prosperity we enjoy, must be obvious to the good Citizens of the United States; it remains, therefore, for them to pursue such a line of conduct, as will insure these blessings, by averting the calamities of war."[29]

Events at home and abroad seemed to conspire against Washington's dream of empire. While Indian forays in the Northwest were finally ended in 1794 as a result of the Battle of Fallen Timbers, Britain continued to hold on to her Western posts, and this, coupled with her violation of American maritime rights, threatened to cause hostilities between the two countries. At the same time, free transit of the Mississippi remained uncertain, and the administration was plagued continually by foreign intrigues along the frontier. Armed rebellion broke out in Pennsylvania against a tax on whiskey. The President's proclamation of neutrality embittered Francophiles who felt the administration was siding with England. When they learned the government had concluded the Jay Treaty with that country, their attacks against Washington became personal and abusive.

The President's reaction was to remind the nation of the destiny it held if neutrality were maintained and internal disunity ended. "Our agriculture, Commerce, and Manufactures, prosper beyond former example," he remarked in his annual message to Congress in December, 1795. "Placed in a situation every way so auspicious," he concluded, "motives of commanding force impel us, with sincere acknowledgment to heaven, and pure love to our country, to unite our efforts to preserve, prolong, and improve, our immense advantages."[30]

The international situation improved somewhat during the first half of 1796, and the future became more hopeful than it had been for the last several years. The successful negotiation of Jay's Treaty momentarily ended the danger of war with England, while Pinckney's Treaty settled major differences with Spain to the great advantage of the United States, particularly by guaranteeing her right to navigate the Mississippi. As his second term drew to a close, Washington could consider retirement without leaving the country facing the dire prospects of war.

At the same time, however, bitter fighting had broken out in the House of Representatives over appropriating funds to put Jay's Treaty into effect. The Anti-Federalists also continued their attack on the administration with unabated fury. This strife made the President even more anxious to leave the inferno of government for the solitude of Mount Vernon. In February he broached the idea of retirement to Hamilton. Soon afterward he asked him to prepare a farewell statement to the nation based on Madison's draft of 1792, with a section he added himself. After much correspondence and revision, Hamilton incorporated Washington's thoughts into an entirely new draft, which was then delivered to the newspapers.[31]

As with the proclamation of neutrality, historians have generally interpreted the Farewell Address as the statement of a policy of independence from European affairs. As evidence they have emphasized that part of the address which calls for neutrality with respect to the struggle in Europe.[32] Others have pointed to the section urging an end to political partisanship and have analyzed the address in light of the political war raging between Federalists and Anti-Federalists.[33] Clearly, however, these ideas were subordinate to the larger view of America's future which Washington had outlined in his draft proposal to Hamilton. Commenting on the bitter House struggle over Jay's Treaty at about the time the address was being prepared, the President remarked in words similar to those in his valedictory:

> Every true friend to this Country must *see* and *feel* that [our] policy . . . is not to embroil ourselves, with any nation whatever; but to avoid their disputes and their politics; . . . Twenty years peace with such an increase of population and resources as we have a right to expect; added to our remote situation from the jarring power, will in all probability enable us in a just cause, to bid defiance to any power on earth.[34]

Attainment of this vision of America's destiny which he had first begun to develop as a youth surveying the frontier, which had become more perceptible during the struggle against England, and which he had worked to achieve following the revolution, had become the major objective of his administration. It was only proper that he should leave this vision in his Farewell Address as his legacy to the country.

During the last years of his life Washington remained confident that his dream of America's future would come true. He was disappointed that political divisions, even within the Federalist party, were accentuated during the administration of his successor, John Adams. He also regretted that affairs in Europe threatened to lead to war between the United States and France, and that he was called by Adams to prepare an army for conflict. As he told the President's son, John Quincy Adams, he had expected after delivering his valedictory "to pass the remnants of a life

(worn down with cares) in ruminating on past scenes, and contemplating the future grandeur of this rising Empire."[35] Instead
of despairing over the nation's future, however, he viewed the
events of these years merely as additional barriers for his country
to surmount before it could attain its destined place in the world.
In urging military preparations in case of attack by France in
1798, he remarked:

> Regarding the overthrow of Europe at large as a matter not en-
> tirely chimerical, it will be our prudence to cultivate a spirit of
> self-dependence, and to endeavour by unremitting vigilance and
> exertion under the blessings of providence, to hold the scales of
> our destiny in our own hands. Standing, as it were in the midst
> of falling empires, it should be our aim to assume a station and
> attitude, which will preserve us from being overwhelmed in their
> ruins.[36]

The next year Washington died. Soon afterward one of the
great distortions in American history began. An apostle of empire
was transformed into an architect of isolationism.

NOTES

1. The full text of the message can be found conveniently in Victor
Hugo Paltsits, *Washington's Farewell Address* (New York, 1935), pp.
139-69.
2. Washington to the Earl of Buchan, Philadelphia, April 22, 1793,
John C. Fitzpatrick, ed., *Writings of George Washington* (39 vols., Washington, 1931-44), XXXII, 427-30.
3. Washington to Francis Dandridge, Mount Vernon, September 20,
1765, *ibid.*, II, 425-27.
4. Washington to Thomas Johnson, July 20, 1770, *ibid.*, pp. 17-21.
For the early correspondence relating to the Potomac scheme, see Grace
L. Nute, ed., "Washington and the Potomac," *American Historical Review*,
XXVIII (April 1923), 497-518. For a discussion of the impact of mercantile views on colonial thought, see William Appleman Williams, "The
Age of Mercantilism: An Interpretation of the American Political Economy, 1763 to 1828," *William and Mary Quarterly*, XV, 3rd ser. (1958),
419-37, and *The Contours of American History* (paperback ed., Chicago,
1966), pp. 77-117. See also Curtis P. Nettels, "British Mercantilism and the
Economic Development of the Thirteen Colonies," *Journal of Economic
History*, XII (Spring 1952), 105-14.
5. Thomas Perkins Abernethy, *Western Lands and the American Revolution* (New York, 1959), pp. 93-7; C. H. Ambler, *George Washington
and the West* (Chapel Hill, 1936), pp. 31-3, 56-8, 126-28, 139-40. For

one aspect of the rivalry between Virginia and Pennsylvania which concerned Washington, see W. Neil Franklin, "Pennsylvania-Virginia Rivalry for the Indian Trade of the Ohio Valley," *Mississippi Valley Historical Review,* XX (March 1934), 463-80.

6. Washington to Thomas Johnson, Mount Vernon, July 20, 1770, and May 5, 1772, Fitzpatrick, ed., *Writings of Washington,* III, 17-20, 82-3.

7. Washington to Capel and Osgood Hanbury, Mount Vernon, July 25, 1767, *ibid.,* II, 465-66.

8. Kate Mason Rowland, *The Life of George Mason* (2 vols., New York, 1892), I, 418-27; Douglas Southall Freeman, *George Washington* (7 vols., New York, 1945-1957), III, 363-70. For Washington's early interest in economic diversification, including his promotion of home manufacturing, see Rose Charlotte Engleman, "Washington and Hamilton: A Study in the Development of Washington's Political Ideas" (doctoral dissertation, Cornell University, 1940), p. 10. Miss Engleman shows how many of the programs of Washington's administration, such as the fostering of manufacturing, which have been associated traditionally with Alexander Hamilton, had actually been long advocated by the first President.

9. *Memorandum,* May 1, 1782, Fitzpatrick, ed., *Writings of Washington,* XXIV, 194-215.

10. Washington to President of Congress, White Plains, September 12, 1778, *ibid.,* XII, 434-36; Washington to John Sullivan, New Windsor, May 29, 1781, *ibid.,* XXII, 131-32.

11. Washington to President of Congress, Fredericksburg, November 14, 1778, *ibid.,* XIII, 254-57.

12. Washington to John Augustine Washington, Newburgh, June 15, 1783, *ibid.,* XXVII, 11-13.

13. Washington to Merchants of Philadelphia, Philadelphia, December 9, 1783, *ibid.,* pp. 262-63.

14. October 4, 1778, John C. Fitzpatrick, ed., *The Diaries of George Washington* (4 vols., Boston, 1925), II, 317-28.

15. Washington to Marquis de Lafayette, Mount Vernon, July 25, 1785, Fitzpatrick, ed., *Writings of Washington,* XXVIII, 205-10.

16. Washington to George Plater, Mount Vernon, October 25, 1784, *ibid.,* XXVII, 482-84. See also Washington to Thomas Jefferson, Mount Vernon, March 29, 1784, *ibid.,* pp. 373-77; Washington to James Madison, Mount Vernon, *ibid.,* XXVIII, 335-38.

17. Washington to Governor Benjamin Harrison, Mount Vernon, October 10, 1784, *ibid.,* XXVII, 471-80; Washington to Henry Lee, Mount Vernon, June 18, 1786, *ibid.,* XXVIII, 459-61; Washington to Richard Henry Lee, Philadelphia, July 19, 1787, *ibid.,* XXIX, 249-50.

18. Washington thus presented Congress with a plan first proposed by the Countess of Huntingdon to give land to emigrants who would come to the New World and perform missionary work among the Indians. Congress, however, refused to appropriate land and nothing came of the project. See James Jay to Washington, New York, December 20, 1784, "George Washington Papers," Library of Congress, Manuscript Division,

Washington, D.C., Microfilm Reel 94; Washington to James Jay, Mount Vernon, January 27, 1785, Fitzpatrick, ed., *Writings of Washington,* XXVIII, 41-44; Washington to Countess of Huntingdon, Mount Vernon, February 27 and June 30, 1785, *ibid.,* pp. 86-8, 180-81. For Washington's plan to settle the West, see Washington to Hugh Williamson, Mount Vernon, March 15, 1785, *ibid.,* pp. 107-08; Washington to James Duane, Rocky Hill, September 7, 1783, *ibid.,* XXVII, 133-40; Washington to Jacob Read, Mount Vernon, November 3, 1784, *ibid.,* pp. 485-90.

19. Washington to Marquis de Lafayette, n.p., June 19, 1788, *ibid.,* XXIX, 522-26.

20. Washington to Sir Edward Newenham, Mount Vernon, August 29, 1788, *ibid., XXX,* 70-4. See also Washington to Reverend Francis Adrian Vanderkemp, Mount Vernon, May 28, 1788, *ibid.,* XXIX, 504-5.

21. "Sentiments on a Peace Establishment" enclosed in Washington to Alexander Hamilton, Newburgh, May 2, 1783, *ibid.,* XXVI, 374-98. See also Washington to Chevalier de La Luzerne, Mount Vernon, February 7, 1788, *ibid.,* XXIX, 404-7; Washington to Comte de Rochambeau, Mount Vernon, January 29, 1789, *ibid., XXX,* 187-88.

22. Thomas Jefferson to Washington, Philadelphia, April 2, 1791, Paul Ford, ed., *Writings of Thomas Jefferson* (10 vols., New York, 1892-99), VI, 235-39.

23. Washington to James Seagrove, Augusta, May 20, 1791, Fitzpatrick, ed., *Writings of Washington,* XXXI, 288-91.

24. Washington to Arthur Young, Philadelphia, December 5, 1791, *ibid.,* pp. 436-40; Washington to David Stuart, Philadelphia, April 8, 1792, *ibid.,* XXXII, 18-19; Washington to Sareh Cary Fairfax, Mount Vernon, May 6, 1798, *ibid.,* XXXVI, 262-65.

25. Washington had continued to foster the development of domestic manufacturing since the end of the Revolution. Even before he became President he corresponded with a number of Europeans about the development of a textile industry in America. See Washington to Annis Boudinot Stockton, Mount Vernon, August 31, 1788, *ibid., XXX,* 75-77; Edmund Clegg to Washington, April 6, 1784, n.p.; Edmund Randolph to Washington, Richmond, January 4, 1786, "Washington Papers," Microfilm Reel 95.

26. Washington to David Humphreys, Philadelphia, March 23, 1793, Fitzpátrick, ed., *Writings of Washington,* XXXII, 398-400.

27. Washington to James Madison, Mount Vernon, May 20, 1792, *ibid.,* pp. 45-9. See also Washington to Attorney General, Mount Vernon, August 26, 1792, *ibid.,* pp. 135-37.

28. Samuel Flagg Bemis, "Washington's Farewell Address: A Foreign Policy of Independence," *American Historical Review,* XXXIX (January 1961), pp. 203-4; John C. Miller, *The Federalist Era, 1789-1801* (New 1934), 250; Esmond Wright, *Fabric of Freedom, 1763-1800* (New York, York, 1960), pp. 128-31; Nathan Schachner, *The Founding Fathers* (New York, 1954), pp. 239-44.

29. Washington to Citizens of Annapolis, Philadelphia, September 18, 1793, Fitzpatrick, ed., *Writings of Washington,* XXXIII, 90-1. See also

Washington to Gouverneur Morris, Philadelphia, July 21, 1791, *ibid.,*
XXXI, 326-30; Washington to Secretary of the Treasury, Philadelphia,
May 7, 1793, *ibid.,* XXXII, 451; Gale William McGee, "The Founding
Fathers and Entangling Alliances," (doctoral dissertation, University of
Chicago, 1947), pp. 222-33.

30. *Seventh Annual Address to the Congress of the United States,*
December 8, 1795, Fitzpatrick, ed., *Writings of Washington,* XXXIV, 386-
93.

31. The pertinent documents leading to the preparation of the Farewell
Address in final form can be found conveniently in Paltsits, *Washington's
Farewell Address,* pp. 238-59.

32. Bemis, "Washington's Farewell Address," pp. 250-68; Wright, *Fabric
of Freedom,* pp. 211-12; Miller, *The Federalist Era,* pp. 196-98.

33. Alexander DeConde, "Washington's Farewell, the French Alliance,
and the Election of 1896," *Mississippi Valley Historical Review,* XLIII
(March 1957), 641-58; Joseph Charles, *The Origins of the American
Party System* (New York, 1961), pp. 46-8; Schachner, *The Founding
Fathers,* pp. 394-405.

34. Washington to Charles Carroll (Private), Philadelphia, May 1,
1796, Fitzpatrick, ed., *Writings of Washington,* XXXV, 29-31.

35. Washington to John Quincy Adams, Mount Vernon, January 20,
1799, *ibid.,* XXXVII, 98-9.

36. Washington to Secretary of War, Philadelphia, December 13, 1798,
ibid., pp. 32-45.

SUGGESTED READING

1. THE FAREWELL ADDRESS

For an excellent discussion of the historiography of the Farewell Address, see Albert K. Weinberg, "Washington's 'Great Rule' in Its Historical Evolution," in Eric F. Goldman, ed., *Historiography and Urbanization: Essays in American History in Honor of W. Stull Holt* (Baltimore, 1941), pp. 109-38. On the eve of America's entry into World War II, Weinberg attempted to destroy the notion that the Farewell Address was a "great rule" for Americans to follow. Remarking that individuals had made of the first President's valedictory what they wanted, he concluded that America's freedom of action should not be restricted by any dogmatic citation of the address.

Other interesting interpretations of the Farewell Address which have not been reprinted or noted in this volume include Boothe Colwell Davis, "The Myth of Washington's No Entangling Alliances," *University of Buffalo Studies*, IV (1923), 22-9; Rupert Hughes, "Washington—And 'Entangling Alliances,'" *New York Times Mag-*

azine (February 18, 1940), pp. 7, 15; Louis B. Wright, "The Founding Fathers and 'Splendid Isolation,'" *Huntington Library Quarterly,* VI (February 1943), 173-95; and Joseph Charles, *The Origins of the American Party System* (New York, 1961), pp. 37-53. Davis, Hughes, and Wright view the address essentially as a statement of independence and a declaration that the United States was not to become embroiled in European struggles. Emphasizing Washington's dependence on Hamilton, Charles interprets the message as a political manifesto prepared by Hamilton to wield the first President's prestige against the Anti-Federalists.

Essential to any study of the Farewell Address is Victor Hugo Paltsits, *Washington's Farewell Address* (New York, 1935). Paltsits outlines the history of the message (including its reception and a nineteenth-century controversy over its authorship), and cites all the documents and correspondence pertinent to its writing.

2. GEORGE WASHINGTON

The literature on the first President is enormous. Useful introductions to the more standard works are Joseph Schafer, "Washington and His Biographers," *Wisconsin Magazine of History,* XI (December 1927), 218-28; Albert Bushnell Hart, "A Study of Washington Biography," *The Publisher's Weekly,* CXIX (February 19, 1931), 820-22; and William Alfred Bryan, *George Washington in American Literature, 1775-1865* (New York, 1952), pp. 86-120. For a listing of pertinent materials consult also Howard F. Bremer, ed., *George Washington, 1732-1799: Chronology, Documents—Biographical Aids* (Dobbs Ferry, N.Y., 1967).

The most comprehensive biography of Washington is Douglas Southall Freeman, *George Washington* (7 vols., New York, 1948-1954). The first five volumes and part of the sixth were written by Freeman. The biography was completed after his death by his aides, John A. Carroll and Mary Wells Ashworth. While their work represents a monumental piece of scholarship, the character of the first President tends to be lost in a myriad of detail, especially on military matters, which constitutes the major part of the narrative.

James Flexner is currently preparing a three-volume study of Washington. The first two volumes—*George Washington: The Forge of Experience, 1732-1775* (Boston, 1965) and *George Washington in the American Revolution, 1775-1783* (Boston, 1967)—are already completed. Though written in a lively style, they are narrow in focus, based as they are almost solely on Washington's own letters and correspondence.

For one-volume assessments of the first President, see Curtis P.

Nettels, *George Washington and American Independence* (Boston, 1951); Esmond Wright, *Washington and the American Revolution* (New York, 1962); and Marcus Cunliffe, *George Washington: Man and Monument* (Boston, 1958). Cunliffe is especially good in his discussion of the myths which have obscured the first President's life and made historical evaluation of him difficult.

An excellent essay which elaborates on this same problem is Curtis P. Nettels, "The Washington Theme in American History," *Proceedings of the Massachusetts Historical Society,* LXVIII (1952), 171-97. Notwithstanding the many biographies of Washington, Cunliffe stresses the lack of adequate historical treatment of the first President. He notes that studying the period 1763-1798 without due reference to Washington is like studying the New Deal without proper consideration of Franklin Roosevelt. Referring to Washington's active participation in the resistance movement against England after 1763 and to his early advocacy of a strong central government, he comments on how little attention has been paid to Washington's activities in the final break with the mother country and the establishment of the new nation. He concludes by calling for a new investigation of Washington's role in history, especially as a political leader, and for an examination of such questions as his relations with Congress, individual states, and other political leaders.

As Nettels points out, historians have generally neglected to note Washington's role in relation to the events, people, and ideas of his time. Exceptions to this are Max Farrand, "George Washington in the Federal Convention," *Yale Review,* XVI (May 1907), 28-87; Harold W. Bradley, "The Political Thinking of George Washington," *Journal of Southern History,* XI (November 1945), 469-86; Samuel Flagg Bemis, "John Quincy Adams and George Washington," *Proceedings of the Massachusetts Historical Society,* LXVII (1945), 365-84; and Marshall Smelser, "George Washington and the Alien and Sedition Acts," *American Historical Review,* LIX (January 1954), 322-34. An important unpublished study is Rose Charlotte Engleman, "Washington and Hamilton: A Study in the Development of Washington's Political Ideas" (doctoral dissertion, Cornell University, 1948). Miss Engleman shows clearly how many of the Federalist programs, commonly associated with Alexander Hamilton, were actually conceived or long favored by Washington.

One aspect of the first President's career that has received considerable attention is his lifetime interest in the settlement and development of the West. The standard work on this subject is Charles H. Ambler, *George Washington and the West* (Chapel Hill, 1936). Thomas Perkins Abernethy's *Western Lands and the American Revo-*

lution (New York, 1959) also contains useful information about Washington's interest in frontier speculation, while Hugh Cleland, ed., *George Washington in the Ohio Valley* (Pittsburgh, 1959), conveniently brings together Washington's own narratives of the seven trips he made to the Ohio Valley between 1753 and 1794. Other interesting works on Washington and the West include Herbert Baxter Adams, "Washington's Interest in Western Lands," *Johns Hopkins University Studies in Historical and Political Science,* III, 3rd ser. (January 1885), 55-77; Roy Bird Cook, *Washington's Western Lands* (Strasburg, Va., 1930); Samuel M. Wilson, "George Washington's Contacts with Kentucky," *The Filson Club Quarterly,* VI (July 1932), 215-60; and Hugh G. Cleland, "George Washington and Western Pennsylvania Politics," *Carnegie Magazine,* XXX (September 1956), 231-36. Washington's interest in connecting the Ohio Valley with the Atlantic seaboard by means of the Potomac River can be followed in Grace L. Nute, ed., "Washington and the Potomac," *American Historical Review,* XXVIII (April and July 1923), 497-519 and 705-22. On the same subject, see Herbert Baxter Adams, "Washington's Interest in the Potomac Company," *Johns Hopkins University Studies in Historical and Political Science,* III, 3rd ser. (January 1885), 79-91.

3. FOREIGN POLICY

Foreign policy of the early Republic has received much attention from historians. A useful bibliography of the important studies is John C. Miller, *The Federalist Era, 1789-1801* (New York, 1960), pp. 290-93.

The most comprehensive treatment of Washington and foreign policy is Alexander DeConde, *Entangling Alliance: Diplomacy and Politics Under George Washington* (Durham, N.C., 1958). DeConde discusses the diplomacy of Washington's administration largely in terms of the domestic struggle between opponents (Federalists) and supporters (Anti-Federalists) of the Franco-American Alliance of 1778. Obviously sympathetic with the latter group, DeConde's assumption that the nation's policy at the time Washington took office in 1789 was based on the maintenance of this alliance is open to serious question. A more recent work, Paul A. Varg's *Foreign Policies of the Founding Fathers* (Lansing, Mich., 1963), also stresses the relationship of domestic and foreign affairs. A useful unpublished study is Gale William McGee, "The Founding Fathers and Entangling Alliances" (doctoral dissertation, University of Chicago, 1947). McGee makes clear that instead of favoring a policy of permanent noninvolvement with regard to European affairs, the Founding Fathers actually envisaged a growing nation which would someday take its place among the great world powers. For Washington's attitude toward the French Revolution, see Louis Sears, *George Washington and the French Revolution* (Detroit, 1960).

Useful articles on the views of Washington's administration toward foreign affairs include Samuel Flagg Bemis, "The Background of Washington's Foreign Policy," *Yale Review,* XVI (January 1927), 316-36, and "John Quincy Adams and George Washington," previously cited; Henry M. Wriston, "Washington and the Foundations of American Foreign Policy," *Minnesota History* (March 1927), pp. 3-26; and Louis B. Wright, "The Founding Fathers and 'Splendid Isolation,' " *Huntington Library Quarterly,* VI (February 1943), 173-78.

4. GENERAL STUDIES

Of the more general studies of the Federalist era the most useful are John C. Miller, *The Federalist Era, 1789-1801* and Esmond Wright, *Fabric of Freedom, 1763-1800* (New York, 1961).

Numerous biographies of the Founding Fathers survey the history of the early republic. Three of the best are Irving Brant, *James Madison, Father of the Constitution: 1787-1800* (Indianapolis, 1950), the third volume of a major study of Madison; Dumas Malone, *Jefferson and the Rights of Man* (Boston, 1951), the second volume of a multi-volume work which treats the establishment of the new nation through Washington's first administration; and John C. Miller, *Alexander Hamilton and the Growth of the New Nation* (New York, 1959), a comprehensive single-volume study of Washington's principal adviser.